24 Hour Telephone Renewals 02(

HARINGEY LIBRARIES

THIS BOOK MUST BE RETURNED ON OR BEFORE
THE LAST DATE MARKED BELOW

To	HORNSEY LIBRARY	
19 AUG 2021		

Online renewals – visit libraries.haringey.gov.uk

Published by Haringey Council's Communications Unit 1149.19 • 11/15

amongst my best men

amongst my best men

African-Americans and The War of 1812

*[Fought by the US in defence of the continuation of the slave trade! Newly enslaved Africans were transported from the Carolinas to the West Indies] **

By: Gerard T. Altoff

With an Introduction by: Jospeh P. Reidy

Maps and Illustration by Robyn Opthoff Lilek

The Perry Group
Put-in-Bay, Ohio

* This trade continued until the late 19C into Cuba when slavery was eventually abolished there.

Copyright © 1996 by   The Perry Group
                       P.O. Box 484
                       Put-in-Bay, OH   43456

The Perry Group—Friends of Perry's Victory & International
Peace Memorial—is a non-profit organization dedicated to
fostering the historical, cultural, and environmental programs of
Perry's Victory & IPM.

Library of Congress Catalog Card Number: 95-069728
ISBN 1-887794-02-6

Printed in the United States of America

Cover art: Battle of Lake Erie: the *Niagara* Strikes Back
               From an original oil painting by Peter Rindlisbacher
               Reproduced through the courtesy of the artist.

For those who fought
For those who fell
and
For those who served

including

Private John Althoff
3rd Regiment of Pennsylvania Militia
1814

and

Private Jacob Sell
5th Detachment of Pennsyvlania Militia
1814

TABLE OF CONTENTS

LIST OF MAPS

PREFACE

The War of 1812 is without doubt one of the least known of all of America's wars. Mere mention of the war conjures in the average American's mind a series of illusions, misconceptions, and false assumptions. Chief among those fallacies is that the United States won the war, closely followed by numerous supposed truisms perpetuated by individuals reluctant to admit that the United States rushed headlong into an avoidable war, blundered through ill-conceived military campaigns, suffered defeat in most of the land battles, and nearly lost the war outright. Thus, it is not surprising that the role of African-Americans in the War of 1812 is as misunderstood as the war itself.

This general ignorance concerning the War of 1812 is often brought to light at re-enactments that I attend. In October, 1994 I participated in a War of 1812 re-enactment at the Mississinewa Battlefield, a few miles north of Marion, Indiana. Outfitted in the uniform of a regular in the United States Infantry, I was standing in front of a row of tents which comprised part of the American encampment. The camp abutted a narrow track on which visitors to the battlefield strolled by. Lounging by the tent-row enjoying the pleasant autumn afternoon, I was watching a steady stream of visitors walk past when an elderly black man and his wife approached. Stopping in front of me, the gentleman studied my uniform for a moment before asking what I represented. His wife muttered something like, "Oh lord, here he goes again," and she walked off. The gentleman informed me that he was a World War II veteran, and he went on to relate in considerable detail his experiences in the military. As he continued it was evident by his manner, bearing, and speech that he was extremely proud of his service in his country's defense. He then demonstrated his knowledge of military history by summarizing the roles of African-Americans in other wars: black soldiers and sailors in the Revolutionary War, service by the 54th Massachusetts Regiment and other black Civil War units, the Buffalo Soldiers of the 9th and 10th Cavalry Regiments along the western frontier, the 10th Cavalry Regiment in Cuba, and black outfits in World Wars I and II. Finally, he said something that left me nearly speechless: "Of course, there were no African-Americans in this war," referring to the War of 1812. I was more than happy to disabuse him of that notion.

Having spent 15 years as the chief ranger and historian at a national park site commemorating a black history theme, I was well aware of black participation in the War of 1812. Also, through my general interest in American military history I was familiar with much of the black military experience in the United States. However, I took that knowledge for granted. Previously, I had presented papers and interpretive talks at various history conferences and symposiums concerning the role of black soldiers, sailors, and civilians in the War of 1812, and I already had visions of writing a small book, but it was not until I encountered an individual well versed in and proud of his military heritage—yet ignorant of a major aspect of that heritage—that I really wanted to see this book published.

In the few works that have heretofore delved into the subject, the role of black Americans in the War of 1812 is usually described in one or two pages buried in the midst of a much broader military perspective. Even then, only a few general details about a few specific battles are mentioned, with little or no attempt at context or continuity. Disclosed in these works is the basic fact that black soldiers and sailors fought in the War of 1812, but little more.

My desire to have this book published is not necessarily to educate African-Americans in what amounts to a small segment of their history; such an aspiration would be presumptuous in any case. Likewise, this work is not intended to be an exhaustively researched, all-encompassing, authoritative social or military history of black participation in the War of 1812, or of the War of 1812 itself. It would be impossible within the context of this work to describe every minor skirmish or incident of the war, or to recount every mention of African-American participation, military and/or civilian. The principal goal of this book as written is two-fold: to acknowledge that African-Americans played a much greater role in the War of 1812 than most people know or suspect, and to place that role in context by providing a concise, capsulized history of War of 1812 campaigns.

One of the individuals who helped review this manuscript prior to publication expressed the opinion that I tackled one of those subjects about which few specific details can be written since recordkeeping procedures during the period lacked attention to detail. He further related that because of the shortage of documentary sources I was forced to embed a few known facts into a larger work of generalities. Sadly, his assessment is all too accurate. Details are lacking, and available information is found in widely scattered sources. It goes without saying that I had neither the time, opportunity, nor means to unearth all of these sources, and information which was uncovered was often incomplete and difficult to evaluate.

Black recruits were not accepted into the U.S. Army at the outbreak of the War of 1812, and when the ranks were finally opened, black soldiers were incorporated into regular regiments beside white troops, where their racial identity was swallowed up. Seldom were the deeds of individual soldiers recorded during the War of 1812, and when specifics were noted, it was usually in a negative sense, such as when a soldier deserted. The U.S. Army enlistment records, which sometimes list an individual soldier's personal traits and characteristics, are often ambiguous. Accounts are more comprehensive where black soldiers fought in organized black units, but during the War of 1812, unlike the American Civil War, few instances occurred where black troops campaigned together in cohesive outfits. The most notable example was at the Battle of New Orleans, where black units fought for both the United States and Great Britain.

Large numbers of black sailors served in the U.S. Navy during the War of 1812; however, crews manning the tiny, crowded naval vessels were integrated, and officers who compiled the ship and station muster rolls did not differentiate between black and white seamen. As with the Army, individual sailors were rarely mentioned in official records or secondary sources.

Because details concerning black soldiers and sailors are so difficult to find, and because those details tend to be very specific in nature, this book is written as a narrative of the War of 1812, with anecdotal insights of African-American participation weaved into the story. In one or two instances it may appear that the focus of the work has been lost, and several pages may pass without a specific reference to black soldiers and sailors. This is particularly true where naval battles are discussed, and the sole reason is because in documentary sources, black sailors were treated the same as white sailors, and where there is mention of particular individuals in official records, reference to race is usually omitted. In the case of land battles, individual black soldiers have often been identified as participants, but their feats are unknown. Since it is often impossible to pinpoint the deeds of individual soldiers and sailors, the battles in which they fought are described instead, and in a few instances, the fiery ordeals that the participants endured and the horrors to which they were exposed are vividly portrayed. The reader can only be reminded that even though there occasionally may be no specific information pertaining to African-American participation, black soldiers and sailors did serve in virtually every land and naval engagement of the War of 1812.

Gerard T. Altoff
Put-in-Bay, Ohio

ACKNOWLEDGEMENTS

A work of this nature cannot be compiled without the assistance of numerous people. By generously sharing their knowledge and resources, the following individuals were instrumental in making this book possible: Tom DeVoe from Flanders, New Jersey; Bob Garcia at Fort Malden National Historic Site; Lance Hatten from the Castillo de San Marcos National Monument; Martin Lake of the Mississinewa Battlefield Society; Tyrone Martin—"The Captains Clerk"—in Tryon, North Carolina; Dave Nathanson of the National Park Service's Harpers Ferry Center Library; Ralph Naveaux at the Monroe County Historical Commission; Larry Nelson from Fort Meigs State Memorial; Brian Nichols at the Toledo-Lucas County Public Library; Ron Potvin from the Newport Historical Society; John Alden Reid of Horseshoe Bend National Military Park; Scott Sheads from Fort McHenry National Monument and Historic Shrine; Charles Tingley of the St. Augustine Historical Society; and David Webb at Fort George National Historic Park.

In addition to several of the individuals listed above, a number of other people either helped to review this manuscript in an effort to eliminate its many blunders, or otherwise contributed their time, abilities, and talents toward the publication of this book. For so doing and for being so accommodating, I would like to thank: Margaret Altoff, Don Cartwright, Paul Ghioto, Dave Guthrie, Bill Gwaltney, Malcolm Hardin, Mike Hoover, Peggy Isaly, Mark Johnson, Jeff LaRock, Marty O'Toole, Harry Schroeder, and Matt Switlik. Extra thanks go to Debra Diroff for her repeated editorial work, and undying thanks for the unflagging and professional editorial efforts of Tracy Quinn, an assistant editor with William Morrow & Company, Incorporated/Publishers.

The above named people were of tremendous help, both in providing sources and information, and correcting my mistakes. However, all errors are my own.

Special thanks are extended to Robyn Opthoff Lilek, whose willingness to donate her time and artistic flair to this project are much appreciated, and whose diligence and attention to detail are evident in her work; and to Peter Rindlisbacher, who generously sanctioned the use his spectacular work of art for the cover. Additionally, I wish to convey my gratitude and appreciation to Joseph P. Reidy at Howard University, who graciously consented to lend his literary talent for the introduction.

I also with to thank Richard A. Lusardi, superintendent of Perry's Victory and International Peace Memorial, whose continued encouragement and support have enabled me to see this project to fruition.

Furthermore, I cannot forget to extend my thanks, appreciation, and also my apologies to Cyndee Altoff and Kristin Heather Altoff for patiently tolerating my historical exuberance, which they do not fully share, and for suffering through (I think) my many absences.

Finally, publication of this book would not have been possible without the support and sponsorship of The Perry Group, and I wish to convey my heartfelt thanks to The Perry Group board and members.

INTRODUCTION

Few accounts of the War of 1812 fail to note the importance of British impressment of United States seamen in prompting Congress to declare war. Most such narratives recall the infamous *Chesapeake* affair of 1807, wherein a British frigate forced the commander of the *Chesapeake* to relinquish four crewmen accused of deserting His Majesty's service. Yet few modern accounts note what one nineteenth century commentator considered the centerpiece of the incident: three of the four impressed seamen were of African ancestry. The abridgement of the liberties of free black "citizens of the republic," Joseph T. Wilson insisted, provided "the key-note and rallying cry" behind the U.S. declaration of war. Wilson, a veteran of the Civil War's fabled 54th Massachusetts Volunteer Infantry, made his observation in *The Black Phalanx* (1890), a pioneering chronicle of the African-American experience in the early wars of the United States. Though he despaired of ever "ascertain[ing] the exact number of negroes who stood beside the guns" during the War of 1812, Wilson did not hesitate to credit them with helping the young nation win "just recognition from the maritime powers of the world."

Publication of Gerard T. Altoff's *Amongst My Best Men: African-Americans and The War of 1812* adds both depth and texture to Wilson's sketchy outline of the War of 1812, which to this day remains the least studied and understood war in the nation's past. Over the past century, sources have come to light that simply were unavailable to Wilson; what is more, over the past generation historians have developed rewarding techniques for assessing both the experiences of ordinary combatants in battle and the impact of warfare on civilian life in the battle zone and on the homefront. Altoff deftly exploits these advances to produce a comprehensive treatment of the African-American role in the war.

Amongst My Best Men does not lack for exciting anecdotes and fascinating details; nor does it negate Wilson's judgment that the African-Americans' service upheld "the honor of the race." It does, however, add a more nuanced perspective than the conventions of nineteenth-century historical narrative allowed. Altoff, in short, resists the temptation toward sweeping statements that homogenize disparate experiences. Taking variety as his point of departure, he carefully explains the differences black servicemen encountered from one branch of service to another and from one theater of operation to another. Moreover, he explores the war's diverse effects upon African-American civilians living in the different war zones.

Black sailors, for example, saw the war in many ways as a continuation, rather than a disruption, of prewar patterns of life and work. From prior experience—in the merchant marine and whaling fleet if not necessarily the Navy—they clearly understood the dangers of maritime service. Yet they also appreciated the egalitarian aspects of shipboard life and the prospects of prize money in addition to their regular pay. Other patriotic motives—among which Wilson identified "Free Trade, Sailor's Rights and Independence on the seas as well as on the land"—also inspired African-American men to volunteer for naval service. By one estimate, some 15 to 20% of the Navy's enlisted personnel were of African ancestry, and on certain vessels that figure exceeded 50%.

The war on the land created a different set of patterns. The passage of time has not proven conducive to unraveling Wilson's mystery regarding the number of African-American men who served, but Altoff's research suggests that the number was significant and, in fact, appears to have increased substantially over the course of the war. By the summer of 1814, as troop shortages affected both regular Army and militia units alike, recruiters for the former began to accept black volunteers routinely and officials in several states placed the loosest possible interpretation upon the federal and state militia acts. The latter measures, most of which were modeled after the federal act of 1792 that obliged white men to enroll for militia service, tended to exempt (if not prohibit) non-whites from serving or to restrict their contributions to fatigue duty rather than combat. In short, the crisis atmosphere produced something of a relaxation of the rules, such that African-Americans who volunteered might as soon have their services accepted as rejected.

Like the American Revolution before it and the Civil War after it, the War of 1812 helped loosen the bonds of servitude between masters and slaves, in some cases briefly but in others permanently. The British assaults against Washington and Baltimore in the summer of 1814 and New Orleans in December 1814 and January 1815 proved especially conducive to this disintegration. With both sides attempting to mobilize black manpower, slaves saw openings for freedom that would have been inconceivable in times of peace. Some fled in the direction of Native Americans while others sought the protection of the Spanish or the British. Free African-Americans also took advantage of rare opportunities to improve their social standing. The free people of color in New Orleans, for instance, persuaded General Andrew Jackson to accept their services in large measure to gain fuller recognition of their citizenship rights.

Altoff's careful depiction of these multifaceted circumstances helps clarify why some African-Americans were willing to volunteer for service in the armed forces of the U.S., why others subordinated national loyalty to their quest for freedom, and why still others attempted to remain neutral. In short, because the War of 1812 presented such a varied face, it is little wonder that African-Americans responded in kind. Altoff's sympathetic study provides both the information necessary to appreciate this variety and the context for understanding its broader significance to both the history of the war and the history of the nation.

Joseph P. Reidy
Howard University

I

Naval Operations

*...no Captain can do very wrong
if he places his Ship alongside
that of an Enemy*

Horatio Nelson

*Our country: in her intercourse
with foreign nations may she
always be right; but our country,
right or wrong!*

Stephen Decatur

1

FREE TRADE AND SAILORS RIGHTS

The origins of the War of 1812 can be traced to the end of the American Revolution. Tensions between the United States and Great Britain remained high even after the Treaty of Paris, which ended the Revolutionary War, was ratified. Relations were further strained during the 1790's and early 1800's, a time when England was fighting for her life against a European continent dominated by Napoleon Bonaparte. During this period the United States aroused British enmity by openly trading with England's enemies. Great Britain countered this implied threat by issuing a series of economic sanctions collectively called the Orders in Council. The Orders in Council empowered the Royal Navy to stop neutral vessels on the high seas and seize those which were transporting contraband goods. During the period between the Revolutionary War and the War of 1812, literally hundreds of American merchant ships were confiscated by the British.

In addition to rigorously enforcing the Orders in Council, the Royal Navy found other ways to breed tensions with the United States. Desperately short of sailors after years of blockading European ports and fighting costly battles against the Napoleonic Navies, the British government authorized its warships to forcibly stop any and all United States ships in international waters and abduct sailors to fight for England. Far from being a new institution, impressment was a long-established practice employed by a number of countries, often against their own citizens; it was an early and crude form of the draft brought about by the crisis of war. Impressment was even exercised by the United States during the Revolutionary War. During the 1790's, as Great Britain's war against Napoleon progressed, huge numbers of sailors were needed to man the ever-expanding Royal Navy. Volunteers quickly dried up, and the navy's press gangs had stripped England's coastal cities and towns of able-bodied men. A new pool of manpower was needed. American ships were a prime target because of Britain's animosity toward her former colonies and because the British Navy was confident that there was little the virtually defenseless United States could do about it.

When Royal Navy captains stopped American ships on the high seas, they were ostensibly seeking to recapture deserters or impress one-time British citizens. Anyone born in the British Isles, regardless of acquired citizenship, was still considered a citizen of Great Britain, but citizenship notwithstanding, British commanders who required a specific number of seamen to fill their watch, quarter, and station bills were not overly concerned about citizenship papers, especially if the overhauled American vessel was outbound from the United States. In such cases, due to slowly traveling communications, no repercussions could be expected for three months or more, by which time the principal characters were difficult to find and the facts of the case were usually muddled or forgotten.

One of the most notorious examples of British impressment, and one that nearly precipitated a declaration of war, occurred on 22 June 1807. The U.S. Frigate *Chesapeake* (38 guns) had just sailed from the Gosport Navy Yard in Norfolk, Virginia when it was confronted in international waters by HMS *Leopard* (50). The *Leopard*'s captain, Salusbury Humphries, dispatched one of his lieutenants to board the *Chesapeak*e and demand that four alleged deserters be returned to His Majesty's service. American Commodore James Barron courteously but flatly refused to submit or relinquish any *Chesapeake* crewmen. When his lieutenant returned on board, the British captain maneuvered the *Leopard* alongside the *Chesapeake* and, without warning, fired a devastating broadside into the unsuspecting American frigate. After a ten-minute engagement, during which the U.S. ship never effectively responded, Commodore Barron hauled down his colors. Captain Humphries, fully realizing the political implications of his hostile action against the American ship, shrewdly refused to accept the *Chesapeake* as a prize of war; still, he did seize the four deserters.

Of the four seamen who were impressed, three actually had deserted from His Majesty's Frigate *Melampus* (36) when that vessel made a port call at Hampton Roads, Virginia a few months earlier. Seamanship being their livelihood, the sailors simply turned around and enlisted in the U.S. Navy. The three, all black sailors, were William Ware, Daniel Martin, and John Strachan; the fourth individual was a white seaman named John Wilson, whom the British accused of deserting from the merchant service. Wilson was later hanged for desertion at Halifax, Nova Scotia. Nearly four years passed before the incident was finally redressed and the British government returned to the United States two of the three remaining seamen; one of the black sailors apparently died in England while in custody.[1]

Impressment was one of three principle reasons the U.S. declared war against Great Britain for the second time in less than forty years. Estimates vary considerably, but during the years preceding the war, between 2,500 and 25,000 seamen were snared from American vessels by the British Navy.[2] Undoubtedly a significant percentage of the impressed sailors were of African descent, especially since for a period of time black seamen serving on U.S. registered vessels did not enjoy the same legal protection as white sailors. Not until 1803 did the U.S. Congress even agree to "enquire into the expediency" of offering black merchant seamen the same right of protection under the law as their white counterparts.[3]

Both impressment and the Orders in Council imposed serious constraints on America's maritime commerce prior to the War of 1812. Vessel captains sailing from American ports faced the uncertainty of reaching their destinations with less than a full crew, or possibly not arriving at all. But the British were not America's sole concern. Trouble with the French Revolutionary government erupted in 1798 and led to the two-year Quasi-War with France. Then, in 1806, Napoleon countered the Orders in Council with his own economic sanctions against Great Britain and the United States when he issued the Berlin Decree. Shortly thereafter Thomas Jefferson pushed an American economic embargo against Great Britain and France through the U.S. Congress. Confusion reigned among maritime nations and the United States found itself confronted by several potential foes. England, however, had been a sworn enemy for years, whereas the France of the Marquis de Lafayette had been a benefactor during the American Revolution. With almost daily accounts of shipping being impounded in Great Britain or seamen being impressed by the British from U.S. registry ships, the United States had a ready antagonist on which to focus its anger.

2

THE MERCHANT SERVICE AND WHALING

In the decade preceding the War of 1812, roughly 90% of all United States imports and exports were transported by both American and foreign merchant fleets plying their trade from east coast and gulf coast ports. Another important economic venture among maritime nations was whaling, although at the time it was just gaining momentum in the United States; at the turn of the 19th century, English ports berthed more than 300 whalers, while the American whaling fleet consisted of about 100 vessels.[4] Along America's coastal plains thousands of young men abandoned what amounted to relatively safe but often plain and unimaginative livelihoods to seek excitement and adventure at sea.

The social fabric of life at sea evolved differently from that on land. Seafaring was "a partly separate subculture with its own mores and traditions" which "could offer minority men opportunities not available in the mainstream."[5] This was a contingency born of necessity due to the unique nature of shipboard existence. Subjected to long absences from home combined with harsh, arduous, and dangerous living and working conditions, sailors were forced to endure perils and uncertainties not readily accepted by the average working man on land. Shipmasters often experienced difficulty recruiting sufficient numbers of men willing to tolerate such an uninviting environment and thankless work; willing hands were a much greater priority than skin color. Yet it was honest labor that offered an opportunity for a good paying job with minimum discrimination; prejudice against free black workers in northern states often precluded the acquisition of jobs and fair treatment on land. One New Englander lamented that, "To drive carriage, carry a market basket after the boss, and brush his boots, or saw wood and run errands, was as high as a colored man could rise."[6] But shipboard labor shortages offered an alternative. A seafaring life was one of the few occupations where a black man in America could achieve a semblance of equality.

Harmony among ship's crews was essentially a product of the sea environment. For all intents and purposes, a ship at sea was an independent and isolated community whose very survival was entirely reliant upon the crew that served her. Every man on board was in varying degrees dependent upon the skills and teamwork of his fellow shipmates. A shirker, regardless of color, was not tolerated, and if the ship's officers failed to resolve a disciplinary problem, the seamen themselves would initiate appropriate, and often harsh action. Fundamentally, it boiled down to the individual sailor's skills and abilities and his willingness to perform his duty and share in the work with his shipmates.

Although the caste system was very much alive at sea, it had little to do with color. In fact, the basic labor and social structure of shipboard life had been clearly delineated for centuries. From the moment an officer, skilled craftsman, or landsman signed on board a vessel his role and his place were defined and clear. Officers worked and socialized together, as did warrant officers, petty officers, and seamen. Rank barriers and social barriers were rarely broken. Opportunities for advancement existed and a sailor's rank or shipboard clique might change, but his social status could not be altered. The social gap between officers and lower ranks was so great that even when a petty officer was elevated to warrant or officer rank he might be accepted professionally, but seldom socially.

Skin color did not invalidate nautical custom and tradition. That is not to say that prejudice at sea was non-existent. Black seamen, conscious of their unique disposition and the ambivalent atmosphere, would often socialize together and eat with other black messmates. Undoubtedly, black messes were segregated to some extent on some vessels, but true segregation was impossible on board a cramped and crowded ship. Ultimately, shipboard operations and the overriding hunger for profit by the owners and crew always took precedence.

Black sailors had been part of the maritime world for as long as ships had been at sea. In a country like the United States where prejudice was the accepted norm, seafaring offered refreshing and unique opportunities. Equally important to black seamen was the effect on pride and self-worth. Black sailors performed the same work, generally received the same pay, ate the same food, and shared the same living conditions as white sailors.

8

AFRICAN-AMERICANS AND THE WAR OF 1812

Advancement most likely was slower, but black seamen who persevered for multiple voyages and gained the necessary experience and skills were promoted, and white sailors were subject to the orders of black officers and petty officers. Black seamen functioned as petty officers, warrant officers, ship's officers, and even captains. In the period prior to the American Civil War, as many as 40 black shipmasters captained American merchantmen and whalers. Several black captains berthed entirely black crews. Among these were Absalom F. Boston, master of the Nantucket-based *Industry*; Pierre Etienne, captain of the *Victoire*, home-ported in New Orleans; and Alvan Phelps, commander of the *Traveller*, out of Westport, Connecticut.

As knowledge, experience, and financial security were obtained, black ship captains and businessmen were able to purchase part or even total ownership of a number of U.S. registered merchant and whaling vessels. For a brief period the sole owner of the *Rising States* was Richard Johnson, who also held part ownership of the *Francis* and the *Washington*, all New England-based vessels. Johnson later sold interest in the vessel to nine other individuals, most of whom were black partners. Paul Cuffee served as master of the Westport-based *Traveller* for one cruise, but he also maintained a one-half ownership of the *Alpha*, the *Traveller*, and the *Ranger*, plus a one-third interest in the *Hope* and the *Hero*. John Updike, of Petersburg, Virginia, owned four merchant vessels.[7]

The numbers of black seamen who crewed American merchant and whaling ships were substantial. A survey of crew lists from Philadelphia, perhaps the busiest of American ports, revealed that of 2,524 seamen registered in that city in 1810, 378 were of African descent, nearly 15% of the total. Two years later the percentage had risen to 17.2. Crew numbers shipping out of New Orleans during this same period totaled 19.3% African-American, while black sailors comprised 17% of the crews sailing from Baltimore.[8] In Providence, Rhode Island, where black citizenry accounted for 8.5% of the population, they comprised 20% of the seamen.[9] All along the east and gulf coasts, at ports like Portland, New Bedford, Newport, Westport, Wilmington, Charleston, Savannah, and Mobile, merchant and whaling ships conducted the commerce of a nation, and free men of color sought berths in order to improve their lives. Some merchantmen were crewed exclusively by black sailors.

Notable among early black seamen was Crispus Attucks who, as a runaway slave, crewed merchantmen and whalers for 20 years before be-

9

coming a victim of the Boston Massacre on 5 March 1770.[10] Although he never went to sea, Frederick Douglass worked in the shipping industry at the port of Baltimore as a shipcaulker, professing that he "knew a ship from stem to stern, and from keelson to crosstrees, and could talk sailor like an 'old salt'."[11] Douglass eventually used his occupation to escape bondage. By donning "a red shirt and tarpaulin hat and black cravat, tied in sailor fashion, carelessly and loosely about my neck," Douglass obtained a protection certificate from a black sailor and boarded a train for Philadelphia and freedom. He subsequently pursued his trade along the wharves of New Bedford, Massachusetts.[12]

In addition to free men of color, a considerable number of slaves served on board merchant vessels, although ascertaining precise numbers is nearly impossible. Ship captains would often increase their profit margin by using their own slaves as crews, while in other cases businessmen would send men in bondage to sea and pocket the slave's wages. It was not unknown for slaves to comprise an entire ship's crew; during the War of 1812, three vessels with all-slave crews put to sea from New Orleans. Whenever possible, slaves would make the most of the situation and use merchant ships to broker their freedom, and a captain might readily find himself short of crewmen in a northern or foreign port. Runaway slaves would occasionally sign on a merchantman if the opportunity presented. Concealing their identity, they would usually, but not always, jump ship as soon as a free port was entered. One escaped Maryland slave found his way on board a merchantman and remained a sailor for more than 20 years. Merchant ships remained an avenue of escape for slaves until the 1820's, when slave states began enacting "Negro Seamen's Laws." One example is the South Carolina laws, passed in 1822. South Carolina decreed that any free black sailor entering a Palmetto State port would be imprisoned until his ship sailed, at which time the vessel's master was required to pay for the seaman's board. If the captain failed to pay, the seaman could be sold into slavery. As the years passed the Negro Seamen's Laws became more and more restrictive.[13]

It was not only black men who went to sea. Black children commonly sailed on merchant and whaling ships, and black women occasionally served in a crew. Boys as young as seven would be employed as cabin boys, stewards or "waiting boys," cook's apprentices, or apprentice seamen. Seldom did members of the same family go to sea together, although there were rare instances of brothers or fathers and sons being on the same ship. At least two families, the Hazards and Gardners, both from the Newport, Rhode Island area, had eight and nine family members, respectively, who were mariners. Black women serving as crewmembers were extremely rare. White shipmasters or officers would occasionally take a black mistress on a cruise, but some black women served on merchant ships in regular capacities, usually as stewardesses, cooks, or seamstresses.[14]

While black seamen might have managed to attain a semblance of equality, life was still characterized by toil, brutality, and deprivation. Black and white sailors alike took their chances if their ship was waylaid by an English man-o'-war on the high seas, but black seamen had more cause to worry and slaves in particular faced an uncertain future, which might include continued slavery, imprisonment, or impressment. The Royal Navy's penchant for impressing American sailors, combined with England's imposed economic embargo and their military aid to America's Indian adversaries in the Old Northwest, induced the United States to declare war on Great Britain on 18 June 1812.

3

THE BLUE WATER NAVY: 1812-1813

Inauspiciously for the United States, overconfidence in the Army's capabilities led to a string of defeats on land during the war's early months. But the U.S. Navy set a different tone, initially winning an impressive array of victories over the pretentious Royal Navy. Though barely past its infancy, the United States Navy was, at this point in time, better trained and disciplined than its adversary. Still, American ship-to-ship successes early in the war were more attributable to superior American firepower and to the small number of available British ships than to any transcendent naval prowess.

When war was declared in 1812, the British Navy embodied more than 650 warships, more than 100 of which were two-decker 74-gun line-of-battle ships. By comparison, the U.S. Navy mustered only 17 ocean-going ships, the largest of which were three 44-gun frigates. British contempt for the American Navy, added to the Royal Navy's resource-consuming naval blockade of Europe, constrained the Admiralty to assign only 25 vessels to the North American Station, headquartered at Halifax, Nova Scotia. Strongest of this number was the 64-gun *Africa*—smallest of the two-decker class—backed up by five 38-, 36-, and 32-gun frigates; the bulk of the North American Station comprised smaller sloops-of-war, brigs, and armed schooners. Collectively, U. S. warships feasibly could contend with such numbers, but when factoring odds against the U.S. Navy, the number of British ships allocated to the North American Station was only one consideration and more than a little deceiving. Royal Navy squadrons were also assigned to other bases in the western Atlantic Ocean: the Leeward Islands Station, with 27 ships based at Antigua; the Jamaican Station, having 19 ships posted to Port Royal; and the Newfoundland Station, which deployed 12 ships from St. Johns. So, even though Great Britain's commitment to the North American Station was small by comparison, the Royal Navy still handily outnumbered the U.S. Navy in the western Atlantic and, so they thought, easily outclassed the upstart Americans.[15]

Despite the greater number of British ships, the U.S. Navy possessed some notable advantages. American frigates were, for the most part, larger and more heavily constructed than British frigates. Also, American 44-gun frigates not only mounted more guns than British frigates, but they also carried heavier guns. Virtually every warship during the period, both British and American, supported more cannon than that for which it was rated. For instance, in 1812 the frigate *Constitution*, a 44-gun 5th rate, actually mounted 56 guns, and the frigate *Essex*, a 32-gun 5th rate, carried 46 cannons. Moreover, British 38- and 36-gun ships were predominantly 18-pounder frigates, so called because they mounted 18-pounder cannon on their gun decks and 12-pounders on their partially armed upper decks. For the most part, British frigates exclusively arrayed long guns in their broadsides. American 44-gun frigates carried 32-pounder carronades on their upper, or spar decks, and 24-pounder long guns on their gun decks; the notable exception was the *United States*, which supported 42-pounder carronades.[16] By the simple expedient of mounting heavier caliber pieces, the weight of broadsides fired by the big American frigates endowed them with a significant firepower advantage over their more lightly-built and lesser-armed opponents.

Further hampering Royal Navy effectiveness was its past triumphs over the European navies. Time and again during England's 20-year conflict with Napoleon the British Navy had confronted superior numbers. Victory was the usual result, and repeated success led to overconfidence within the Admiralty, the high command, and among the Royal Navy officer corps. By 1812, the Royal Navy had become dangerously complacent. When war erupted with the United States, nothing less than victory was expected from Royal Navy captains, and the mere thought of defeat was unacceptable to the Navy and the British public. But long years of tedious and dreary blockade duty, combined with a shortage of material and manpower resources, had eroded the Royal Navy's formidable abilities. Also, the lubberly ships and poorly trained sailors of the French and Spanish Navies could not compare with the stoutly-built, heavily-gunned, and aggressively commanded American warships the British Navy would face during the American war.

In the first few months of the war, a string of American ship-to-ship victories stunned the British Admiralty and the Royal Navy. Equally confounded was a disbelieving English public. The United States Navy's initial success, occurring on 13 August 1812 off Newfoundland's Grand Banks, was a modest one. Mistaking the U.S. Frigate *Essex* (32) for a merchant vessel, His Majesty's Sloop-of-War *Alert* (16) smugly attacked the superior American warship, only to surrender ignominiously when her captain, facing frightening odds, discovered his blunder. Then on 19 August the U.S. Frigate *Constitution* (44), captained by Isaac Hull, defeated H.M. Frigate *Guerriere* (38) in a two-hour exchange of gunfire south of Newfoundland. The ravaged British ship, dismasted and sinking, was set on fire and blown up by her exultant captors after the British wounded were carefully transferred. HMS *Guerriere* was only the first of many prizes that fell to what would become the most successful American warship of the frigate navy era.

Also contributing to the American cause was the shallow water navy. Two small British brigs, the *Detroit* and *Caledonia*, were boarded and captured on Lake Erie when a cutting out expedition (a boat or landing party assembled to capture, or cut-out, a vessel anchored or hove-to near shore) from the Black Rock Naval Station near Buffalo, led by Lieutenant Jesse D. Elliott, boldly crept under the guns of Fort Erie on the night of 8 October. Less than a fortnight later, on 18 October, the U.S. Sloop-of-War *Wasp* (18), five days outbound from Delaware Bay, overwhelmed H.M. Brig *Frolic* (18) in a bloody 43-minute yardarm to yardarm engagement. Unfortunately for the *Wasp*, her luck ran out just a few hours after the victory. By sheer chance, cruising in the same vicinity was the British two-decker *Poictiers* (74). When the big line-of-battle ship hove into view, the *Wasp* was prevented from escaping because her sails had been shredded during her fight with the *Frolic*. Both the damaged American ship and her prize were forced to surrender. Seven days later, midway between the Azores and the Cape Verde Islands, Captain Stephen Decatur, commanding the U.S. Frigate *United States* (44), bested H.M. Frigate *Macedonian* (38). Jubilant citizens at New London, Connecticut were afterwards regaled by the spectacle of the *United States* towing her vanquished prize into port.

Victory followed victory, but the ocean war was not entirely one-sided. On the evening of 22 November, the 12-gun U.S. Brig *Vixen* stumbled into a fight with H.M. Frigate *Southampton* (32); the outcome was never in doubt. *Vixen*'s loss was counterbalanced by the *Essex* (32), which easily overpowered the British packet *Nocton* (10) on 12 December. The positive

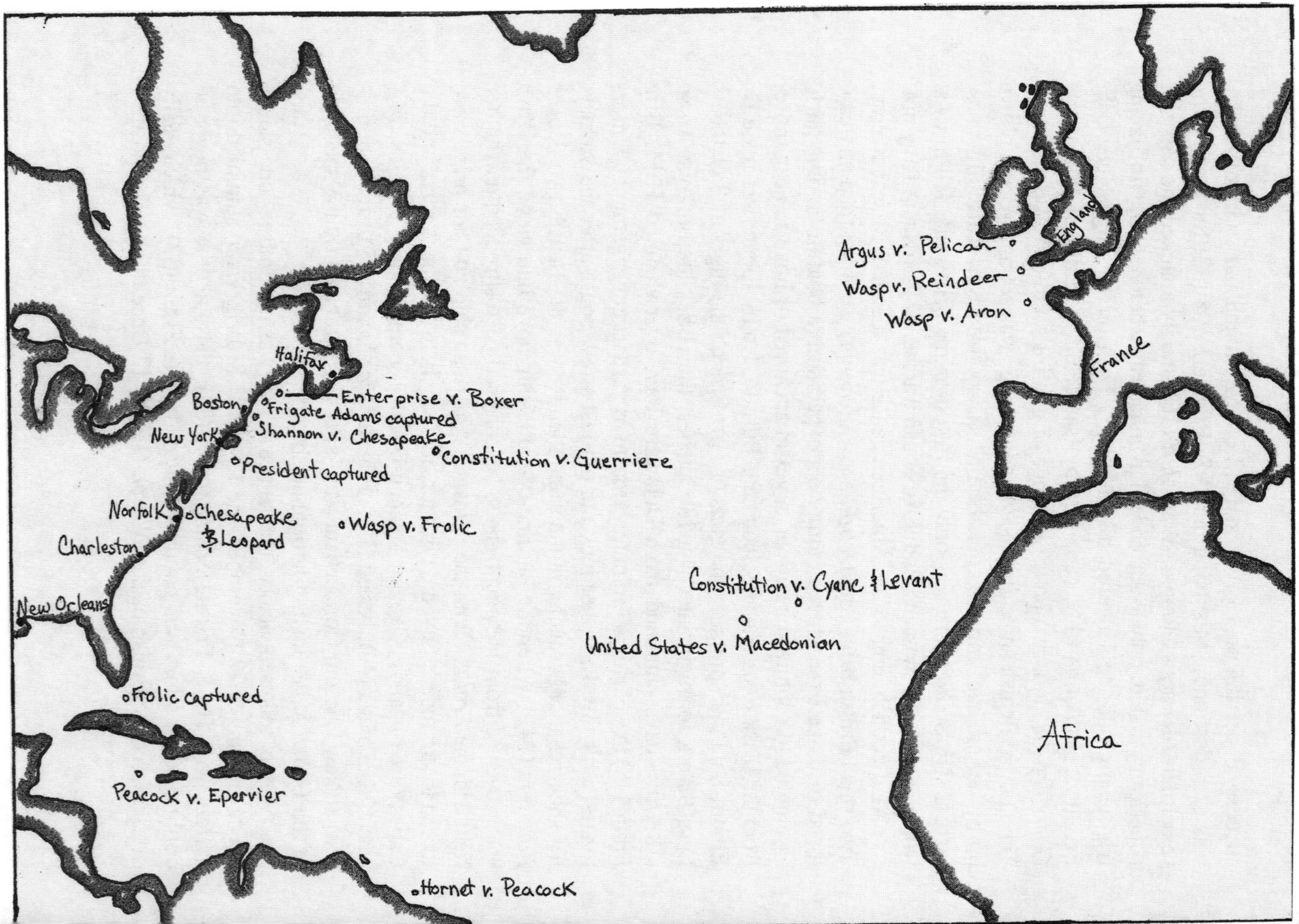
Argus v. Pelican
Wasp v. Reindeer
Wasp v. Avon
England
France
Halifax
Enterprise v. Boxer
Boston
Frigate Adams captured
New York
Shannon v. Chesapeake
Constitution v. Guerriere
President captured
Norfolk
Chesapeake
& Leopard
Wasp v. Frolic
Charleston
New Orleans
Constitution v. Cyane & Levant
United States v. Macedonian
Frolic captured
Africa
Peacock v. Epervier
Hornet v. Peacock

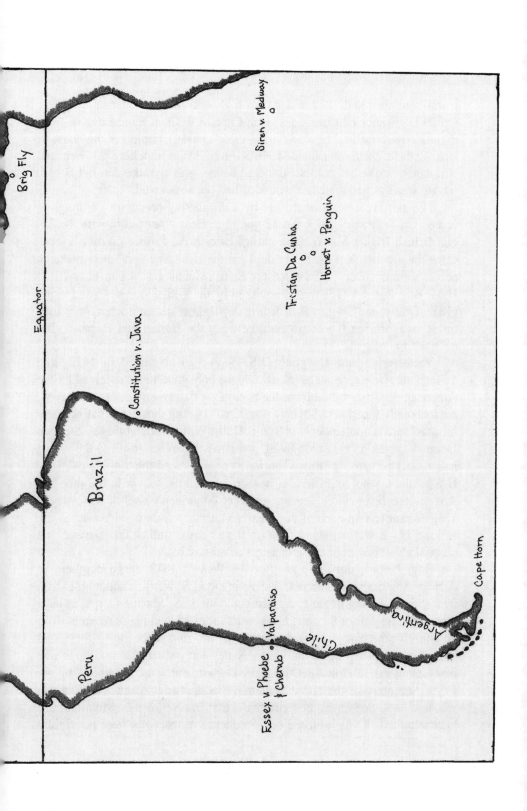

trend continued and 1812 ended on a high note for the young U.S. Navy. On 29 December Old Ironsides, with Captain William Bainbridge in command, struck again. In a withering close quarters battle off the coast of Brazil, the *Constitution* mauled HMS *Java* (38), compelling the wrecked Britisher to strike her colors. Battered beyond salvage, the derelict British frigate was torched after her wounded had been removed.

The new year was ushered in by a disquieting precursor of things to come. On 17 January 1813, the 12-gun U.S. Brig *Viper* fell in with the 32-gun British frigate *Narcissus*, a clash in which the former predictably became the victim. Yet the heady days for the U.S. Navy and the American people were not over. Off the coast of British Guiana on 24 February 1813, H.M. Brig *Peacock* (18) was vanquished by the U.S. Sloop-of-War *Hornet* (18). Oddly, the 18-gun British brig *Espiègle* rested at anchor only four miles away during the entire fight between the *Hornet* and *Peacock*, but declined to engage.

Victories for the fledgling U.S. Navy had abounded in 1812, and through the war's early stages practically the only good news received by the American public stemmed from the triumphs of a few small, outnumbered, but inherently superior U.S. Navy warships. During those stimulating early months such commanders as Isaac Hull, William Bainbridge, Stephen Decatur, David Porter, Jacob Jones, and James Lawrence inspired the young nation, and the names of their victorious vessels graced the tongues of every U.S. citizen who could read a newspaper. Little known is the fact that African-American sailors, serving on every American vessel of war, played a significant role in each of those early victories. Side-by-side with white sailors, black seamen stood firm on flayed decks amidst the carnage and unspeakable horrors of close quarters naval combat.

Both before, during, and after the War of 1812, large numbers of African-Americans volunteered to serve in the U.S. Navy. Although barred by law from serving in the U.S. Army and the U.S. Marine Corps, at least in the opening year of the war, few constraints precluded black recruits from enlisting in the Navy. However, this was not always the case. Steps had been initiated to segregate the United States Navy when the naval arm was first established. Shortly after the Navy Department was formed in August, 1798, Secretary of the Navy Benjamin Stoddert advised one ship captain who was recruiting for his new command that "no Negroes or Mulattoes are to be admitted."[17] As it turned out, Stoddert's instructions were not rigidly followed, and the seagoing service's very nature during this time period insured that any concerted effort to exclude black seamen from the Navy would not endure. Cornelius Howard, a black seaman and one of the U.S Frigate *Constitution*'s original crew members, was signed on by Captain Samuel Nicholson less than two months after Stoddert's order was issued.[18]

Black seamen fought on board U.S. warships during the Quasi-War with France and during the Tripolitan Wars against the Barbary pirates. One of those fighting sailors who shed blood for the United States was Perow Newzer. Wounded in action off Tripoli harbor in 1803, Newzer received no benefits from the government, so the neglected seaman attempted to rectify the injustice by writing to the Secretary of the Navy on 10 November 1806:

> You will be so good as to excuse the liberty I take in writing you, but having been one of the party who burned the Frigate *Philadelphia* on the Shores of Tripoly [sic], & not having received any pay or compensation for that Service, I have to request you to order payment to me in Philadelphia, for I am too poor to go to Washington for it.
>
> My name is Perow Newzer, a black man, which you will find on the Muster Roll.
>
> Please to direct to me at N[umber] 12 Arch Street, Philad'a.
>
> Having received a considerable Hurt in my left leg in the Service, it disables me a good deal & I want my money to pay for my Board.
>
> I was one of the Crew of the Brig *Syren*, Capt. [Charles] Stewart.
>
> In confidence of your kind attention to a poor fellow, who has faithfully served the U. States, in the war with Tripoly [sic].[19]

Despite the fact that many African-American sailors served on board United States warships, the Navy still retained its official doctrine of excluding black and mulatto seamen during the first decade of the 1800's. Some influential ship captains like Edward Preble heeded the policy and specifically instructed their recruiters to reject black recruits, while other captains ignored the strictures.[20] Ultimately, the presence of African-American seamen on board U.S. warships during this period seems to have been entirely arbitrary.

Official U.S. Navy policy was not altered until 3 March 1813, when Congress passed:

An Act

For the regulation of seamen on board the
public and private vessels of the United States.

Be it enacted by the Senate and house of Representatives of the United States of America in congress assembled,

That from and after the termination of the war in which the United States are now engaged with Great Britain it shall not be lawful to employ on board any of the public or private vessels of the United States any person or persons except citizens of the United States or persons of color, natives of the U. States...[21]

Official policy notwithstanding, discrimination in the Navy was not the norm prior to the War of 1812, and the declaration of war obviated any such conventionalism. Life at sea on board a merchant or whaling ship offered few luxuries, but a berth in a U.S Navy vessel promised an even bleaker outlook. Harsh discipline, low pay, poor food, austere living conditions, endless hard work, long periods at sea removed from hearth and family, plus the ever-present prospect of death or mutilation in battle, rendered it difficult to enlist recruits. Understandably, in a time when vessel commanders were forced to vie with merchantmen and privateersmen for qualified crewmen, the majority of navy captains were less concerned about the color of a prospective recruit's skin than about enrolling healthy able-bodied individuals.

Crews were, of necessity, integrated due to cramped and limited living space, but black sailors in the Navy, like the merchant service, were unavoidably subject to varying degrees of prejudice. Although racial tension could not be totally eliminated, a ship's captain, vested with near god-like authority and power, could readily quell any discontent. Overt prejudice was for the most part minimal and controllable, although latent discrimination was a different story. Not unexpectedly, the proximity of mortal danger —the certain knowledge that by their actions fellow crewmen, be they black or white, literally possessed the power of life and death—did much to eliminate any predilections toward bias!

Most black seamen who served in the Navy were free men, products of the numerous northern port cities where decent jobs for free black workers were scarce. In some instances, sailors and officer's servants were slaves, and it was an occasional practice for slave owners, including some naval officers to arrange for their charges to be inducted into the Navy. Between 1799 and 1801, Commodore Silas Talbot shipped at least two slaves on board the *Constitution*.[22] The "property" owners would garner the slaves wages, benefits, and prize money.[23] Such a transaction proved lucrative unless the unlucky slave-cum-seaman was wounded, fell ill, or suffered an accidental debilitating injury. In that event:

> ...[the slave's] master shall allow out of his wages a reasonable compensation for such medical and hospital aid as he may receive, and if the injury [or] disability shall be likely to continue, the master shall cause such Slave to be removed from the public hospital.[24]

One eminent naval historian has estimated that black seamen constituted 15 to 20% of enlisted sailors in the United States Navy before, during, and after the War of 1812.[25] On some warships the numbers appear to have been considerably higher. Following one notable success during the war, the crew of a triumphant New York berthed vessel was extended an invitation to attend a theatrical performance presented in honor of their bravery in battle. As reported, the entire crew "marched together into the pit, and nearly one half of them were negroes."[26]

Ascertaining a precise number or percentage of African-Americans who served in any one U.S. Navy ship or station is virtually impossible since the Navy itself made no differentiation between the races on official documentation such as vessel or station muster rolls. In most respects, black sailors were considered no different, no better, and no worse than white sailors. Yet the Navy's impartiality when compiling official records has deprived modern historians of the ability to identify black seamen. Pension records provide one of the best sources for detecting black sailors, but only a small percentage of sailors who served actually applied for pensions, so any statistical extrapolation is pure guesswork. Contemporary accounts of black participation in the War of 1812 are widely scattered and not easily found. Many references are so general as to be useless except to state that African-Americans did serve in the Navy, while others are very specific to one or more individuals and give no hints as to overall service of black sailors. Occasionally a conspicuous exception offers tantalizing hints, such as the letter written by Surgeon Usher Parsons in 1862:

> In 1816, I was surgeon of the [U.S. Frigate] *Java*, under Commodore [Oliver Hazard] Perry. The white and colored seamen messed together. About one in six or eight were colored.
>
> In 1819, I was surgeon of the [U.S. Frigate] *Guerriere*, under Commodore [Thomas] Macdonough; and the proportion of blacks was about the same in her crew. There seemed to be an entire absence of prejudice against the blacks as messmates among the crew. What I have said applies to the crews of other ships that sailed in [U.S. Navy] squadrons.[27]

Tracking down just one individual can often prove extremely frustrating. For example, in Martha S. Putney's book *Black Sailors, Afro-American Merchant Seamen and Whalemen Prior to the Civil War*, the author relates that a man named:

> Freeman, no given name, was on board the British ship *Java* when she was captured by the *Constitution*. Freeman, who claimed American citizenship, had been pressed by the British. He subsequently became a member of the crew of the *Constitution*.[28]

Commander Tyrone G. Martin, USN (Retired), former commanding officer of the U.S. Frigate *Constitution*, has amassed an impressive amount of data pertaining to the frigate's history and the men who served her. When queried, Martin wrote that according to his copy of the H.M. Frigate *Java*'s muster rolls at the time of her defeat by the *Constitution*, John Freeman was a "presst" American from New York who had been a landsman in *Java*'s crew since 22 October 1812.[29] Freeman may have joined the *Constitution* after being freed from the *Java*, but the muster rolls for Old Ironsides during the late months of 1812 no longer exist, and Freeman does not show up on any of the frigate's muster rolls for June 1813 through September 1815. Commander Martin speculated that Freeman might have shipped aboard Old Ironsides, and he may have been one of the 150 *Constitution* seamen who were transferred to Commodore Isaac Chauncey's command on the Great Lakes in April, 1813. A number of Chauncey's men were eventually dispatched to Lake Erie during the summer of 1813, and a John Freeman did serve as an ordinary seaman on board the U.S. Brig

Niagara during the Battle of Lake Erie. The trail appears logical, but vital links are missing, and since John Freeman is a common name, much of the story cannot be verified.

Although pinpointing individual black sailors is virtually impossible, their deeds were acknowledged collectively. The U.S. Navy's ship-to-ship conquests provided a backdrop for black seamen to both showcase their skills and prove their courage to any skeptical white officers and sailors, and victorious commanders readily hailed the fighting qualities of the Navy's black sailors. Captain Isaac Hull, commanding officer of the *Constitution* when she prevailed over the *Guerriere*, later voiced his approbation. Although Hull employed the degrading lexicon of the day, his message was nevertheless clear and undeniable:

> I never had any better fighters than those niggers, they
> stripped to the waist and fought like devils, sir, seeming to
> be utterly insensible to danger and to be possessed with a
> determination to outfight the white sailors.[30]

Sufficient evidence does exist to state that African-American seamen fought in most, and probably all, of the Navy's engagements during the War of 1812. It is unfortunate that most of their deeds have been lost to history. Black sailors, like their white counterparts, were heroes and cowards, fighters and skulkers, hard workers and malingerers. Black sailors endured the same privations, diseases, tedium, back-breaking labor, harsh conditions, cruel discipline, and gut-wrenching fear as their white counterparts. Black sailors suffered the same ghastly wounds and died as horribly as their white counterparts. But unlike their white counterparts, black sailors were subjected to varying degrees of racism and were denied unconstrained liberty and equality because of their color. Black seamen merit tremendous credit for persevering under the millstone of prejudice, for serving their country so capably, and for remaining loyal under such adverse conditions.

Engrossed by the war in Europe, England was nevertheless dismayed by the untimely and humiliating naval reverses it suffered during the early months of the American War of 1812. Still, the loss of a few frigates and brigs proved trifling to the indomitable Royal Navy. Recognizing the fundamental strength of the big American frigates, the Admiralty responded to the threat by first augmenting the North American Station with bigger and stronger ships to blockade American ports harboring warships, and then by implementing a change in strategy. To preclude future defeat and embarrassment—a tremendous hue and cry had been raised against the Royal Navy by the English press—British captains were ordered not to engage the larger class of American frigates without at least a two-to-one advantage. Furthermore, British commanders were instructed that "no 18-pounder frigate was voluntarily to engage one of the 24-pounder frigates of America."[31]

The Admiralty's tough stance yielded immediate results. Less than one year into the war many U.S. Navy warships found themselves bottled up in port by an ever-strengthening British blockade. By mid-1813 squadrons of British warships, similar to latter day hunter-killer groups, lurked about American harbors like packs of hungry wolves anxiously waiting for their prey to bolt from closely-watched warrens. For the remainder of the war, American captains found it exceedingly difficult to break the British chokehold.

One impulsive commander who did challenge the blockade was Captain James Lawrence. An early hero of the war, it was Lawrence who commanded the *Hornet* (18) when it humbled the British *Peacock* (18) on 24 February 1813. Lawrence's victory earned him a promotion to the rank of captain and command of the *Chesapeake*, a powerful 38-gun frigate. Although a formidable vessel, the *Chesapeake* had developed a reputation for being a hard luck ship. Uncharacteristically for a U.S. warship during the War of 1812, she was also an unhappy ship. It was the *Chesapeake*, as previously related, that had ignominiously surrendered to HMS *Leopard* in 1807, a mortifying and disgraceful incident to the rest of the Navy. The vessel had also suffered a protracted string of unexplained accidents and mishaps which had inflicted damage to the ship and injuries to her crew. She had just returned from a long, unproductive cruise, during which her captain had been ill for most of the voyage and only four small prizes were captured. When Lawrence assumed command on 18 May 1813, the *Chesapeake* was shorthanded and many of her crewmen were raw, untrained recruits. Her remaining veteran seamen had not been paid nor had they received prize money, and morale was at rock bottom.[32]

Despite such ominous indicators, Lawrence ill-advisedly sortied on 1 June 1813 to fight what turned out to be the best drilled and most efficient British frigate on the North American Station, HMS *Shannon* (38). Having foolishly violated orders to avoid British warships and prowl instead for merchantmen, Lawrence rashly sailed with a frazzled crew that was undermanned, poorly trained, and near mutiny. The impetuous Lawrence compounded his mistakes by engaging in a chivalrous battle, yielding crucial tactical advantages in order to offer his opponent a fair fight, which turned out to be anything but fair. Well-aimed, rapidly-fired British broadsides cut a bloody swath of destruction, decimating *Chesapeake*'s gundeck and unhinging her crew. Lawrence himself was shot down early in the battle, struck by musket balls in his leg and groin. As he was being carried below, the mortally wounded captain purportedly uttered the now famous phrase, "Don't give up the ship." Nevertheless, the thoroughly demoralized crew of the ravaged *Chesapeake*, many of whom were cowering below deck or intoxicated, or both, did give up the ship. Lawrence lost his life and his vessel in one of the briefest, most deplorable naval defeats in American history; the action lasted only thirteen minutes.[33] In the wake of disaster, the adoring, unsuspecting American public, in one of those ironies of history, idolized the brave Lawrence for his tragic, heroic death.

The frigate's loss was a disaster, and blame had to fall on someone's shoulders. Lawrence, who should have been censured, was instead regaled as a hero, so a scapegoat was needed. William S. Cox, the *Chesapeake*'s youthful third lieutenant, proved a likely candidate. Cox was charged with five specifications, the most serious of which included deserting his post and cowardice. During his court-martial Cox testified that when Lawrence was shot down, the mortally wounded commander ordered Cox to help carry him below to the surgeon. For supposedly following orders, Cox was charged with deserting his battle station. The ill-fated lieutenant was also accused of cowardice for not cutting down American seamen—his own men—who were fleeing below deck when disaster loomed. Eventually exonerated of four of the five specifications, Cox was convicted only of neglect of duty, for which he was ruthlessly cashiered from the service.[34]

Harsh as this punishment may seem, it could not possibly compare with what was meted out to another scapegoat. William Brown was a black seaman who had been hand-picked by Lawrence to blow a bugle in the event the *Chesapeake* was boarded; the bugle call would rally the *Chesapeake*'s crew to repel boarders. A few days before the engagement Lawrence had gathered all hands on the *Chesapeake*'s deck. Using the bugle as an inspirational symbol, he called for a brave volunteer to sound the alarm if and when the crucial time arrived. Not exactly certain of what was transpiring, but nonetheless enamored with the brass instrument, Brown proudly stepped forward and volunteered. Lawrence, overconfident and arrogant, unconscionably failed to ascertain that the hapless seaman did not know how to blow the bugle.[35] Not surprisingly, when the crucial moment arrived the unsuspecting Brown failed to do what was required, for which he was subsequently charged with cowardice and neglect of duty. During his trial Brown's counsel pleaded for mercy, avowing:

> God has made the prisoner too insignificant a being on whom to visit the loss of the *Chesapeake*. If his accidental exertions might have saved the ship, he would not have had the credit of it, nor would he have been entitled to it. And if you decide otherwise, and charge the whole misfortune to one who could barely comprehend his simple duty, other nations will laugh at the little subterfuges to which we resort, and instead of enlarging our naval fame we shall belittle our national character.[36]

Unmoved by the eloquence of Brown's advocate, the court sentenced the seaman to forfeit all pay and to receive 300 lashes with the cat-o'-nine-tails. Reviewing the verdict, President James Madison took pity on the wretched sailor and reduced his punishment to a nonetheless blood-chilling 100 lashes.[37]

In 1952, through the unflagging efforts of a descendent, William S. Cox was absolved of his alleged misdeeds. Legislation was passed and subsequently signed by President Harry S. Truman posthumously restoring Cox to the rank of lieutenant in the U.S. Navy.[38] There have been none to plead for Seaman William Brown.

By the summer of 1813, U.S. commerce raiders were finding it more and more difficult to penetrate the ever-tightening cordon of enemy warships. The harsh example of James Lawrence and the *Chesapeake* served to illustrate just how dangerous and costly it could be to challenge overtly the pernicious British blockade.

4

PRIVATEERS

Craving combat, United States warship captains were reluctant to admit that ships of the U.S. Navy were far too few and precious to waste on glory-seeking, ship-to-ship engagements with the Royal Navy. In fact, ship captains were often instructed to avoid British warships since the loss of even one American warship constituted a severe blow to the fighting capabilities of, and dramatically reduced the efficiency of, the numbers-parched Navy. Even if the frantic and belated shipbuilding program instituted by the Navy managed to cast a few more frigates or even one or two 74-gun ships-of-the-line into the fray, the U.S. Navy simply could not compete should England deploy additional resources across the Atlantic. The Navy's role was multi-faceted, and while victories over enemy ships served as valuable morale boosters, the British Navy's mastery of the oceans would not be diminished by the defeat of an odd frigate, sloop-of-war, or brig.

Brash and eager U.S. Navy captains sought recognition and glory through victory in battle, but it was the mundane business of disrupting British commerce and not high profile ship-to-ship engagements where the Navy was most effective. However, if a U.S. Navy fighting ship declined to engage in battle when there existed a reasonable expectation of success, then the commander of that vessel could anticipate being subjected to justifiable censure by the public and his peers, and quite possibly face charges for cowardice. Good judgment had to be applied when choosing to risk the loss of a precious warship in battle, but the unwritten code of the period seldom permitted running from a fight. Paradoxically, sound judgment also enjoined that the United States could not realistically hope or expect to cripple the awesome British war machine. Even so, if American ships could interdict and impede English commerce, then the furor raised by the British economic community would certainly force the Admiralty to take notice and take action.

Warships were highly effective commerce raiders and it was in this endeavor that the Navy needed to focus, but the oceans were not the sole domain of British and American warships. In addition to the opposing navies, large numbers of private ships also stalked the seas in search of deeply laden merchantmen and prize money. Privateers were sleek, fast, heavily manned vessels bristling with guns, looking for all the world like the predators they were. During a period when warships were too few and overextended with a myriad of duties and responsibilities, owners of private vessels could take up the slack by obtaining a letter of marque, an official government sanction to sink or capture enemy ships. For all intents and purposes, a letter of marque equated to a license for legal piracy.

Despite the publicity privateers received, naval vessels were much more effective at commerce raiding than letters of marque. By comparison, during the War of 1812, U.S. warships captured an average of 7.5 prizes each, while privateers managed to average only 2.5 prizes each. Striking as those figures may appear, it was the ratio of warships to privateers that made the latter such a compelling factor. Fewer than 25 U.S. Navy warships were available to roam the oceans in search of prizes, whereas the number of warranted privateers totaled 526.[39] Although sailors who crewed privateers were skilled, professional mariners, they were still merely amateurs-at-war seeking to fill their purses. A number of factors rendered privateers less effective than U.S. Navy commerce raiders, but sheer numbers alone made them a force with which to contend.

Sailors of African descent often comprised a large percentage of privateer crews, both on British and American letters of marque. On 7 November 1812, an American naval officer at Savannah, Georgia informed the Secretary of the Navy that off the coast of Georgia and South Carolina:

> ...there is now, and has been for a Number of days, a
> British Cutter [similar to a sloop, but having its single mast
> located farther astern] Privateer, Mounting But 8 Guns and
> mand [sic] Chiefly with Blacks about 70 in Number,
> Cruizing [sic] between Savannah and Charleston—and [the
> privateer] has already done a great deal of mischief.[40]

The British privateer *Mars* was gunning for careless American prey off the coast of North Carolina in the fall of 1813. Spotting two small coasters close inshore near New Inlet, the privateer's captain launched two small boats to pursue the unarmed Americans. Straying too close to shore, one of the British small boats struck a sand bar and broached, allowing its 17-man crew to be captured by a group of North Carolina militiamen. Of the 17 British seamen who were taken prisoner, 13 were black sailors.[41]

On 1 January 1813, Nathaniel Shaler, commander of the American privateer *Governor Tompkins*, penned to his agent an account of a deadly duel he survived against a British frigate. Mistaking the warship for a transport, Shaler barely managed to outsail and elude his opponent:

> At 3 P.M. [on 25 December 1812] a sudden squall struck us from the northward, and the ship not having yet received it, before I could get our light sails in, and almost before I could turn round, I was under the guns, (not of a transport) but of a large frigate!...I immediately...commenced a brisk fire from our little battery, but this was returned with woeful interest. Her first broadside killed two men, and wounded six others....The name of one of my poor fellows who was killed ought to be registered on the book of fame, and remembered with reverence as long as bravery is considered a virtue. He was a black man, by the name of John Johnson; a twenty-four-pound shot struck him in the hip, and took away all the lower part of his body. In this state the poor, brave fellow lay on the deck, and several times exclaimed to his shipmates, 'fire away boys, neber haul de color down.' The other [man killed] was also a black man, by the name of John Davis, and [he] was struck in much the same way: he fell near me, and several times requested to be thrown overboard, saying he was only in the way of others. While America has such sailors, she has little to fear from the tyrants of the ocean.[42]

Another engagement involving a letter of marque was both remarkable and unusual in that it was rare for a privateer to engage, not to mention defeat, an enemy warship. Even less frequently did such clashes involve boarding and hand-to-hand fighting. On 5 August 1813, the American privateer *Decatur* (7), home-ported at Charleston, South Carolina, captured H.M. Sloop *Dominica* (14) in a vicious little battle which left three out of every four British crewmen dead or wounded. After exchanging tentative broadsides, the *Decatur* maneuvered astern of the *Dominica* and punched her bowsprit through the Englishman's mainsail. *Decatur*'s captain then called away boarders:

> A terrible scene of slaughter and bloodshed then ensued;
> the men fought with swords, pistols, and small arms....
> Both parties fought with unparalleled vigor and desperate
> courage. The decks were covered with the dead and
> wounded.[43]

Nearly the entire complement of the *Decatur* was composed of black sailors, and the British apparently were not appreciative of the privateersmen's fierce fighting qualities. Charles R. Simpson, a British agent for prisoners in the United States, proclaimed that the American privateer:

> ...with a very large Crew...who amounted in Number I
> believe to be 93 chiefly if not all Blacks. & Mulattoes. and
> in Ferocity and cruelty exceeded by none...and after a most
> desperate Discharge of Musketry succeeded in Boarding
> when a Scene of Cruelty was exhibited which has perhaps
> been never equalled. the Boarders Killing in the most
> merciless manner all the Wounded on the Decks.[44]

The fighting was viewed differently from the American perspective. South Carolina District Judge John Drayton reported to Secretary of State James Monroe that the *Decatur*'s "whole Crew fought nobly: took the Sloop by boarding: and treated the prisoners with the utmost humanity."[45] Later captured by a British frigate, the *Decatur* was the largest privateer to sail from Charleston during the War of 1812.

Sailors of African descent were encountered in every aspect of the naval war, their presence being so common as to seldom elicit special notice or mention. Occasionally a keen observer would record minute details, and a journal maintained by a crewman on one letter of marque relates just how normal it was to encounter black seamen on warships, privateers, and merchantmen. The appropriately named privateer *Yankee* was a 168-ton brig based in Bristol, Rhode Island. Mounting 15 small cannons and quartering a crew of 120 men, *Yankee* completed six successful voyages during the war, capturing 40 prizes. When she set sail for her second cruise on 17 October 1812, *Yankee* berthed an astute and observant young man by the name of Noah Johnson. Johnson's journal is valuable for its attention to detail and its mention of black sailors:

> 6th day. Spoke [to] the American ship *Ariadne* of
> Boston...17 days out. Captain [Bartlett] Holmes informed
> us, that on the 11th instant he was boarded by an officer

from the American frigate *United States*, Commodore
[Stephen] Decatur; that the *Ariadne*'s crew having mutinied
he requested Commodore Decatur to take six of the ring-
leaders on board the frigate, which he did accordingly....
Whilst on board the *Ariadne* our lieutenant observed the
disorderly conduct of her crew, particularly of the cook, a
stout Negro fellow, who not only abused but struck his
captain and mate, and moreover called our bargemen a set
of pirates and villains. On being informed of this circumstance [*Yankee*] Captain [Oliver] Wilson requested permis-
sion of Captain Holmes (which was of course granted) to
punish said Negro as an example to the rest of his crew.
Accordingly Mr. Cuffy was tied to the windlass and each
of the boat's crew as well as the *Ariadne*'s officers, gave
him a dozen [lashes] to teach him his duty and good
manners in [the] future.

47th day. At meridian [noon] continued in chase of the
sail ahead....Found we came up rapidly with the chase,
which appeared to be a privateer built schooner...opened a
brisk cannonade on the starboard side, which the enemy
returned....Observed the enemy's vessel to be on fire....
The scene that now presented itself...was shocking beyond
description. The vessel was still in flames, the quarterdeck
was blown off, the captain was found near the mainmast,
naked, mangled, and burnt in the most dreadful manner,
one of the seamen lay near him bruised and burnt equally
bad; a black man was found dead on the cabin floor and
five others lay around him apparently dying. All these
wounded men were carefully brought on board the *Yankee*,
where they received every possible attention....Dr. Miller
dressed their wounds, but found the captain and several
black seamen in the most dangerous condition....A small
black boy presented a most singular yet distressing appearance. He was literally blown out of his skin. For some
time after he was brought on board we thought he was
white. The anguish and sufferings...must have been inde-
scribably painful and excrutiating [sic]....During the night

the five black seamen died and were thrown overboard....
The blacks whom we found dead were employed in filling
cartridges in the magazine...

53rd day. The day commences with light airs, inclin-
ing to calm. Continued in chase of the sail ahead. At 1
P.M. made out the chase to be a large armed brig, showing
ten [gun]ports on a side with English colours flying at her
main peake....At 1/2 past 1 P.M. the enemy commenced
the action...1/2 past 3 P.M. having approached, under a
most galling fire, within good musket shot of the enemy,
we gave three cheers and opened our whole battery upon
him....20 m[inutes] past 4 P.M. observing that the enemy's
fire became extremely faint...our commander gave orders
to cease firing....Found our prize to be the English letter of
marque brig called the *Andalusia* of Gibraltar...navigated
by 100 men, including 80 free Africans, who assisted at the
great guns or acted as marines....Captain [Anthony Yates]
Kendall was wounded in the leg, the boatswain in the face,
and one seaman in the shoulder, besides several blacks....

61st day. At 10 A.M. discovered [a] brig...under the
guns of Fort Apollonia [near Port Bouet on the Ivory Coast]
at anchor. 1 P.M. piped for volunteers to man the barge
and cut her out....According to...plan at 4 P.M we rounded
to within musket shot of the enemy....In six minutes [we]
were alongside and took possession of the prize. Not a shot
was fired....We find our prize to be the English copper
bottomed brig *Fly* of London, Jonathan Tyderman, master
...navigated by eleven men, besides blacks...of all the
monsters which a seafaring life engenders, the captain of
the *Fly* is the most brutal. Ignorant yet presumptuous,
assuming, without merit, prejudiced, passionate, cowardly,
his person corresponding to his mind, large, rawboned,
harsh features, dark complexion, and speaking with the
uncouth accent of a real cockney. He disgusted every
officer on board the *Yankee* by his boasting swaggering
conduct. He even had the daring presumption to introduce
his black mistress into our cabin. No one except Captain

Wilson, whose forbearance is truly astonishing, could have overlooked so gross a violation of decorum.

72d day. Spoke [to] the little Portuguese schooner or boat (14 tons burthen) called the *Antonia de Santa Rosa de Lima*...5 days out from St. Thomas bound to Prince's Island with 27 slaves on board and manned by 9 black seamen. This black navigator had lost himself and was steering N.W. instead of E. by S., which was his true course.[46]

People of color from every imaginable country crewed ocean-going vessels. Among the many ships that became prizes of the *Yankee* was an East Indiaman named the *General Wellesley*:

The East India ship *General Wellesley*, 16 guns, 86 men, 500 tons...with a valuable cargo of 18,000 bars of iron... outward bound, namely, for Calcutta...was captured by the privateer *Yankee*, after a running fight. She was manned [with a prize crew] and ordered to proceed to Charleston, but unfortunately, while entering that port, she was lost on the bar. Her original crew consisted of 36 Englishmen, [and] 50 Lascars [sailors and soldiers from the East Indies], all of whom were drowned, but seven.[47]

The *Yankee* was atypical in that her cruises were so successful. Privateering involved tremendous risks and by extension incurred tremendous profits for both owners and crews. Only 207 of the officially sanctioned 526 privateers captured one or more prizes, meaning that more than 60% of all letters of marque returned empty handed. While many achieved notoriety, few attained notable success, and a considerable number of privateers themselves were destroyed or became prizes to marauding British warships.[48]

One such privateer was the 9-gun *General Armstrong*. Commanded by Samuel C. Reid, the *General Armstrong* floated at anchor at Fayal harbor in the Azores on 26 September 1814 when HMS *Plantagenet* (74), *Rota* (38) and *Carnation* (18) loomed on the horizon. Deciding to cut out the pesky privateer, the British assembled 180 men from the *Plantagenet* and *Rota* and crammed them into seven smallboats. Splitting their attack force, the boarders attempted to overwhelm the *General Armstrong* at both bow and stern, but the American privateer refused to yield pliantly and a spirited and ruthless defense ensued. The heavily-armed boarders were fended off at the privateer's stern, but the determined British managed to gain a foothold over the little schooner's bow. In furious and merciless hand-to-hand fighting, all three of *General Armstrong*'s lieutenants and many of her forward division sailors were cut down. The boarding party was on the verge of over-powering the defenders when Reid, after repelling the first attack at the *General Armstrong*'s stern, counterattacked with his aft division and bloodily repelled the attackers. Their gallant effort cost the British 34 killed and 86 wounded. A half-hearted attack by *Carnation* the next day was also rebuf-fed, but the privateer's position, blockaded by overwhelming numbers with no hope for escape, was clearly hopeless. Having made his defiant gesture, Reid abandoned and scuttled his truculent little ship.

Since the British blockade focused almost exclusively on those ports harboring American naval warships, swarms of privateers were able to sail from less conspicuous anchorages up and down the east and gulf coasts. The fast, streamlined letters of marque also faced fewer difficulties slipping past enemy naval pickets at larger ports. On the other hand, U.S. Navy warships were under constant scrutiny. Few escaped to harass English merchant shipping, and as the months passed and the British blockade grew stronger, it became increasingly more difficult to evade the burgeoning oaken wall of British ships. United States losses mounted as additional British vessels were dispatched to bolster the North American Station. By mid-1813, the Royal Navy's intrinsic sovereignty was manifesting itself along the east and gulf coasts, where the pitifully few U.S. frigates and their smaller consorts huddled forlornly in their harbors, helpless prisoners caged in watery jails. With the eastern and southern ports corked, the focus of naval operations shifted to the Great Lakes.

5

THE INLAND SEAS

During the War of 1812, United States strategy hinged upon the annexation of Canada. As a result, the northern lakes arena witnessed the hardest and bloodiest fighting of the war. If the waterways comprising much of the border between the United States and British Canada could be controlled by the U.S. Navy, American forces would have ready made avenues for invasion attempts. Conversely, the lakes and rivers could just as easily serve as a back door for the enemy—vulnerable passageways allowing the British to slash through to the soft underbelly of the United States. Whoever wielded power on the lakes possessed a powerful strategic and tactical advantage.

Early in the war, the lack of United States military resources in the Great Lakes region caused the American frontier to be perilously undefended. The British, unhindered by the U.S. Navy, used the lakes as transportation routes for troops and supplies during the latter half of 1812. But leaders in Washington, D.C. recognized that warships were required to form a protective shield along the country's northern and northwestern border, and by late 1812 a furious ship-building program had been inaugurated. By the summer of 1813, through new construction and the conversion of purchased merchant vessels, U.S. naval flotillas were cruising Lakes Erie, Ontario, and Champlain, and, like their counterparts on the Atlantic, warships on the lakes berthed large numbers of African-American seamen.

For the most part, general references about black seamen on the lakes are scarce. Specific citations concerning individuals are even more rare, such as the grim diary entry recorded by Surgeon's Mate Usher Parsons at the Black Rock Naval Station on 7 April 1813: "James Smith a coloured man died today."[49] However, the role of black seamen on the lakes served as the focal point of a bitter controversy which erupted during the summer of 1813 between the overall Great Lakes commander and his subordinate on Lake Erie.

AMONGST MY BEST MEN

In March of 1813, Master Commandant Oliver Hazard Perry was assigned by Commodore Isaac Chauncey to finalize construction and take command of the Lake Erie flotilla, based at Erie, Pennsylvania. By mid-July, the 11 vessels comprising Perry's squadron were built, fitted out, and ready to sail, save for one major stumbling block. Needing approximately 700 men to man his ships, Perry could muster only 120 men fit for duty.[50] Due to limited resources at Erie, Perry was forced to depend upon his superior for reinforcements. The majority of naval resources destined for the lakes were channelled through Sackets Harbor, New York, the Lake Ontario headquarters for the Great Lakes Command, and Chauncey, as the overall commander of Great Lakes naval operations, was obligated to responsibly allocate those resources. On several different occasions the Lake Erie commodore communicated with Chauncey to request reinforcements, but without success. Uncertain why Chauncey was unresponsive to his queries and willing to pursue whatever methods necessary to man his ships, Perry bypassed his immediate superior and communicated his concerns directly to the Secretary of the Navy. When Chauncey discovered that Perry went over his head, an acrimonious correspondence was initiated between the principals. Chauncey felt, not without some justification, that Perry wished to rid himself of his superior's authority and gain an independent command.

The Lake Erie commodore's flagrant breach of military etiquette infuriated Chauncey, but his impolitic ploy nevertheless worked. Pressure from sources in Washington, D.C. and elsewhere ruptured the logjam of seamen, prompting Chauncey to dispatch from Sackets Harbor to Lake Erie two drafts of sailors comprising nearly 150 men. Although desperate for seamen, Perry was still less than delighted with the quality of his reinforcements. Giving little thought to his actions, Perry artlessly penned to Chauncey an indictment that asserted:

> The men that came...are a motley set, blacks, Soldiers, and boys, I cannot think that you saw them after they were selected. I am however, pleased to see anything in the shape of a man.[51]

As might be expected, the Great Lakes commander was "mortified" when he discovered that Perry ignored the chain of command and complained directly to the Navy Department. Already piqued by his subordinate's blunder, the blatant impudence of Perry's latest grievance about the

36

reinforcements caused an incensed Chauncey to retort:

> I regret that you are not pleased with the men sent you...
> for to my knowledge a part of them are not surpassed by
> any seamen we have on the fleet, and I have yet to learn
> that the Colour of the skin, or cut and trimmings of the
> coat, can effect a man's qualifications or usefulness. I have
> nearly 50 Blacks on board of this Ship [the *General Pike*],
> and many of them are amongst my best men....[52]

Most of Chauncey's statement was undoubtedly true, but Perry was not diverted by Chauncey's seeming artifice, and he once again communicated directly with Navy Secretary Jones. Referring to the hodgepodge of soldiers and sailors that Chauncey forwarded to Lake Erie, Perry asserted, "...they may sir, be as good as are on the other Lake, but if so, that squadron must be poorly manned indeed."[53]

This unseemly interchange has occasionally been used to insinuate that Chauncey was a progressive and Perry a bigot. Chauncey may have been truly liberal-minded, but labeling Perry as racially biased based on this one exchange is rash. Perry's words and actions must be placed in context with his own frustration and anxiety, fostered by the immediacy of the strategic situation on Lake Erie. British incursions into northwest Ohio in late April, and again in late July of 1813, generated urgent pleas for assistance from William Henry Harrison's beleaguered army, heightening Perry's distress and compelling him to initiate unorthodox measures to man his flotilla in order to assist the harried American ground forces. The circumstances do not excuse Perry's imprudence or impetuousness, but they may help to explain his behavior.

Although he had reason to be nettled, much of the grief that came Perry's way was self-inflicted. Perry was plagued with an impulsive personality and throughout the course of his dispute with Chauncey—and for that matter during most of his career—he seemed self-absorbed and oblivious to everything other than his own problems. Among other faults, Oliver Hazard Perry exercised more than a modicum of myopia in dealing with his superiors, disregard for Chauncey's situation on the lower lake, and ill-considered use of the vernacular when referring to the men from Lake Ontario as "blacks, Soldiers, and boys."

Some fault for the controversy must also attach itself to Chauncey, either directly or indirectly. The fact that none of the 50 black sailors from

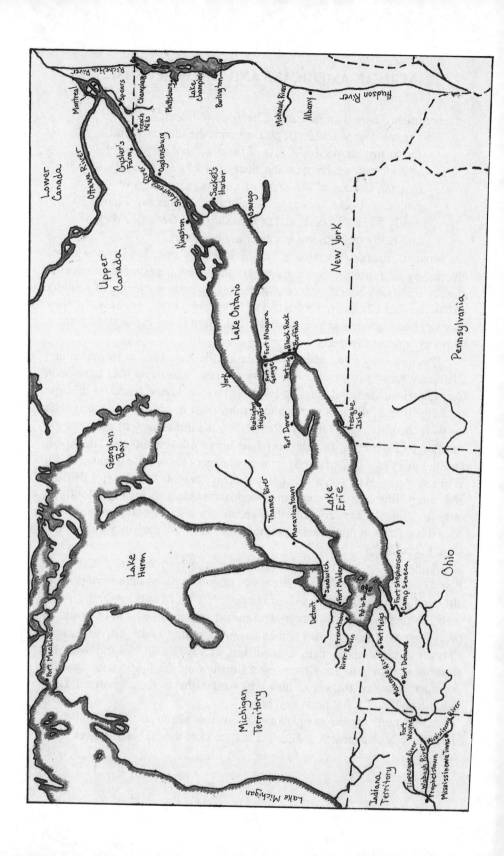

the *General Pike* were sent to Lake Erie—seamen who Chauncey described as "amongst my best men"—is evidence of the Lake Ontario commodore's desire to retain the veteran seamen for his own ships. More than likely, the task of selecting men for transfer to Lake Erie was delegated by Chauncey, and even if the individual designated for that chore did not receive specific instructions, a junior officer was not about to incur the wrath of his superior by arbitrarily consigning the Lake Ontario squadron's most highly trained and disciplined sailors to another command. Instead, human nature motivated the selecting officer to rid Chauncey's flotilla of its undesirable elements: the sick, the least trained, and those who experienced disciplinary problems.

There can be no doubt that a number of African-American seamen were among the men transferred from Lake Ontario to Lake Erie, but it was not "the Colour of the skin" that so concerned and discouraged Perry. Since black seamen had constituted a significant percentage of the naval rank and file since the institution of the U.S. Navy in 1794, and since Perry was a 13-year veteran of the Navy, he could not have been surprised that black sailors were included among the drafts of men sent from Lake Ontario. In fact, a number of black seamen were among the 150 men who not only volunteered but were welcomed by Perry to accompany him from his previous command at Newport, Rhode Island when he transferred to the lakes.

What the Lake Erie commodore actually deplored about the Lake Ontario men was the lack of training, poor discipline, and ill-health of all the sailors, not just the black seamen. Perry was not the only individual at the Lake Erie Naval Station who noted the poor condition of the newly arrived men. When writing about the health of the crewmen sent from Lake Ontario, Sailing Master William Taylor lamented that many "were barely able to assist themselves,"[54] while Purser Samuel Hambleton complained, "Our force consisted principally of the refuse of Commodore Chauncey's fleet...."[55]

Despite the deficiencies of his reinforcements, Perry had no choice but to accept their services, white and black, and their efforts more than sufficed. On 10 September 1813, Perry won a decisive victory, capturing Commander Robert Heriott Barclay's six-ship British Lake Erie squadron in a frenzied three-and-a-half hour battle near Put-in-Bay, Ohio. But the victory did not come easily. Two hours of incessant broadsides transformed Perry's stately flagship, the 20-gun brig *Lawrence*, into a blasted hulk with nearly 80% casualties. Just when defeat seemed inevitable, Perry hauled down his battle flag, upon which were emblazoned James Lawrence's dying words—Dont [sic] Give Up The Ship—and transferred to the U.S. Brig *Niagara*, *Lawrence's* sistership. With a fresh 20-gun brig under his feet, Perry broke the chaotic British battle line, hurled broadsides from *Niagara's* larboard and starboard sides, and forced the entire enemy squadron to capitulate. Perry's victory, in addition to sweeping the British from Lake Erie, conclusively altered the balance of power in the Old Northwest.

Whatever his feelings towards his African-American crewmen, Perry nevertheless praised his victorious black seamen to Chauncey, who in turn wrote:

> Perry speaks highly of the bravery and good conduct of the negroes, who formed a considerable part of his crew. 'They seemed to be absolutely insensible to danger. When Captain Barclay came on board the *Niagara*, and beheld the sickly and partly-colored beings around him, an expression of chagrin escaped him at having been conquered by such men'[56]

Little information has passed into history pertaining to the black sailors who fought with Perry, and few have been identified. Jesse Williams was an ordinary seaman on the flagship *Lawrence*, where he was wounded in action. Before being sent to Lake Erie, Williams served on the U.S. Frigate *Constitution,* where, as the 1st sponger (assigned to "sponge" the gun tube to extinguish sparks before loading) on number 3 long gun, he participated in Old Ironsides' victory over HMS *Java* on 29 December 1812. In 1820, while a resident of Philadelphia, Williams was awarded a silver medal from the State of Pennsylvania for his role in the battle.[57] Also wounded on the *Lawrence* was Newport Hazard, one of the seagoing Hazard family from Newport, Rhode Island. Hazard served under Perry at the Newport Naval Station and he was one of 150 volunteers from the Newport station to accompany Perry to the lakes.[58] Anthony Williams, a native of Salem, Massachusetts, fought on board the schooner *Somers*. Williams moved to Meadville, Pennsylvania after the war, where he died in either 1833 or 1834.[59] Cyrus Tiffany may be the best known black seaman from the Lake Erie fleet because of his close personal association with Perry. Tiffany, variously recorded as a seaman and a musician, also served with Perry at Newport. Perry apparently took a personal interest in Tiffany's well being. According to one account:

When the engagement approached, the Commodore, in as far as he could to put [Tiffany] out of harms way, placed him on the berth deck [of the *Lawrence*] with a musket & bayonet, with orders to charge upon any one attempting to skulk below. Shortly after the battle began the men fell so thick & fast that the Commodore observed the hatchway crowded with wounded, where passage below seemed to be obstructed. On going there he found them charged upon by 'old Tiffany,' who swore they were a set of skulkers, and should not come below....In the [U.S. Frigate] *Java* he sometimes took great liberties, which the Commodore bore in the greatest good humor, & was much incensed on one occasion when a Lieutenant had punished him with a ropes end [a thickly knotted rope's end, called a starter, was used by boatswain's mates to galvanize shirkers]. He was a 'hanger on' to the Commodore to the day of his death, who always took the most humane care of him.[60]

In some instances, references relating to individuals on board the Lake Erie flotilla are peripheral or obscure, making it difficult to ascertain their race. On the prize money list can be found the name of Jack Russell, a ship's boy who served on board the U.S. Brig *Lawrence*. Russell's prize money was paid to "George Mason, his master," but it is uncertain whether Russell was a slave or an indentured or apprenticed white boy.[61] Isaac Hardy was an ordinary seaman killed in action on board the U.S. Brig *Niagara*. Hardy's wife later applied for a widow's pension from the government. To demonstrate her relationship to Hardy she was required to provide proof of marriage, and the marriage certificate for Isaac and Diane Hardy was signed by John Gloucester, Pastor of the First Presbyterian African Congregation in Philadelphia. Diane Hardy also retained the same lawyer as Jesse Williams when she requested her husband's silver medal from the State of Pennsylvania.[62] The name of Jesse Walls, or Wall, not scribed on the prize money list or any other official source, can be found in three separate accounts of the dedication of the Oliver Hazard Perry statue in Cleveland, Ohio in 1860, and in other works. Benjamin Lossing, author of the comprehensive *Pictorial Field-Book Of The War Of 1812*, wrote that Wall was a colored man who was a fifer on board the brig *Niagara*. Wall was about 74 years of age when he attended the 1860 event.[63]

AMONGST MY BEST MEN

Another confusing chapter of the Lake Erie story is that of the African-Americans who, like Jesse Wall, claimed to have fought in the Battle of Lake Erie, but whose names do not appear on the list of men who served on board the fleet. Muster rolls for the Lake Erie Naval Station during the period in question have not been found, so the most referred to source for determining the names of Battle of Lake Erie participants is Samuel Hambleton's prize list. Hambleton was the U.S. fleet purser who, in 1814, was detailed to compile a list of participants so that prize money appropriated by Congress could be accurately disbursed. Yet Hambleton's list is not complete; some names were omitted and numerous other errors were made.

Years later, a number of survivors and widows claims were filed at the pension office on the basis that their spouses fought at the Battle of Lake Erie. At least three of these claims emanate from African-American families. Mary Brown, wife of Robert Brown [or Bronen] filed a widow's pension application after her husband passed away. From Bedford, Pennsylvania, Brown apparently served in the Army—possibly the militia —supposedly fought on board the fleet, was wounded in action, and was discharged because of his wounds. He died in Bedford on 18 January 1865. Mary Brown's pension application was granted and she received $12.00 per month until her death in Bedford on 4 December 1895.[64] Elizabeth Brown, wife of James Brown, filed a claim in 1871. She attested that her husband, who was originally from Somerset, Pennsylvania, where they were married in April of 1812, served with Perry in the battle. After the war, James and Elizabeth Brown made their home at Erie, Pennsylvania, where James died in August 1857. The claim was rejected because Elizabeth Brown had lost her marriage certificate and could not prove her relationship to James Brown.[65] Margaret Boone filed a similar pension application upon the death of her husband. Brown Boone was a native of Hartford County, North Carolina, and he reportedly enlisted in the North Carolina Militia in August of 1812. At that time he was 22 years old, 5'9", and a farmer by occupation. He was sent to Norfolk, Virginia and, according to the pension application, somehow ended up on the Lake Erie fleet. Brown Boone died in Franklin County, Ohio on 9 September 1843. Margaret Boone, who was 78 when she filed her application in June of 1878, could remember no clarifying details. Her claim was denied because no official corroborating information could be found.[66]

Then there is the case of Hannibal Collins. The Fall, 1994 issue of

Newport History, the bulletin of the Newport, Rhode Island Historical Society, proclaims that Collins was a freed slave from Newport, that he fought with Perry on Lake Erie, and that he was among the smallboat crew that rowed Perry from the *Lawrence* to the *Niagara* when the commodore transferred his flag at the crucial point of the battle. Yet the name of Hannibal Collins is not found on either Samuel Hambleton's prize list or the list of men who accompanied Perry from Newport to the lakes.[67]

Any or all of these men may have served with the American squadron on Lake Erie, and if they did, it is not known why their names were omitted from Samuel Hambleton's prize list. Since Hambleton also excluded the names of more than fifteen white participants, there seems to have been no contrived effort to discriminate against black seamen. It seems likely that Hambleton simply did not possess detailed muster rolls or other official information necessary to compile a comprehensive list.

Since there is no supporting documentation, it can only be estimated that between 10 to 20% of the sailors on board the Lake Erie squadron were African-Americans. This estimate does not represent the total fleet complement since roughly 40% of the men who served on Perry's fleet were not sailors, but soldiers and marines. In other words, of the roughly 550 or so men who served with the flotilla, about 200 should be deducted before the percentage is calculated. Even the 10 to 20% figure might be called into question. In 1862, one of the Lake Erie squadron's surgeons, Doctor Usher Parsons, recalled:

> In 1814 [approximately one year after the Battle of Lake Erie], our fleet sailed to the upper Lakes to co-operate with Colonel [George] Croghan [in an attempt to recapture Fort] Mackinac. About one in ten or twelve of the crews were blacks.[68]

At the time, Parsons was responding to a specific inquiry, and he obviously estimated his figure. It must also be remembered that nearly 50 years had passed to cloud his memory. Although the exact numbers probably will never be known, it is an indisputable fact that African-Americans did fight on board the United States flotilla during the Battle of Lake Erie, and they served with courage and distinction.

Unfortunately for the United States, operations on Lake Ontario did not experience the same success as those on Lake Erie. Commodore Isaac Chauncey and his British rival, Captain Sir James Lucas Yeo, lapsed into a counter-productive shipbuilding superiority contest; neither would risk their squadron before attaining a decided numbers advantage. Yeo's actions might be viewed as less ineffective than Chauncey's since the British commander was attuned to Great Britain's official strategy of defending and holding British North American possessions. Chauncey had the greater imperative to be aggressive because U.S. strategy was offensive instead of defensive.

The naval war on Lake Ontario was characterized by maneuver, with the opposing fleets constantly dodging and shifting about to gain the upper hand. Rather than a single decisive battle, numerous small engagements were fought at little known places with names like York, Fort George, False Duck Islands, the Gennessee, the Niagara River, and the "Burlington Races." In these less than strategically significant actions, poor management by both commanders caused the loss of more vessels than did any action on the part of an enemy.

Black seamen were spread throughout the Lake Ontario flotilla, but, as in every other theater of operations in the war, there is a dearth of detail concerning their efforts. Of the 14 vessels comprising Chauncey's squadron during the summer of 1813, sources do provide information pertaining to at least two. The *General Pike* was a small frigate mounting 28 guns and berthing nearly 300 sailors. If Chauncey's previously quoted statement is accurate, then 50 black seamen were quartered on the *General Pike*—17% of the ship's complement, exluding U.S. Marines.

The *Scourge* was one of eleven smaller gunboats attached to the Lake Ontario flotilla. In the pre-dawn hours of 8 August 1813, Chauncey's squadron, hove-to off Twelve Mile Creek, was caught unawares by a sudden and severe squall accompanied by gale force winds. The *Scourge* and another unlucky gunboat broached, guns and equipment broke loose, and both vessels capsized and foundered in 300 feet of water. Of 32 *Scourge* crewmen, all but eight perished.[69]

One *Scourge* survivor's exploits were later made famous by the James Fenimore Cooper work, *Ned Myers; or, A Life Before The Mast.* Myers was an old salt with service on several ships under his belt. When assigned to the *Scourge* in 1813 he was appointed captain of the forecastle and served as gun captain of a small 6-pounder cannon. "My gun crew were five negroes" recounted Myers, and "The gun was called the Black Joke."[70] Myers puckishly referred to his gun crew as the "Black Jokers." The

AFRICAN-AMERICANS AND THE WAR OF 1812

Scourge disaster was related in detail by Myers, and his memoir mentions three black crewmen in addition to his five-man gun crew. Even if these eight men were the only black sailors of the *Scourge*'s complement, which is doubtful, they would still constitute 25% of the total ship's crew. In a poignant footnote to the incident Myers chronicled, "All my Black Jokers were drowned, and nothing remained of the craft and people with which and whom I had been associated all summer."[71]

Black crewmen were also in evidence on board British and Canadian ships on the Great Lakes, an area that still requires research. British ships on the oceans berthed as many and possibly more black sailors than U.S. ships; however, fewer British seamen served on the Great Lakes since many lake vessels were crewed by Canadians. One such Lake Ontario crewman was a black seaman by the name of James Long, who became a prisoner of war when the small merchant vessel *Elizabeth* was captured by the Americans on 11 November 1812. Imprisoned in the United States, Long, either by escape or by exchange, made his way back to York, Upper Canada, by 1813.[72]

By the end of 1813, operations on Lake Ontario slumbered in stalemate, and while Perry's victory on Lake Erie buttressed American morale and furnished ammunition for the U.S. peace commissioners at Ghent, Belgium, little tangible impact was felt in other theaters of operation. Yet the Great Lakes were not the only inland seas to experience the horrors of naval warfare. Another fresh water lake in upstate New York was to witness the only other fleet action fought during the War of 1812.

Napoleon's abdication in 1814 led to a temporary cessation of hostilities in Europe, which released large numbers of British troops for service across the Atlantic Ocean. Many of the Duke of Wellington's best regiments were shipped to Canada. In late August of 1814, General Sir George Prevost, Governor General of Canada, crossed the St. Lawrence River and marched up Lake Champlain with more than 11,000 battle-hardened British veterans. Prevost's army was poised to brush aside the ill-trained and heavily outnumbered Americans and strike at the heart of the United States: the Hudson Valley and New York City. A small flotilla of warships and galley gunboats, commanded by Captain George Downie, rendezvoused with Prevost in the lower reaches of Lake Champlain. Prevost's plan called for a coordinated assault at Plattsburg, New York: the British Army would overwhelm U.S. defenses arrayed along the south bank of the Saranac River while Downie would decimate the American naval force. If Downie could neutralize his adversary's flotilla, then the entire American line would be exposed to a crippling enfilade fire from the British squadron's heavy guns, thereby compelling the U.S. units to withdraw.

Awaiting Downie's ships at Plattsburg Bay was an American squadron commanded by Master Commandant Thomas Macdonough. Because Macdonough's ships anchored the right flank of the Army's Saranac River line, the commodore chose to fight utilizing a static defense, an unusual tactic for a flotilla of warships. Consequently, Macdonough devoted considerable thought to his flotilla's alignment inside the bay. Plattsburg Bay is formed by Cumberland Head, a narrow protrusion of land jutting from Lake Champlain's west bank and curving gently in a south-southeasterly direction. The bay itself runs in a nearly direct north-south line. Almost in the center of the bay's mouth and bisecting the harbor entrance lay Crab Island. By anchoring his four larger vessels in a line perpendicular to Cumberland Head, the commodore astutely blocked the center of the main channel between the headland and Crab Island. Macdonough's ten galley gunboats were placed in a supporting position inside his cordon of larger vessels. The American commodore's shrewd tactics compelled his adversary to round Cumberland Head from the north and then beat upwind into the bay, all the while exposed to the broadsides of Macdonough's anchored ships.

Early in the morning of 11 September 1814, Downie cleared Cumberland Head and tacked into Plattsburg Bay. Displaying superior seamanship and discipline, Downie, under fire, maneuvered his ships into position opposite the Americans, anchored, and opened fire. Commencing the battle for the British was a devastating double-shotted broadside fired from 16 long 24-pounders on the *Confiance*, Downie's flagship. Wood splinters and British iron engulfed the *Saratoga*, Macdonough's flagship, cutting down at least 40 American crewmen. Responding in kind moments later, an American broadside killed Downie when a heavy shot dismounted a British gun; the heavy cannon barrel struck Downie squarely in his mid-section. But the commodore's death failed to stop his unswerving crews from hurling repeated broadsides into the equally hard-fighting Americans. British shot shredded the American flagship and Macdonough was twice flung violently to the *Saratoga*'s deck, though he was not seriously injured either time. One by one the American cannons were silenced by the accurate British gunners, until every gun on the flagship's engaged side was disabled. Amazingly, as if prescient, Macdonough had rigged a spring line on *Saratoga*'s anchor cable, and now, in the furor of battle, his seamen heaved on the ship's capstan bars and slowly pivoted the flagship completely about, bringing *Saratoga*'s larboard [left side] guns to bear. Unable to match Macdonough's maneuver, the *Confiance* was inundated by fresh broadsides and forced to strike her colors. It was not long before the *Linnet*, *Finch*, and *Chubb* followed suit, although the British galley gunboats did manage to slip away. In the two-and-a-half hour engagement, Thomas Macdonough had won what was arguably the most decisive victory of the War of 1812 for the United States.

The value of Macdonough's victory became evident that same day. Despite losing his fleet, British General Prevost's army still outnumbered the American infantry by nearly four to one, but Macdonough's success so unnerved the hesitant British leader that he made only a perfunctory attack on Plattsburg before deciding to retreat, thus ending one of the most formidable British threats of the war.

As on Lakes Erie and Ontario, a large number of black sailors crewed the Lake Champlain squadron. One of Macdonough's sailors was a West Indian named Peter Joe, who had previously served as a gun crewman on board the 44-gun frigate *President*.[73] Another, a man known simply as Cookie, was killed while manning a gun on board the flagship *Saratoga*.[74] Seaman John Day fought on the galley gunboat *Viper* and later served with the U.S. Mediterranean squadron in 1816.[75] Also with Macdonough was Seaman Charles Black, a Pennsylvanian whose father fought at Bunker Hill. Black reportedly served on an English vessel before the war, was later exchanged, and subsequently joined the U.S. Navy.[76]

A large percentage of the men who comprised the Lake Erie, Lake Ontario, and Lake Champlain flotilla crews were not sailors but soldiers. A shortage of manpower among the various lake squadrons was a never-ending concern. One method of relieving the shortage was to seek volunteers from Army units serving in the vicinity. On the Lake Erie flotilla, soldiers comprised approximately 40% of the crews, though few black soldiers served with William Henry Harrison's army in the summer of 1813. But by 1814 black recruits were more commonly accepted into the Army's ranks, and one of Macdonough's black crewmen on Lake Champlain was Cato Williams, a private from the 11th U.S. Infantry Regiment.[77]

The Battle of Lake Champlain put an end to the final British invasion of the United States via the northern frontier, saving numerous northeastern manufacturing centers and port cities from possible capture and destruction. However, the peril to the east coast was far from over. Since the Royal Navy's illustrious fighting squadrons were no longer needed to blockade Europe, many of the veteran ships were dispatched across the Atlantic Ocean to join the growing British effort to punish the unruly Americans.

6

THE BLUE WATER NAVY:
1813-1815

Following the *Chesapeake*'s loss on 1 June 1813, the U.S. Navy found it increasingly more difficult to conduct the war at sea. The Admiralty continued to reinforce its western Atlantic Ocean naval stations, strengthening the American blockade to the point where U.S. warships faced great hazards simply clearing their home ports. Some never made it. The U.S. Frigate *Constellation* (38), having set sail from the Gosport Navy Yard at Norfolk, Virginia in early January 1813, was passing through Hampton Roads en route to the Atlantic when a powerful British squadron rounded Cape Henry and entered the Chesapeake Bay. Hurriedly kedged (move a ship by dropping the anchor ahead of the vessel and then heaving on the windlass to move forward) up the Elizabeth River, *Constellation* was barely saved from capture.

Thwarted of their chance to destroy one of the detested American frigates, the British squadron proceeded to raid villages and towns up and down the Chesapeake and Delaware Bays. Despite having rendered the American frigate *hors de combat*, the specter of the *Constellation* so worried the British that in mid-April Admiral Sir John Borlase Warren returned to the Chesapeake Bay's mouth with the intention of capturing Norfolk and the blockaded frigate at the same time. On the morning of 21 June 1813, Admiral Warren landed 2,500 men on the Virginia shoreline a little to the north of Craney Island, the American stronghold that guarded the entrance to the Elizabeth River and the Gosport Navy Yard. After a short march to the south, the landing force effectively blocked the now isolated island from mainland support. Warren then dispatched 50 barges carrying 1,500 men from his fleet to overrun Craney Island.

Tiny Craney Island held a small earthwork fortification supporting batteries of light and heavy artillery. Crammed with about 2,500 mostly inexperienced militiamen, the garrison was augmented by a contingent of *Constellation* crewmen who manned some of the heavy artillery pieces. The British assault force, completely exposed on the open water, was given no opportunity to gather momentum. Craney Island's artillery, firing grape and canister shot, churned the Chesapeake Bay waters into a bloody froth, felling about 200 of the attackers before the British barges pulled back. Contributing significantly to the British defeat were Craney Island's stout earthworks, mostly dug and erected by Virginia slaves. Included among the workers was a long-time Virginia resident known simply as Pomp, whose wife managed to purchase the elderly slave's freedom nearly 50 years later in order to allow him to die a free man.[78]

The British failed to capture *Constellation*, but she remained blockaded for the remainder of the war, and the frigate's predicament seemed to mirror that of the entire U.S. Navy in 1813. Warships that did manage to evade the blockade were hounded by the enemy, making any success problematic. In June 1813, the U.S. Brig *Argus* (16) sidled past the port of New York blockade and roamed freely for two months, racking up 21 prizes, many of them along the coast of England itself. Causing great consternation, *Argus* made a considerable impact on commerce in the British Isles until she encountered H.M. Brig *Pelican* (18) at dawn on 14 August off the western tip of Wales near St. David's Head. *Argus* Captain William Allen probably could have escaped his larger and more heavily armed opponent and continued with his highly successful commerce raiding mission. But victory in battle against the enemy was a sure road to peer esteem, public adulation, and early promotion. Besides, any captain worth his salt simply did not run from an enemy, whether it was the right thing to do or not. Four minutes into the action Captain Allen lost his leg to a British cannonball. Bearing unimaginable pain, the unflinching Allen refused to be carried below, retaining command until loss of blood caused him to faint. After 45 minutes, pummeled into a veritable wreck, *Argus* struck her colors. Captain Allen did not survive.

Loss of the *Argus* was avenged, though not offset, when the U.S. Brig *Enterprise* (16) throttled H.M. Brig *Boxer* (14) off Penguin Point, Maine on 5 September 1813, although even victory was beginning to prove bitter and hollow. Another valuable commander was lost to the U.S. Navy when *Enterprise*'s senior officer, Lieutenant William Burrows, was mortally wounded. *Enterprise* herself experienced a similar fate. The brig was so cut up that after limping back to the Charlestown Navy Yard in Boston, she was fit only for conversion to a guard ship.

Continued give and take heralded the early months of 1814. In spite of constant enemy pressure, U.S. warships occasionally contrived to escape the British tormentors during a pitch black night when a storm would blow the blockaders out of position, or when captains of blockading vessels became frustrated and temporarily abandoned their stations. American seagoing raiders inspired dread among English merchantmen and incurred the Admiralty's wrath, yet the marauders could not forever avoid the ocean-wide net cast for them. British squadrons and lone warships scoured the Atlantic, eager for the glimpse of an American sail.

As earlier related, black seamen sailed on each and every U.S. Navy vessel that put to sea. Free men of color were more than willing to serve their country, and many felt that they should be allotted greater roles and responsibilities. One such patriotic individual was Augustus Thomas. On 29 January 1814, while a resident of New Haven, Connecticut, Thomas addressed a plea to the Secretary of the Navy:

> sir [sic] although i [sic] am a man of colour i [sic] have taken the boldness upon myself to address your honour this letter that i [sic] have a little ambitious spirit for a small navy to [be] compose[d] of free men of colour of the united states [sic] wishing that the government would authorise [sic] and give unto the free blacks a certain number of vessels of war to be maned [sic] and officered with thare [sic] own colour and that they should be station [sic] at any fronts or front to repel a [sic] invading enemy and that they shall serve during the war or sooner discharged and be under the marshal laws of the union i [sic] see that the united states [sic] have black armies and i [sic] think they aught [sic] to have a black navy to display thare [sic] talents by water as well as land perhaps [sic] sir your honour may think that my request is not worthy [of] your honours notice but i [sic] think it is the duty of every man to stand in defence [sic] of [his] country wether [sic] black or white sir [sic] if your honour see [sic] fit to notice this letter i shall be verry [sic] happy to receive an answer[79]

Thomas's suggestion was not acted upon. No United States Navy ships put to sea with all black crews, and no black officers served in the Navy during the War of 1812. But the U.S. Navy did recognize, if somewhat reluctantly, that its warships would be better served with black seamen than without them, and, as previously noted, between 15 to 20% of all Navy crews were composed of black sailors. The individual and collective courage of both black and white seamen for the most part went unrecorded by those who filed official reports of great victories and grim defeats. Since the names and valorous deeds of those stalwart black and white seamen are little remembered, history can recount only the names and tales of the ships on which they served.

On 1 January 1814, the *Constitution* (44) again put to sea. Six weeks later, on 14 February, she effortlessly nabbed the *Pictou*, a 14-gun British schooner. But overall, the famous frigate's cruise proved relatively unproductive. After snaring only a few small prizes, Old Ironsides returned to port, nearly being trapped herself by two British frigates. Then, on 28 March, the U.S. Navy suffered a severe blow when the remarkable cruise of the U.S. Frigate *Essex* (32) was terminated off Valparaiso, Chile.

Irrefutably one of America's premier commerce raiders, the *Essex* had departed Delaware Bay on 27 October 1812. For the next year and a half the *Essex* was an American fox in a British chicken coop. After ravaging British merchant shipping up and down the east coast of South America, Captain David Porter then used his discretionary authority to round Cape Horn and wreak havoc among the British whaling fleets in the Pacific Ocean. As Porter reported to the Secretary of the Navy:

> I had completely broken up the British navigation in the Pacific; the vessels which had not been captured by me, were laid up, and dare not venture out....The valuable whale fishery there is entirely destroyed, and the actual injury we have done them may be estimated at two and a half millions of dollars independent of the expense of vessels in search of me.[80]

Unfortunately for Porter, the hunters eventually sniffed the spoor, and the vessels pursuing *Essex* ultimately tracked the raider down. After searching for *Essex* for several months, H.M. Frigate *Phoebe* (36) and H.M. Sloop-of-War *Cherub* (18) finally cornered their prize in Valparaiso harbor. For six weeks, the two English warships cruised patiently outside the Chilean seaport, knowing that Porter in due course would have to sail.

Easing out of Valparaiso on 28 March, the overmatched Porter prudently attempted to evade his persistent shadows. He nearly succeeded by sailing *Essex* into the protective cover of a rain squall, but then the swirling winds ripped away the frigate's main topmast. Slowed by the ugly gap in his ship's majestic sail plan, Porter's only option was to engage. Two-and-a-half hours and 75 broadsides later, with 153 bloodied crewmen littering his ship's blasted and splintered deck, the redoubtable Porter surrendered his valiant ship and crew, thus ending one of the most incredible commerce raiding cruises of the war.

It was in early 1814 that the U.S. Government's accelerated shipbuilding program—too little, too late—began to bear fruit. In addition to several new sloops-of-war, the U.S. Navy was authorized to build 74-gun line-of-battle ships, and add to the small number of 44-gun frigates (two of each were launched in 1814). None of the larger vessels were fitted out before war's end, but first among the new sloops-of-war to put to sea was the *Frolic* (22), named for the British vessel captured by the *Wasp* in 1812 (it was and is common practice to name vessels after enemy ships taken as prizes during victorious engagements, or after other successful vessels of the same name). Her career was all too brief. After collaring only two prizes, *Frolic* was patrolling the Straits of Florida when she stumbled upon H.M. Frigate *Orpheus* (36) and the 12-gun schooner *Shelburne*, becoming a prize in turn after a 13-hour chase. Another of the newly built sloops was more successful. Eight days after *Frolic* was lost, the 18-gun *Peacock* encountered the 18-gun British brig *Epervier* southwest of Jamaica. The *Epervier* yielded following a 45-minute exchange of gunfire.

In late spring, the U.S. Brig *Rattlesnake* (16) prospered temporarily, preying upon British merchant shipping until she was chased and run down by HMS *Leander* (50) on 22 June. Three weeks later, the U.S. Brig *Siren* (16) was caught by HMS *Medway* (74) after an 11-hour pursuit off the west coast of South Africa, despite frantic attempts to lighten *Siren* by the oft-used desperation measure of heaving all spare gear, including guns, overboard.

During that bleak year of 1814, American victories in the Atlantic were all too often followed by disaster, with the sloop-of-war *Wasp* (22) providing the perfect example. *Wasp* was a sistership of the newly built *Peacock* and *Frolic*, named for her predecessor which defeated the British brig *Frolic* in October, 1812, and was, in turn, captured by HMS *Poictiers* (74). Taking her first prize on 2 June 1814, *Wasp* ranged the middle reaches of the Atlantic, snatching up four more Britishers in the next three-and-a-half weeks. On 28 June, *Wasp* sighted the 18-gun brig *Reindeer*. Losing no time, Master Commandant Johnston Blakely attacked. In a brisk 30-minute duel, *Wasp* inflicted 57% casualties upon *Reindeer*'s 118-man crew and captured what was left of the sinking wreck. Blakely's damaged ship—*Wasp* lost 11 killed and 15 wounded—pulled into L'Orient, France for repairs, but not before seizing two more prizes en route. It was two months before the sloop's canvas again blossomed to the ocean breezes, but *Wasp* had not lost her sting. At sea once more, Blakely, in only a few short days, lured three more prizes into the *Wasp*'s nest. Then, on the evening of 1 September, the 18-gun brig *Avon* hove into view. A furious 30-minute cannonade ensued before *Avon*, horribly cut up, struck her colors. Just as Blakely was lowering a boat to take possession of his prize, the sails of two more British warships eased over the horizon. Blakely made off, but the appearance of friendly vessels could not help the ruined *Avon*, which soon slipped beneath the cold and unfeeling waves. *Wasp* continued the mission, capturing her 15th prize on 21 September. On 9 October the doughty little commerce raider encountered a Swedish vessel off the Cape Verde Islands and made some exchanges. Then the U.S. Sloop-of-War *Wasp* loosed her canvas, turned toward the vast empty wastes of the Atlantic Ocean, and sailed into oblivion. She was neither seen nor heard from again.

The small frigate *Adams* (28) was another unlucky American warship. Two long cruises in 1814 netted 10 prizes, but she was dogged by the Royal Navy at every turn. On 17 August, *Adams* ran aground in heavy fog off the coast of Maine. Efforts to refloat her were successful, though not before she was spotted by H.M. Brig *Rifleman* (18). While *Rifleman* sped off to notify a large British fleet nearby, Captain Charles Morris sailed the *Adams* 27 miles up the Penobscot River in an attempt to elude possible pursuit. It was a forlorn hope. Embodying 18 ships, the British fleet included two 74-gun line-of-battle ships and ten troop transports. Opposed by only 30 American regulars and 300 hapless militiamen, the British cautiously but confidently moved up the Penobscot, covered by 750 soldiers and marines marching along the riverbank parallel to the warships. His position hopeless, Captain Morris burned the *Adams* on 3 September to keep her out of British hands.

Also on 3 September, the U.S. Schooner *Tigress*, veteran of the Battle of Lake Erie, was captured by a British ruse on Lake Huron. Next morning the schooner *Scorpion*, sister to the *Tigress*, suffered the same humiliation. Such small actions were not unusual since seven gunboats of what was once Oliver Hazard Perry's proud Lake Erie flotilla were either captured or burned during 1814. What singled out these vessels was the fate of their crews. Prisoners captured on the lakes were normally marched to Montreal and held in captivity until exchanged for British sailors or soldiers being held by the United States, but for some reason the two gunboat crews were treated differently. The *Tigress* and *Scorpion* crewmen were instead transported to a place so notorious that its very name conjured sinister images in the minds and terrifying dread in the hearts of every American sailor: Dartmoor Prison. Constructed in 1809, Dartmoor was situated on 30 acres in a lonely and desolate section of Devonshire, England. By 1815, the prison's double walls incarcerated more than 6,000 American prisoners, including 2,500 impressed seamen who had refused to fight against their countrymen. Confined in dank and despairing gloom, hundreds of Dartmoor's crowded and undernourished captives perished from disease. When the Treaty of Ghent was finally signed on 24 December 1814, more than three months were allowed to pass before the prisoners were informed of the war's end; possibly the British were awaiting the treaty's ratification before spreading the word. In any event, on the evening of 6 April 1815, having discovered the news and frustrated by the delay of their release, some of the prisoners attempted to convey their dissatisfaction by refusing to return to their cells after a brief exercise period in the prison yard. Fired upon by the guards, five prisoners were killed and another 33 were wounded.

Among Dartmoor's large number of black inmates was Richard Seavers, a black sailor from Massachusetts. Standing a powerful 6'5" tall, Seavers was a natural leader and a former boxing teacher who ruled prison block four with an iron but fair fist, dispensing his own brand of justice. Block four was where most black prisoners were consolidated, and Seavers regulated all block activities. Known throughout the prison as King Dick, Seavers was often seen strolling through the prison toting a large club followed attentively by two white prisoners. Seavers' scrupulous impartiality reportedly generated many requests for transfer to block four.[81]

With the exception of Lake Champlain in September, the Royal Navy suffered few serious losses during the latter months of 1814; their only other setback occurred on 15 September at Mobile Bay, Alabama. A British attack on Fort Bowyer by a four-ship squadron and a corresponding landing force was aborted when H.M. Sloop-of-War *Hermes* (20) was struck by the fort's guns and blew up, suffering a loss of 25 killed and 24 wounded. In uneven trade, the United States forfeited gunboat flotillas on the Patuxent River in Maryland during the Chesapeake campaign in August, 1814, and on Lake Borgne in December, 1814 during the New Orleans campaign.

Tidings of the 8 January 1815 victory at New Orleans electrified the American people, but the new year's first month was anything but auspicious for the U.S. Navy. Further disaster and glory were not prevented by the signing of the Treaty of Ghent on 24 December 1814 since nearly a month passed before word crossed the Atlantic, and in some cases many months would elapse before ships at sea heard the news.

On 15 January 1815, the U.S. Navy suffered a crippling setback when the 44-gun frigate *President*, one of only three of the American Navy's largest class of warships (none of the new 74's or 44's were yet fitted out) was snagged by HMS *Majestic* (56), *Endymion* (40), *Tenados* (38), and *Pomone* (38) while attempting to sidestep the blockade of New York harbor.

Even though her efforts could not compensate for the *President's* loss, Old Ironsides, having exploited a gap in the Boston blockade on 17 December 1814, continued her amazing success. While cruising about 180 miles off the coast of Portugal on 20 February 1815, a sail was spotted and *Constitution* gave chase. Soon a second sail was observed, and it was not long before the ships were identified as H.M. Sloop-of-War *Cyane* (22) (nominally a 6th rate with 22 guns, *Cyane* was actually frigate-built and carried 34 guns) and H.M. Sloop-of-War *Levant* (18). Around sunset both British warships bravely, and maybe a little foolishly, turned to fight. Broadsides flashing in the moonlight briefly illuminated ghostly silhouettes of hulls, sails, and rigging before billowing clouds of dirty, acrid gunsmoke enshrouded the contenders. Several more broadsides, combined with some deft maneuvering by *Constitution* Captain Charles Stewart, soon forced the outgunned *Cyane* to strike. *Levant* adroitly sparred for a while longer before trying to escape, but she too surrendered after a short pursuit.

Providing powder for the *Constitution*'s #14 long gun during her battle with the *Cyane* and *Levant* was young David Dibias (or Debias). After the engagement, Dibias and a small number of *Constitution* crewmen were appointed to serve as the *Levant*'s prize crew and sail the captured British sloop to the nearest American port. But the British managed to recapture *Levant* en route, and Dibias was transported to the West Indies as a prisoner

56

of war. Since the war was already over, Dibias was returned to the United States in June of 1815. He rejoined the *Constitution* and served on board the frigate during her cruise to the Mediterranean between 1821 to 1824. Following his naval service, Dibias signed on as a merchant seaman. In 1838 he was arrested in Mississippi as a suspected fugitive slave. Dibias engaged an attorney to write to the Secretary of the Navy, and it was his confirmation of naval service that verified the former seaman's status as a free man and secured his release—an early example of veteran's benefits.[82]

Eight days after the *President* was taken on 15 January 1815, *Hornet* (20) escaped the New York blockade during a gale. While *Hornet* was preparing to anchor off the coast of Tristan da Cunha on 23 March, H.M. Brig *Penguin* (20) hove into sight. Both ships closed to fight. After only 20 minutes of close-quarters broadsides, with her foremast toppled, mainmast wavering, bowsprit shot away, hull riddled, guns dismounted, and a third of her crew killed or wounded, *Penguin* submitted. A wasted hulk, the British ship had to be destroyed.

Despite the Treaty of Ghent having long been signed and ratified, *Hornet*'s engagement was not the final naval engagement of the war. The U.S. Sloop-of-War *Peacock* (18) met up with the *Hornet* shortly following the latter's victory over the *Penguin*. After cruising together for a brief period, *Peacock* turned eastward, rounded the Cape of Good Hope, and sailed into the Indian Ocean. On 30 June 1815, *Peacock* was passing through the Sunda Strait when the British East India Company brig *Nautilus* (14) was spotted. *Nautilus*'s captain hailed *Peacock* and asked if the American vessel had heard about the peace treaty. Suspecting a trick, *Peacock* commander Lewis Warrington opened fire, loosing the last broadside of the war. Realizing the futility of the situation, the commander of the *Nautilus* quite properly surrendered—a perfectly senseless end to what many would argue was a perfectly senseless war.

II

Land Operations

*....the wonder should be, not that we
blundered, but that we did not blunder
more, and that our talented and veteran
enemies should have out-blundered us.*

Thomas Jesup

*War is as much a punishment to
the punisher as to the sufferer.*

Thomas Jefferson

7

THE ROAD TO WAR

In the years preceding the United States declaration of war, American citizens found themselves continually provoked. Great Britain's impressment of sailors from U.S. registered vessels, combined with the confiscation of U.S. merchant ships, had incensed the residents of cities and towns up and down the Atlantic seaboard. Anger and indignation directed at the British Navy filled newspaper columns, but America's western frontier was aroused by a different matter entirely.

Manifest Destiny had yet to be proclaimed official American dogma, but its doctrine was already unfolding. Settlers moved west at a prodigious rate, seeking to relocate on land which had long been occupied by Native Americans. On rickety flatboats down the Ohio River, through the rugged mountains pierced by the Cumberland Gap, and inland from the southeast coastlines poured land-hungry pioneers, toward inevitable confrontation with those whose territory they coveted.

One conflict, the American Revolution, had barely been resolved before another was started along the expanding western frontier; this one would be a bitter undeclared war savagely fought in tangled wilderness with an implacable foe. Unfortunately for those settlers who would soon need military protection, United States legislators handicapped any future military venture after independence had been gained in 1783. The country's new political leadership feared that a strong standing army might conspire to create a military state, so they over-reacted and disbanded the Continental Army. When hostilities between Indians and whites erupted in Kentucky and southern Ohio during the late 1780's, a whole new military establishment had to be created. Fiscal considerations and that same dread concerning a potent standing army caused the new military force to be composed at first of a single infantry regiment only. Poorly led, supplied, and trained, the infant army was a recipe for disaster.

President George Washington's Indian War commenced in the fall of

AMONGST MY BEST MEN

1790 when the first in a series of battles was fought by a 1,500-man force of regulars and militia commanded by General Josiah Harmar. Encountering warriors from a loose Indian confederacy led by Miami Chief Little Turtle and Shawnee Chief Blue Jacket, Harmar's army was soundly defeated near present day Fort Wayne, Indiana. One year later, another United States force of nearly the same size, guided by General Arthur St. Clair, was abjectly routed by the same Indians on the site of present day Fort Recovery, Ohio. St. Clair's defeat remains to this day, in the ratio of casualties suffered to numbers engaged, one of the worst disasters ever suffered by a United States military force. It was not until August, 1794 that the Indians met defeat at the hands of General "Mad Anthony" Wayne at the Battle of Fallen Timbers, near present day Maumee, Ohio. Wayne's victory sired the August, 1795 Treaty of Greenville, in which the tribes agreed to relinquish Indian lands in southern Ohio. Just a few months earlier, on 19 November 1794, the U.S. signed Jay's Treaty with Great Britain, causing the British to evacuate their last remaining occupied outposts in United States territory.

America's relations with Great Britain had been fragile at best during the Ohio Indian wars. Wishing to maintain their monopoly in the lucrative fur trade, officials in the United Kingdom were sympathetic with Indian desires to prevent American expansion. In order to support Indian operations and to further their own political and financial interests, the British had provided weapons, ammunition, supplies, and occasionally military advisors, when American armies led by Harmar, St. Clair, and Wayne advanced into the Ohio country. Britain's military aid to the Indians further taxed already strained British-American relations. At one point, after Wayne's victory at Fallen Timbers, open warfare between British and American troops was just barely averted. The Treaty of Greenville and Jay's Treaty temporarily alleviated much of the discord, but underlying tensions remained.

Prior to Fallen Timbers, U.S. encroachment had consolidated Indian efforts in the Old Northwest, but defeat left the tribes in political and military disarray. Rising to prominence to fill the void at this critical juncture in Native American history was the great Shawnee Chief Tecumseh. Tecumseh's ambition was to bridge the enormous tribal gaps and to unite all tribes into an enormous and enduring Indian confederacy. His strong, unified Indian nation could then, by peaceful means if at all possible, stave off white advancement onto Indian lands. To achieve his dream, the charismatic chief traveled extensively throughout the northwest, midwest, and southeast, exhorting other tribes to join his coalition.

Tecumseh's movement was anchored by a village he established along the Tippecanoe River in Indiana Territory near present day West Lafayette, Indiana. Tecumseh named his village Prophetstown after his brother Tenskwatawa, who was known as the Prophet because of alleged visionary powers. The village was conceived by Tecumseh as a retreat where all Indians could live in harmony with each other. Peace was the great chieftain's desired goal, yet his philosophy advocated Indian land for Indian people, a policy incompatible with land acquisition measures already implemented by the United States. While many tribesmen with whom Tecumseh communicated agreed wholeheartedly with his concept of Indian land for Indian people, many did not necessarily embrace his principle of utilizing peaceful methods to achieve that objective.

In an ongoing effort to strengthen his union, Tecumseh journeyed south to negotiate with the different Creek factions in the spring of 1811. When Tecumseh's absence from Prophetstown was discovered, William Henry Harrison, then Governor of Indiana Territory, decided the time was ripe to take action. Harrison and Tecumseh had been adversaries for many years, and their previous confrontations had been bitter and contentious. One of the major obstacles between the two was Prophetstown itself, situated on land which the governor had been instructed to acquire for white settlement. Harrison knew that without Tecumseh in residence to rally his people emotionally, he would have no better opportunity to eliminate this impediment. Using Indian attacks carried out against white inhabitants in Illinois Territory as an excuse, Harrison gathered a 900-man army and marched to the Tippecanoe River.

Before heading south, Tecumseh designated his brother as caretaker of the village, instructing his sibling that he should not antagonize Harrison or the white inhabitants of Indiana Territory under any circumstances. With this admonition in mind, the Prophet met with Harrison when the latter's troops arrived before Prophetstown on the evening of 6 November 1811. The Prophet convinced Harrison that the Indians wished no trouble from the whites. He suggested that the Americans camp nearby, and they would resume discussions the following morning. But the Prophet, a pretentious and ambitious man, wished to demonstrate his spiritual medicine to the inhabitants of Prophetstown. Completely disregarding Tecumseh's instructions, the Prophet decided to attack Harrison's encampment along the Tippecanoe River in the pre-dawn hours of 7 November. Knowledge of Harrison's strength had been coerced from a captured black wagon driver who also relayed to the Prophet that Harrison intended to attack the Indian camp after negotiations were completed the next day.[1] Surprise gave the Prophet's followers an initial advantage when the warriors attacked, but Harrison's troops rallied and eventually prevailed, defeating the Indians and destroying Tecumseh's dream for peace once and for all.

The origin of many of the muskets found in the Indian camp after the battle infuriated Harrison's men, and ultimately incited the rest of the country. Bearing the stamp of the British government, the weapons provided proof that England was arming America's Indian enemies and provoking them to attack the United States. Such a contention was certainly open to argument, but truth was very much the War of 1812's first casualty. When the group of southern and western congressmen collectively known as the War Hawks discovered details of the incident, they used the British weapons found at Tippecanoe as an excuse to further their own aims. Though war fever was far from rampant in most of the country, the decision-making power-brokers in Washington now possessed all the ammunition they needed: British agitation among the Indian tribes, impressment of American seamen, and the restrictive Orders in Council. What the War Hawks did not consider fully when they conspired to declare war was the woeful lack of readiness on the part of the institution which would have to fight their battles—the United States Army.

In 1812, it was the regular army that formed the backbone of the United States military machine. However, as previously stated, following the American Revolution, U.S. leaders lived in dread that a large standing army might overthrow the elected government and establish a military state. Their fear constrained legislators from establishing a powerful or effective military force. Rather than maintain a standing army, the country instead relied on the militia system, which depended upon untrained and undisciplined citizen soldiers to answer the call-to-arms during national crises. The Indian War in the Old Northwest during the early 1790's underlined the militia's inadequacy and forced the government to expand the regular Army. But by early 1812, the United States Army still could muster fewer than 7,000 soldiers out of an authorized strength of only 10,000.[2] Imminence of war induced Congress to expand the regular army once again, but throughout the war's duration, U.S. Army regiments experienced endless difficulties finding recruits to fill their ranks. Another problem that Congress and the military failed to anticipate was the objections that American militiamen would raise when ordered to fight outside the bounds of the United States.

As ordained by America's political leadership, the U.S. military's primary objective during the War of 1812 was the annexation of Canada. Though the United States lacked a strong, professional army, the politicians and the amateur military strategists in Washington were little concerned. In the three decades preceding the war, large numbers of U.S. citizens had emigrated to Upper Canada, present day Ontario. In fact, an estimated 65% of the Upper Canadian population in 1812 was U.S. born. As a result, many congressmen erroneously believed that the majority of Canadians covertly desired to be assimilated by the United States, and they fully expected the Canadian people to welcome an invasion with open arms! Overconfidence was enhanced by the fact that the United States population dwarfed that of Canada by more than ten to one, so it stood to reason that Canadians would not dare to contest such odds. Also, with England's resources strained by its life-and-death struggle against Napoleon's armies in Europe, few British regiments could be spared to garrison the Canadian frontier, and the Canadian militia was considered to be unreliable. Hence the desire among the War Hawks to annex Canada, combined with a false confidence in American military might and arrogant ignorance concerning Canada's determination to remain an individual entity, gave ready credence to the axiom, "On To Canada."[3]

During the War of 1812, African-Americans were prominently involved in land operations, although the Army was slower to accept black soldiers than the Navy had been to recruit black sailors. In early 1812, United States fighting units were organized into two basic categories: the regular army and the militia. Because the regular army comprised fewer than 7,000 men, state militia units formed the bulk of America's military units and thus could be relied upon to form the country's first line of defense—or so the American public was led to believe. Based on federal legislation, every white male between the ages of 18 to 45 served in the militia compulsorily, so theoretically the country could mobilize tens of thousands of soldiers in the event of national emergency. But state militia units, as would soon be discovered, were deplorably ill-prepared and virtually worthless in a stand-up battle. While often called out, militia regiments were rarely used, especially against

British regulars. Poor training and even worse discipline engendered contempt for the militia by both the U.S. Army hierarchy and the British. That disdain was eventually justified when many militia outfits displayed a deplorable unwillingness to fight.

The status of African-Americans within the various state militia systems is sometimes difficult to determine. When the United States passed the act establishing the federal militia system on 9 May 1792, the wording merely stipulated:

> An act more effectually to provide for the National Defense by establishing a uniform Militia throughout the United States...
>
> That each and every free able-bodied white male citizen of the respective States, resident therein, who is or shall be of the age of eighteen years, and under the age of forty-five years...shall, severally and respectively, be enrolled in the Militia...[4]

That color-conscious phrase—"free able-bodied white male citizen"—is often repeated. The state of New Jersey followed up the federal act that same year with its own, parroting the federal phraseology by mandating the service of "free and able-bodied white male citizens."[5] Similar wording characterized the Vermont Militia Act of 1797 and the New Hampshire Militia Act of 1808.[6] In the spring of 1812, when units of the Ohio Militia were being mobilized, one militiaman remembered that:

> ...the able-bodied white male inhabitants between the ages of eighteen and forty-five, residing on the three eastern tiers of townships of the present county of Portage, and subject to military duty, constituted the Second Regiment, Fourth Brigade, Fourth Division, Ohio Militia...[7]

"Male white citizens" is clearly stipulated, but neither the federal militia act nor many state militia acts specifically prohibit the enlistment of black soldiers, although several states chose to interpret it that way. Ironically, it was mostly the northern states that limited enrollment of black militiamen before the war. Connecticut banned black enlistment in its state militia in 1784,[8] and the 10 March 1785 act for regulating and governing the militia of the Commonwealth of Massachusetts contained two relevant provisions:

> II. That the said Militia shall be formed into a train-band and alarm-list; to contain all trained and ablebodied men,

from sixteen to forty years of age, and the alarm-list, all other men under sixty years of age, excepting in both cases such as shall be hereafter by this act exempted.

XLIII. Negroes, Indians, and Mulattoes, shall be, and hereby are exempted from both the train-band and alarm-list aforesaid.[9]

Michigan Territory proved an exception among the northern states and territories. On 23 December 1808, a committee commented on a number of resolutions placed before the Michigan Legislature two months earlier by Chief Justice Augustus B. Woodward. The fourth resolution referred to the authority imposed by Governor William Hull when he raised a black militia company in 1807 (see Chapter 8). Part of the recommendations put forth by the committee included:

The committee further observes, that the 1st section of an act concerning the militia of this Territory, provides, that every free, able bodied, male inhabitant, of an age described in said act, shall be enrolled and made liable to do military duty, and the ordinance of congress [Ordinance of 1787], which is the constitution of this Territory, contains the following article:

'There shall be neither slavery, nor involuntary servitude in the said Territory, otherwise than is punishment of crimes, whereof the party shall have been duly convicted.' This is an article of compact declared to be unalterable unless by the common consent of the original States and the people of the Territory.

Under this view of the subject, the committee is of the opinion that the conduct of the executive in availing the country of the services of their black people, was not only proper but highly commendable; especially as it was at a period when the safety and protection of the Territory appeared to require all the force which could be possibly collected.[10]

In addition to Michigan Territory, several southern states and territories enlisted free men of color before the war. Louisiana in particular maintained a long and proud tradition of black fighting men and units (see Chapter 12). Virginia's General Assembly passed a Militia Act in 1784 requiring all free persons between the ages of 18 and 50 to be enrolled, including free men of color. Provision II of the Virginia act denoted qualifications, "Here follow [sic] a list of exemption, in which Negroes, or persons of color, are not included."[11] Nevertheless, Virginia amended its Militia Act on 1 August 1788, specifying limited types of service to be performed by free men of color:

> V. And be it further enacted by the authority aforesaid, that every person, so as aforesaid listed, (except free Mulattos, Negroes, and Indians) and placed or ranked in horse or foot, shall be armed and accoutred in [the] manner following:...
>
> VI. And be it further enacted, that all such free Mulattos, Negroes, or Indians, as are or shall be listed, as aforesaid shall appear without arms; and may be employed as drummers, trumpeters, or pioneers, or in such other senile labour, as they shall be directed to perform.[12]

On 10 May 1794, the state of South Carolina likewise authorized that "Negroes and Mulattoes":

> ...shall be obliged to serve in the said Militia as fatigue men and pioneers, in the several regimental beats in which they reside; and upon neglect or refusal to attend when summoned on duty, they, and every one of them, shall be liable to the like penalties and forfeitures as privates in the same regimental company are made liable by law.[13]

Most black militiamen, as specified by the various state militia acts, were free men of color, but it was not unheard of for slaves to accompany militia units. Virtually all slaves serving with state militias were relegated the roles of waiters and servants, though rare exceptions exist. One such exception was a man referred to as Boy Chatham, who rode as a trumpeter with the Chatham Light Dragoons, an elite Georgia unit comprised of "gentlemen volunteers." Boy Chatham was:

> ...a slave purchased by some of the [unit] members on a shareholding basis and [he] was hired out when not blowing military calls. Most of the troop orders and notices printed during this period carried his picture.[14]

AFRICAN-AMERICANS AND THE WAR OF 1812

After the declaration of war, when soldiers were most needed, states such as Georgia and North Carolina passed legislation banning black recruits from enlisting, although some states such as North Carolina did allow African-Americans to serve as musicians.[15] Many southerners undoubtedly feared the prospect of armed black troops either inciting or assisting with slave insurrections.

With the exception of Louisiana, and possibly one or two others, black militiamen serving with state units were relegated to menial tasks. Occasionally, a muster roll or pay roll, such as the field and staff receipt roll for the 17th Pennsylvania Militia Regiment, will provide a specific notation: "Jonathan (a Blackman) waiter to [the Lieutenant Colonel]."[16] Several black militiamen are found on New Jersey muster rolls: "Samuel (a negro)," "Jack (blackman)," "Will (a black man)," "Jupiter Boy of headquarters company," "Dick Negro," and so forth.[17] All of the black militiamen listed were identified as either waiters or servants, although whites also served in these same capacities. Nevertheless, New Jersey, like most states, did not allow black militiamen to serve in a combat role.

Attitudes regarding black enlistment changed as the war progressed and the country's fortunes declined. By the latter half of 1814, several states were actively recruiting black soldiers. In North Carolina, where African-Americans had been restricted to serving as musicians, the revised Militia Act of 1814 permitted free men of color to enlist on the condition that their color was specified. Yet many willing black recruits were rejected even after North Carolina amended its militia act.[18]

Pennsylvania initiated efforts to raise entire units of black troops in 1814,[19] as did New York, which approved "An Act to authorize the raising of Two Regiments of Men of Color; passed Oct. 24, 1814."[20] To consist of 1,080 men each, the general provisions for raising the two New York regiments were laid down in Section 1 of the act:

> Sect. 1. Be it enacted by the people of the State of New York, represented in Senate and Assembly, That the Governor of the State be, and he is hereby authorized to raise, by voluntary enlistment, two regiments of free men of color, for the defence of the State for three years, unless sooner discharged.[21]

While Section 1 clearly specified that the regiment was to be comprised of free men of color, Section 6 of the act was undoubtedly of particular interest to many potential recruits:

> Sect. 6. And be it further enacted, That it shall be lawful for any able-bodied slave, with the written assent of his master or mistress, to enlist into the said corps; and the master or mistress of such slave shall be entitled to the pay and bounty allowed him for his service: and, further, that the said slave, at the time of receiving his discharge, shall be deemed and adjudged to have been legally manumitted from that time, and his said master or mistress shall not thenceforward be liable for his maintenance.[22]

Dire consequences resulting from the British Chesapeake Bay campaign in late August and September of 1814, which included the burning of government and public buildings in Washington, D.C. (see chapter 11), were motivating factors behind the Pennsylvania and New York efforts. These same circumstances also prompted a prominent Georgia citizen to pen an intriguing letter to the U.S. Secretary of War:

> The lamentable news of the destruction of our Capitol has this moment reached us...
>
> In the prosecution of a savage war such as the enemy is now waging against us, all the means of defense which are not injurious to our probity or courage [should be] allowable...
>
> My motive for [the] Liberty I am taking, is to offer a suggestion for the benefit of our country which I fear your Excellency will think a little wild if not dangerous.
>
> This is the employment of Negroes in the present war.
>
> We already believe that the enemy is training Negroes for the purpose of arming them against us [see Chapter 11], and we already know that he has armed the ruthless savage, not only against our warriors, but against our women and children.
>
> If the practice can be justified by honour, the following considerations will fix the economy and safety.
>
> The bounty and pay for a soldier for five years is not less than $900. His clothing must be regularly furnished,

his pay regularly made up, his rations good and in full quantity, or he becomes mutinous.

A Negro man can be purchased for a little more than half of this sum. If he is half as well fed and half as well clad as a white man, he will be satisfied. With regard to our safety; the employment of such force so far from endangering of us, will be greater means of lessening our danger in the Southern States. Let an offer of liberty be made to those who are willing to serve during the war, and I think it will not fail to call amongst us all those from whom we apprehend an insurrection. Let this force be sent against Canada and it would enable us to increase our defense on the sea coast.

The greatest difficulty which offers in the present case is the disposition of those slaves at the termination of the war. Might they not colonize some part of Louisiana and be made a territorial part of our government.

Though I scarcely dare to think of it, yet I dare to ask; is it not probable that the termination of new feuds may put it in our power to offer them a settlement still farther from home? There are numbers of freed Negroes in the Northern States, who if they were permitted would probably strengthen our lines when the soldiery was to be colonized, would furnish them with wives and citizens. Many of the more industrious of those who survived the war would in a series of years be able to purchase their progeny from their former masters, by which the interests of humanity would be greatly promoted. If in addition to this, there was a country to which freed slaves might be sent, it would be a great inducement to the benevolent to free them.

At a moment like this, when the feelings of your Excellency and of every American are burning with indignation, these suggestions may claim your considera-tion. With full assurance that they will meet all the respect which they deserve...[23]

Whether or not the Secretary of War gave credible consideration to this rather rambling proposal is not known, the war ended before any action could be implemented. As mentioned, efforts to raise new black militia units were begun in states like Pennsylvania and New York after Washington, D.C. was burned, but not one of those outfits was fully organized and none saw action before the Treaty of Ghent was signed.

Overall, it appears that the 1792 Federal Militia Act laid down general guidelines governing militia service, and the states thereafter interpreted those precepts to accommodate their own needs and desires. As far as the majority of state militias are concerned, black enlistees were sometimes accepted, but their services were, for the most part, restricted to non-combat roles and only rarely were black militiamen permitted to fight alongside their white counterparts.

As for the regular Army, African-Americans were barred from joining the ranks at the war's outset. Black Americans were most likely displeased with the restriction, but the prohibition may have been providential. During the early part of the war, the United States Army, due mostly to poor guidance, was better known for the incompetence, ineptitude, and mismanagement of its leaders than for its ability to fight and defend the country. The painful reality was that during the first two years of the War of 1812, United States troops were, more often than not, defeated in battle. It was about the time that the U.S. Army came of age as a professional fighting force in the spring of 1814 that black recruits became readily accepted in the regular ranks. Among other campaigns, black regulars served in the bloody fighting along the Niagara River during the summer of 1814, in the 1814 Chesapeake and Plattsburg campaigns, and at New Orleans.

Precisely when black recruits were first allowed to enlist in the regular army, or how many actually served, is uncertain. Some evidence exists to indicate that a few black regulars may have been enrolled as early as 1812 and 1813. By January, 1814, there is no doubt that black recruits were being accepted in the regular ranks. Sources point out the fact that black Americans served in at least 18—and most likely more—of the 48 regular infantry regiments raised during the War of 1812, in addition to the U.S. Corps of Artillery, the U.S. Light Artillery, and the 2nd U.S. Rifle Regiment. In the case of the 26th U.S. Infantry Regiment, indications are that Captain William Bezean enrolled as many as 247 black volunteers at Philadelphia in late 1814 and early 1815, although some of those recruits may have been white. Most black enlistees joined regiments that were just being formed during the final months of the war; consequently, many of the units in which they enlisted never saw action.[24]

The population of the United States in 1812 totaled 6,000,000, of which 1,700,000 were non-white.[25] A large number of the non-white citizens were free men of color, and since the U.S. Army was prohibited by law from enlisting black recruits in 1812, the country failed to take advantage of a huge reservoir of willing and able fighting men. Instead, the role allocated to black Americans early in the war was principally one of labor. For the most part, forced labor was not involved. During British invasion scares, the black populaces of Boston, New York City, Philadelphia, Baltimore, and Washington, D.C. were urged, often by their own leaders, to dig trenches and erect fortifications to help safeguard their homes. Black civilians and white civilians alike poured forth with picks and shovels to dig entrenchments, not only eager to protect their cities, but to serve their country in whatever fashion possible. In the south, instances did occur in which slave owners either offered those in bondage or had their slaves commandeered to perform labor for the state or federal government—sometimes for a fee, sometimes not. Slave or free, black Americans throughout the United States labored to protect their homes, towns, and fellow citizens from marauding British forces.

Unlike wars in some countries, campaigns of the War of 1812 were not waged over vast tracts of the United States and Canada. Strategic importance and difficulty of access to many parts of North America confined the action to theaters of operation—specific locations and crucial areas which would see intense action over limited periods of time. Generally speaking, War of 1812 operations can be divided into four major theaters: the ocean war, the northern lakes, the Chesapeake region or mid-Atlantic states, and the gulf coast region.

First among equals was the northern lakes theater. Since the principal effort of the United States involved wresting Canada from the British, it naturally followed that the heaviest and bloodiest fighting of the war occurred in sections of the Old Northwest—particularly along western Lake Erie—in the north along the Niagara River and the shores of Lake Ontario, and in the vicinity of the St. Lawrence River and Lake Champlain. It was through these regions that the United States planned three major invasions of Canada when war was declared on 18 June 1812.

AMONGST MY BEST MEN

The analogy of a tree and its roots is often used to illustrate U.S. operations against Canada. The St. Lawrence River comprised the roots and trunk of the tree, with the upper lakes forming the branches. Interspersed all along the tree and branches were British installations guarding key points, posts that required supplies and materials of every imaginable type to sustain them. These wilderness forts were singularly difficult to support because supplies had to shipped all the way from England, making for an extremely long and tenuous line of communications. For instance, stores slated for Fort Malden on the Detroit River had to first travel across the Atlantic Ocean. Once in Canada the supplies were hauled up the St. Lawrence River, shipped across Lake Ontario, portaged over the Niagara peninsula, and finally transported along Lake Erie's north shore. Altogether the distance amounted to about 5,000 very difficult and dangerous miles. The Niagara region and Lake Ontario straddled a slightly shorter, but no less arduous, supply line.

Considering the obstacles Great Britain would face with supplying its distant outposts, logic should have dictated American military strategy: capture Montreal, which would sever the St. Lawrence supply artery and isolate British fortifications on the upper lakes to wither on the vine. Instead, American military strategists opted to scatter its resources and hack away at the entire tree instead of sawing exclusively on the trunk or digging out the roots, and it was one of the tree's middle branches that was to feel the first blow from America's dull axe.

8

WESTERN LAKE ERIE AND
THE OLD NORTHWEST

America's initial invasion of Canada occurred along western Lake Erie, with Fort Malden and the Amherstburg Navy Yard—the British installations located at the mouth of the Detroit River—serving as the primary objective. Elimination of Fort Malden and the adjacent navy yard would secure control of Lake Erie, open the way for U.S. troops to occupy all of western Upper Canada, and allow the Americans to strike British military bases along the Niagara River from the rear.

Months before it occurred, political leaders in the United States knew that war would be declared. Advance knowledge enabled President James Madison to plan accordingly. In February 1812, William Hull, the 59-year-old governor of Michigan Territory and former Revolutionary War army officer, was convinced by Madison to raise an army to invade western Upper Canada. At the President's direction, Hull assembled a combined force of regulars and militia, totaling approximately 2,500 men, at Dayton, Ohio. The aging general set out for Fort Detroit, Michigan Territory, in early June.

Fort Detroit was one of very few military posts within the United States sphere of influence to have garrisoned organized black troops before the War of 1812. Michigan had been organized as a territory within the Northwest Territory in 1805. The Northwest Territory included the present states of Ohio, Indiana, Illinois, Michigan, Wisconsin, and part of Minnesota. The Ordinance of 1787, sometimes referred to as the Northwest Ordinance or the Ordinance of Freedom, established the Northwest Territory and served as its territorial constitution. Since its tenets proscribed slavery within territorial bounds, the Ordinance of 1787 abolished institutional bondage in Michigan when it was officially carved out as an individual territory within the overall Northwest Territory.

AMONGST MY BEST MEN

Just across the Detroit River from Michigan lay Upper Canada. Legislation passed in 1793 prohibited slaves from being brought into Canada in the future, and that same legislation manumitted the children of all Canadian slaves. For all practical purposes, the institution itself was being slowly phased out, but in 1805 slavery was still legal in Canada. This meant that the only barrier separating slaves in western Upper Canada from freedom in Michigan was the Detroit River. A wide strip of deceptively calm water, the treacherous river proved far too tempting for many slaves, who risked life and limb to escape to the opposite shore.

At Detroit, escaped slaves who survived the Detroit River's swift current arrived at a slow but steady rate, leaving Governor Hull in a quandary. Jobs in the tiny settlement were not plentiful in 1805-1806, so rather than have unemployed and indigent ex-slaves roaming the country-side looking for work, Hull formed some of the escapees, plus a few local free men of color, into a militia company.

Commanded by a free black man named Peter Denison, the company rose to notoriety in the summer of 1807 when, as a result of HMS *Leopard* firing on the U.S. Frigate *Chesapeake* (see Chapter 1), the threat of war cast a shroud over the United States, Canada, and Great Britain.[26] Area resident and British sympathizer James Askin, alarmed by Detroit's martial preparations, communicated his concerns to his brother, a serving British officer:

> At Detroit they are making great preparations [for war]. The Town of Detroit is Picketed in from the Water Side untill [sic] it joins Fort Lernoult, A Company of Negroes mounting Guard, The Cavalry Patroling [sic] every night, Batries [sic] Erecting along the Settlement, and the Militia called out frequently.[27]

The commanding officer of nearby Fort Malden also took note of troop mobilization at Fort Detroit, and he dashed off a situational analysis to his superior in Montreal:

> The Militia of Detroit have been constantly assembled for the purpose of Drill, they amount to about 400....There is, besides, a company formed of Renegade Negroes who deserted from Captain [William] Elliott and several Gentlemen at this side. This company consists of, I am informed, 36 in number, and [they] are kept for such

desperate services as may be required at this side, they being well acquainted with it.[28]

While diplomatic intervention managed to prevent the outbreak of hostilities in 1807, Governor Hull had unknowingly inaugurated a furor of his own simply by establishing the black militia company. The presence of armed black troops just across the Detroit River unnerved and alarmed many Canadians along with some Americans living in close proximity to Detroit, and they made their reservations known. Also, Canadian slave owners like William Elliott wished to have their property returned. Unmoved by the protestations, Hull avowed that the escapees were now free and loyal citizens of Michigan Territory and, as such, they were fully entitled to bear arms. Opposition nonetheless remained strong, and, unable to withstand the continued pressure, the governor was forced to disband the group.[29] Consequently, Detroit's black militia company was no longer in service when Hull's newly-raised army marched into Fort Detroit in late June of 1812, a circumstance for which the ex-soldiers could be very thankful.

Outnumbering the British regulars at Fort Malden by nearly ten to one, Hull crossed the Detroit River and slowly moved southwest toward the bastion. On 16 July, the Americans handily defeated a small British and Indian force defending a bridge over the Aux Canard River. From the west bank of the Aux Canard, Hull need only march three miles to Amherstburg, surround Fort Malden, and await a British surrender. Instead, the 17 July British capture of Fort Mackinac on the upper lakes introduced the threat of significant Indian reinforcements being sent down from the north. Hull panicked when he intercepted a message about the approaching Indian horde. Abandoning even the pretext of an invasion of Canada, Hull retreated to Fort Detroit, where the unnerved general took counsel of his fears. Failing to take proper preventative measures, Hull apprehensively awaited the Indian host. About 1,000 Indian warriors were serving with the British at Fort Malden, but the message Hull captured, along with the menace of thousands of Indian reinforcements, turned out to be little more than a clever British ruse to stall the American general. It worked.

Shortly thereafter, Major General Isaac Brock—Lieutenant Governor of the Canadas, administrator of Upper Canada, and the most competent British general officer serving in the colony—arrived at Fort Malden with reinforcements. Aggressiveness characterized Brock's every action, and even though he was still outnumbered, the British general contrived to cross his forces over the Detroit River, sever the American supply artery, surround Fort Detroit, and open fire with his artillery. On 16 August 1812, after firing only a few shots in defense of his stronghold, Major General William Hull ignominiously surrendered Fort Detroit and the entire United States northwest army.

Unfortunately for the United States, the consequences of Hull's timidity extended far beyond Fort Detroit. To the west, on Lake Michigan, lay the small outpost of Fort Dearborn, present day Chicago, Illinois, which guarded the mouth of the Chicago River. The little outpost was garrisoned by 58 U.S. regulars, although a number of civilians, including military dependents, also lived in the immediate vicinity. Disregarding the fact that the tiny bastion was well armed and supplied, Hull, within whose command purview the post lay, ordered Fort Dearborn to be evacuated. Captain Nathan Heald, the fort's commander, decided to obey orders despite being warned about imminent danger by a friendly Indian. On the morning of 15 August 1812, the 58 soldiers, plus 14 civilian men, 9 women, and 18 children, nervously shuffled through the fort's open gates and crept south along the Lake Michigan shoreline. Less than one-and-a-half miles from the fort the small column was attacked by 500 Indian warriors, mostly Potawatomis. Resistance was offered by the soldiers, but it was desperate and futile, and the outcome was inevitable. Brutally killed and mutilated were 28 soldiers, 13 civilian men, 2 women, and 13 children, many after the fighting ceased. One of the few survivors of the disaster was an individual simply referred to as "Mrs. [Nathan] Heald's Negro Woman."[30]

Mrs. Heald also survived with the aid of some timely assistance. The Indians had allowed the family of highly regarded local trader John Kinzie safe passage to depart by boat instead of on foot. Still nearby when the killing started, the Kinzie family watched the slaughter in numb horror. Just as an Indian was preparing to kill Mrs. Heald near the Kinzie's boat, the family intervened and managed to purchase the terrified woman's temporary safety with some whiskey. After her harrowing escape, Mrs. Heald was placed under cover in the boat's bottom, but moments later another warrior approached. With pistol in hand the Potawatomi was preparing to search the boat when Black Jim, one of two Kinzie servants:

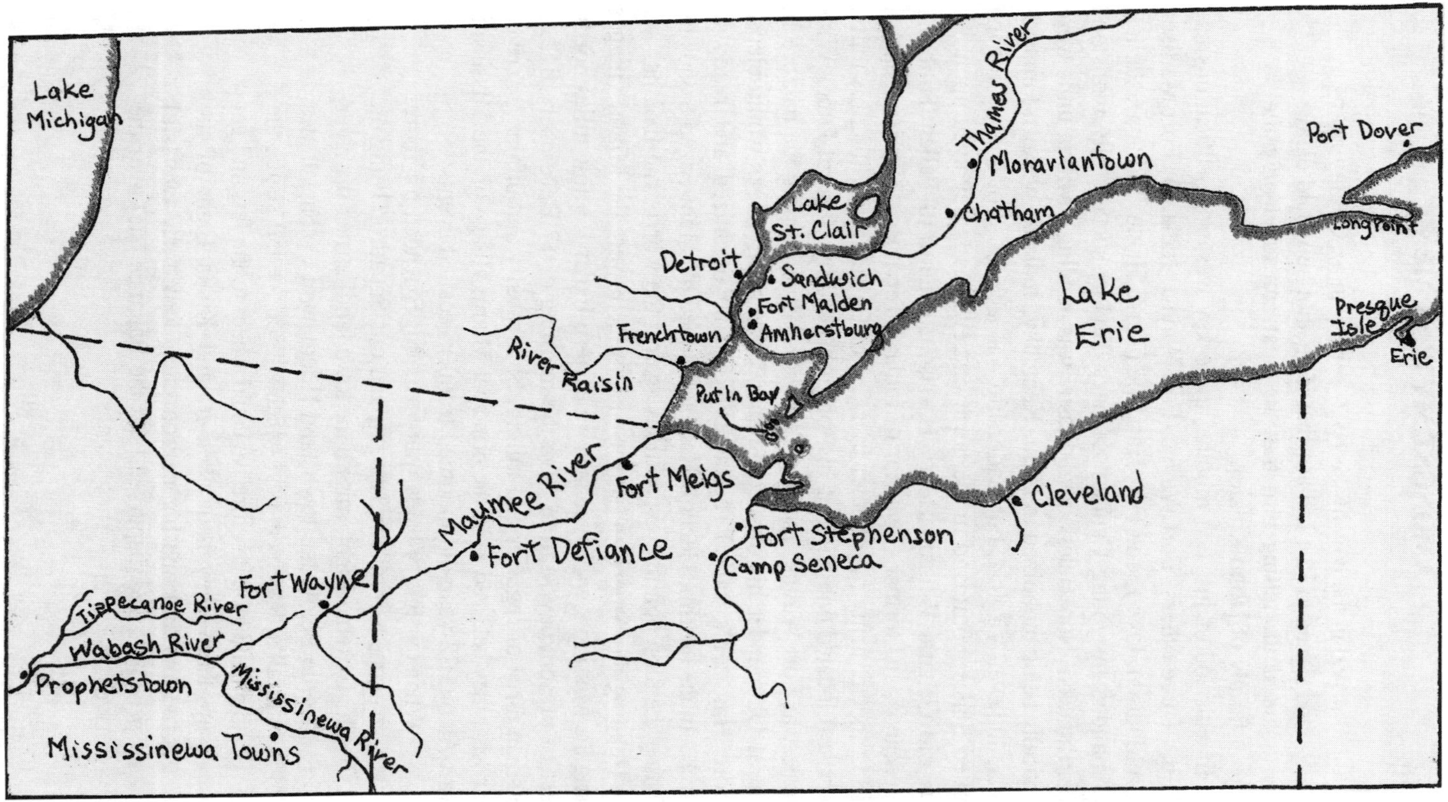
Lake Michigan
Thames River
Port Dover
Moraviantown
Lake St. Clair
Chatham
Longpoint
Detroit
Sandwich
Fort Malden
Amherstburg
Lake Erie
Presque Isle
Erie
Frenchtown
River Raisin
Put In Bay
Maumee River
Fort Meigs
Cleveland
Fort Stephenson
Camp Seneca
Fort Defiance
Fort Wayne
Tippecanoe River
Wabash River
Prophetstown
Mississinewa River
Mississinewa Towns

...stood in the bow of the boat, seized an ax that lay near
and signed to [the Indian] that if he shot he would cleave
his skull, telling him that the boat contained only the
family of [John Kinzie].[31]

In a period of just two months, three key western fortifications had
fallen. Three others, Fort Wayne (Fort Wayne, Indiana), Fort Madison
(Fort Madison, Iowa), and Fort Harrison (Terre Haute, Indiana), the last
commanded by young Captain Zachary Taylor, successfully withstood
Indian attacks. Nonetheless, total disaster was pending. Militia units were
frantically being mobilized in Ohio, Kentucky, Indiana, western Pennsylvania, and even Virginia, but leadership was lacking. Fortunately for the
United States, command in the northwest eventually devolved upon 39-
year-old General William Henry Harrison, veteran of Fallen Timbers,
Tippecanoe, and former Governor of Indiana Territory. Harrison started
raising another army for another invasion of Canada. Dividing his units,
Harrison located one wing of his force, headed by General James Winchester, at Fort Wayne, Indiana Territory, while keeping the balance in
central Ohio under his own command. Still, many weeks would elapse
before Harrison's varied regiments could be organized and ready to
march. In the interim, General Harrison honed his blunt-edged troops by
sending them on punitive expeditions against the worrisome Indians.

Heading the American list for chastisement were the Miami villages
lining the Mississinewa River in northeastern Indiana, a few miles northwest of present day Marion. On the morning of 17 December 1812, a
600-man force of regulars and militia, both cavalry and infantry, arrived
near what they believed to be the principal Miami village on the Mississinewa. As one 22-year-old mounted trooper recalled events:

When our line of battle was formed it Extended for more
than one half mile in Length, and our Squadron being on
the Extreme Right, missed the town [and] struck the river
a little Below the town, and [Lieutenant Colonel James
Simrall's] Rigement [sic] which was on the left struck the
town and took it before we could wheel to the left and get
up there—they had taken it, and Killed Eight of the
Indians and one big negroe [sic], took forty two [sic]
prisoners and dispursed [sic] the Ballance [sic] over the
river.[32]

AFRICAN-AMERICANS AND THE WAR OF 1812

Capturing the dwellings, the troops found to their chagrin that what they had overrun was not the main village but only the first in a string of Indian towns. The soldiers were attacked in turn the next morning by the infuriated Miamis, who were repelled only after severe fighting. With many horses dead and dozens of soldiers suffering from frostbite, the expedition commanders decided to turn back for Ohio, their mission unfulfilled. One of those forced to endure the long trek back while suffering from the agony of frostbite was "Troy Waugh, servant," who accompanied Kentucky Captain William Garrard's Company of Volunteer Light Dragoons.[33]

Mention of the "one big negroe" who fought with the Indians at the Mississinewa River raises an interesting topic. An undetermined number of runaway slaves eventually ended up living with indigenous tribes. How many actually escaped westward with the intent of seeking freedom with the Indians, or simply encountered tribesmen by accident while fleeing, cannot be known. In fact, it is impossible to even begin estimating the number of slaves who evaded bondage and were absorbed by or lost among Native American tribes in the wilderness. Some succeeded only in exchanging one set of chains for another since Indians themselves often kept black runaways as slaves. Other escaped slaves undoubtedly were adopted into tribes or otherwise assimilated as equals, many to fight and die for their own liberty and for the freedom of those who accepted them. Enough references exist to know that such occurrences were not infrequent. A prime example would be the relationships in the southeast that evolved between runaway slaves and the Creek and Seminole Indian tribes (see Chapter 12).

Harrison's order initiating another invasion of Canada in late December, 1812 diverted American attention from the Mississinewa River setback. The first stage of Harrison's campaign was initiated when General Winchester at Fort Wayne was directed to march to the rapids of the Maumee River, located at present day Perrysburg, Ohio, about one mile northeast of the Fallen Timbers battlefield. Harrison would meet Winchester at the rapids, and after consolidating the army he would proceed to invade Upper Canada.

Winchester was first to reach the rapids. While awaiting Harrison's arrival he received some alarming reports from residents of nearby Frenchtown, present day Monroe, Michigan. Tormented by British and

Indians raiding their town, the settlers implored Winchester to drive the enemy away. Winchester obliged and sent more than half of his nearly 1,000-man force to Frenchtown, where, on 18 January 1813, the enemy was evicted from Frenchtown after a headlong assault and a sharp skirmish. But then, instead of retiring to the rapids to await Harrison's arrival, Winchester settled in at Frenchtown, exposing his army on the north bank of the frozen River Raisin and failing to take adequate precautions against attack. In the early morning light of 22 January, the heavily reinforced British and Indians attacked, surprising Winchester's cold and ragged army just as reveille was sounding in the American camp. Struck from front and flank, the U.S. regulars on the American right broke and ran; the resulting bloodbath was ghastly as warriors chased down and killed the panicked soldiers like frightened sheep. On the American left, Winchester's Kentucky militiamen, protected by Frenchtown's palisade wall, succeeded in repulsing three British attacks. However, surrounded and low on ammunition, militia Major George Madison surrendered the remnant of his command at the prodding of Winchester, who had been captured himself early in the fight.

Immediately following his victory, Colonel Henry Proctor removed his own wounded and the unwounded American prisoners to Fort Malden. Under a promise of British protection, the American wounded were left at Frenchtown for later transport to Amherstburg. Proctor's promises notwithstanding, about 200 of the roughly 800 Indian warriors who fought at the River Raisin entered Frenchtown the following morning, set fire to the cabins housing the American wounded, and mercilessly killed approximately 60 helpless prisoners. Most Americans cared little that the Indians were acting in retribution for having their own families, homes, and crops destroyed during raids by U.S. soldiers just weeks earlier. Instead, the enraged American population only considered the fact that 60 defenseless prisoners were massacred, and of 934 U.S. troops engaged at the River Raisin, only 33 escaped being killed, wounded, or captured.

Here also, black Americans were fortunate that the U.S. Army did not yet permit them to fight, but a number of African-Americans still found their way to the field of battle. Troops engaged at the River Raisin were mostly from Kentucky, and many of the officers included slaves among their retinue. One of those heavy-hearted officers was Major George Madison, who fought valiantly and was persuaded to surrender the Kentucky militiamen holding Frenchtown. When he first left the Bluegrass State:

> Major Madison took with him a very black servant named Peter—or Peter Williams as he was commonly called. Peter had the good fortune to be in the battle, and he came home one of the greatest men who had ever been on a stricken field....He claimed all the indulgences due a veteran and had them.[34]

Whether or not Peter Williams was "fortunate to be in the battle" is debatable, but he did become a prisoner of war and in that respect he can be counted among the luckier River Raisin participants. Other slaves who accompanied their masters to the River Raisin were not so fortunate, ending up not as British prisoners, but as slaves to the Indians:

> Two other prisoners of the Indians when last heard from, in April, 1813, were acting as valets to the Indian chiefs. These were Solomon, Colonel John Allen's servant, and that of Colonel William Lewis. Captain [Nathaniel] Hart's servant at the same time was reported alive but his whereabouts uncertain.[35]

With a little timely help, Solomon's servitude among the Indians was short-lived. Ironically, following the Fort Dearborn calamity, the family of trader John Kinzie made their way to Detroit to live out the war among friends. The home in which the Kinzie family resided was turned into a hospital after the River Raisin battle, and every possible action was taken to aid the wretched survivors:

> Everything available among the effects of the [Detroit] citizens was offered to ransom their countrymen....The last bargain made by the Kinzies was effected by black Jim and one of the children, who had permission to redeem a negro servant of the gallant Colonel Allen with an old white horse, the only available article that remained among their possessions.[36]

Colonel Allen's brother was allowed to travel to occupied Detroit to reclaim Solomon, who reportedly chose to return to Kentucky rather than remain with strangers. William Henry Harrison on the other hand, was unable to retrieve his loss. With half of his army wiped out at the River Raisin, Harrison faced a difficult choice. He could easily withdraw his remaining forces back to Franklinton, present day Columbus, Ohio, but such a drastic move would leave the northern Ohio and Indiana frontier vulnerable to British attack and Indian raids. Rather than retreat, Harrison favored the bolder course. He started construction of an advanced supply base at the rapids of the Maumee River. Named in honor of Ohio Governor Return Jonathan Meigs, the large wood palisade fort was nearing completion by mid-April 1813. With the summer campaign approaching, Harrison required large numbers of troops to garrison the new fort, shield his lengthy supply line, and protect the huge frontier. Instead, their terms of enlistment having expired, most of Harrison's militia returned home to plant crops for their needy families. At a point where he clamored for troops, Harrison was reduced to just three understrength regiments of regulars, a company of artillerymen, and a few companies of militiamen who succumbed to the general's appeal to patriotism.

In late April, British General Proctor, who had been promoted after his River Raisin victory, discovered Harrison's predicament. Loading troops and artillery on board the British Lake Erie flotilla, Proctor crossed Lake Erie, sailed up the Maumee River, and surrounded Fort Meigs. Inside the crude fort, Harrison's wet and bedraggled troops suffered through a week-long bombardment, seeking safety from the steady and deadly passage of artillery projectiles by burrowing like moles into the mud of hastily dug traverses. On the evening of 4 May, 1,200 Kentucky reinforcements, unnoticed by Britain's vaunted Indian allies, arrived on the scene. Harrison schemed to relieve the siege by throwing his Kentucky infantry against the British artillery pieces, destroying the troublesome guns, and then consolidating his troops inside Fort Meigs.

In the pre-dawn hours of 5 May, 800 Kentucky militiamen, commanded by Lieutenant Colonel William Dudley, assaulted the British positions. With surprise on their side, the Bluegrass soldiers initially were successful, but Dudley's troops soon lost cohesion. The undisciplined militiamen wasted valuable time while the British and Indians regrouped and prepared a cunning trap. Dudley and his men blundered into the ambush and were soundly defeated. Although Dudley was killed and his troops were bested, about half the Kentuckians fought their way into the fort, enough to enable Harrison to continue resisting. Proctor sustained the siege for another week, but he was unable to entice Harrison out of the fort where superior British numbers and firepower would prevail. Finally, exasperated with his disgruntled Indian allies and equally frustrated by the complaints of his unhappy Canadian militiamen, Proctor withdrew to Fort Malden.

General Proctor nevertheless remained undeterred, and in late July he again sailed up the Maumee River and surrounded Fort Meigs. Once again, the Maumee River bastion proved impervious to British and Indian efforts, leaving Proctor confronted by large numbers of cheerless and rebellious Indians who wanted a victory—any victory. To assuage his mercurial allies, Proctor moved his forces 35 miles to the east in order to assail Fort Stephenson, a small post located about 15 miles up the Sandusky River from Lake Erie, at present day Fremont, Ohio. Only one acre in size and garrisoned by 160 Americans, Fort Stephenson should easily capitulate with little or no fight, or so hoped General Proctor. A British ultimatum to surrender the encircled fort was rebuffed by the American defenders, after which Proctor pounded the post with a day-long artillery bombardment. Finally, at 5 p.m. on the afternoon of 2 August, three long lines of British regulars from the 41st Regiment of Foot assaulted the tiny stockade. As the orderly red files neared the stockade, accurate American musketry whittled away at the courageous infantrymen, hacking ragged gaps in their finely dressed ranks. Pressing resolutely forward, the fearless Englishmen, Scotsmen, and Irishmen of the 41st Foot sought shelter in the ditch fronting the northwest corner of the fort. When the second line of red-coated infantry reached the ditch, the stronghold's single 6-pounder cannon, positioned to enfilade (from a side angle, sweep the entire length of an enemy line with fire) the exposed trench, belched convulsive charges of lethal iron into the unsuspecting foot soldiers. Like giant shotgun blasts, the 6-pounder grape and canister shot cut a murderous swath of destruction. Even the disciplined British regulars could not endure the deadly hail of shot. Bloodily trounced, Proctor had no choice but to retreat once again to his Fort Malden base, opening the way for the Americans to resume the initiative.

African-American participation in northwest operations during the spring and summer of 1813 was limited, with only occasional references surviving to document their presence. The ranks of regular regiments in the Old Northwest had yet to be opened to black enlistees, and few were allowed to serve with Kentucky or Ohio militia units. Occasionally a muster roll notes a black regular or militiaman as a servant or a waiter. While some black Americans involved in the campaign may have been free men, most were slaves. One such individual was mentioned by Captain Daniel Cushing of the 2nd U.S. Artillery Regiment, although it is uncertain as to whether the man was Captain Cushing's personal slave or a volunteer otherwise attached to the unit as a waiter. On 1 January 1813, Cushing, whose company was in the midst of a difficult march from Franklinton to Upper Sandusky, Ohio, recorded in his diary:

> Rained very hard, became very dark, no tent pitched, no fire, nothing to make fire with, hemmed in with a very steep hill on one side and a very wet and muddy bottom on the other. I sent all the officers and men to two houses in the neighborhood, except two wagoners, my black boy Ferguson, and four soldiers that stayed with me.[37]

Another man similarly mentioned was the servant of Lieutenant Joseph Larwill, a member of Cushing's company of the 2nd U.S. Artillery. On 1 March 1813, after a day of trudging through winter snows, Larwill wrote in his journal:

> I forgot to mention that yesterday my black boy Lewis was tomahawked by a Private in Lieut. Maddis Company while he was engaged [in] transacting his business [sic] [At] one of the sleds some misunderstanding took place between them which occasioned words between them. The private, named Patrick, struck [Lewis] on the side of the head with [a] tomahawk which cut him considerable [sic]. Lieut. Maddis corrected Patrick for the offense. The boy was much hurt.[38]

Lewis's wound, while undoubtedly serious, did not prove fatal since Larwill penned another journal entry two weeks later:

> ...having made arrangements to start this morning after breakfast, I have my horse saddled and having paid my waiter (Lewis, a Black Boy) for his services until this day, my company being ready...I got three miles from the lines.[39]

Steadfast resistance by Harrison's troops at Fort Meigs and Fort Stephenson in the spring and summer of 1813 gained valuable time for the United States and opened the way for Oliver Hazard Perry's flotilla to sail onto the scene. As previously stated, the role of black sailors on board the

AFRICAN-AMERICANS AND THE WAR OF 1812

United States fleet was crucial to Perry's overwhelming success on 10 September 1813, which swept the British Navy from Lake Erie. With the Americans in control of Lake Erie, Harrison's army was transported in stages to the Canadian mainland. British General Proctor, his fleet eliminated and supply situation desperate, torched Fort Malden and retreated up the Thames River. Harrison's army followed, pressuring the harried British and Indians to turn and fight near a Christian Indian village called Moraviantown, near present day Thamesville, Ontario. A brief but frenzied engagement on 5 October 1813 routed Proctor's 800 demoralized British regulars, and when the great Shawnee chief Tecumseh was killed, the disheartened Indians melted into the woods. After the battle of the Thames River, as far as the Old Northwest was concerned, the Indians faded into the history books.

Dual victories by Oliver Hazard Perry on Lake Erie and William Henry Harrison at the Thames River virtually ended active campaigning in the Old Northwest. Many of Harrison's regulars were subsequently shipped eastward, where they were needed to augment other U.S. armies and operations. As a result, new regiments had to be raised in the northwest in the event active campaigning resumed. One of the newly constituted units was the 2nd U.S. Rifle Regiment, among whose ranks was black musician Samuel Looks. After enlisting at Chillicothe, Ohio on 4 July 1814, Looks remained with the 2nd U.S. Rifles for the war's duration.[40] Neither Looks nor the 2nd U.S. Rifle Regiment participated in the joint army and navy expedition to recapture Fort Mackinac during the summer of 1814. A miserable failure for the United States, the Fort Mackinac attack was one of the last American attempts to regain lost territory on the upper lakes. Otherwise, the brunt of active campaigning veered to the east.

9

THE NIAGARA REGION
AND LAKE ONTARIO

The Niagara region of the United States and Canada encompassed a picturesque strip of land separating Lakes Ontario and Erie, with the raging Niagara River serving as a conduit, both connecting the lakes and delineating the boundary between the two countries. Populated by similar peoples with common threads often spliced by family bonds, the Niagara River theater of operations would experience, either because of or despite its close cultural ties, the harshest campaigning and the most savage and ruthless fighting of the entire War of 1812.

The ugly face of what approximated a malicious civil war first frowned upon the Niagara region on 13 October 1812. In the weeks prior to that date, an army of nearly 4,000 Americans under the direction of New York Militia General Stephen Van Rensselaer had been consolidated at Lewiston, New York. Composed mostly of New York militiamen, Van Rensselaer's force also included about 800 regulars. Encamped at Black Rock near Buffalo, within supporting distance of Van Rensselaer's force, loitered another brigade of American regulars led by Brigadier General Alexander Smyth.

Across the river from Van Rensselaer's army, opposite Lewiston, lay the American objective, Queenston and its nearby heights. Defending the village of Queenston were two companies of the 49th Regiment of Foot and a detachment of Lincoln County Militia. Combined they numbered about 300 men. Altogether Major General Isaac Brock had nearly 2,000 troops scattered in defensive positions up and down the river's west bank, but most were concentrated at either Fort George or Fort Erie, the bastions guarding the Canadian entrances to the river. From either of those locations Brock could hastily summon reinforcements to any threatened point. Included among the units based at Fort George was a small company of Canadians composed exclusively, except for its white officers, of black militiamen.

The concept of black troops serving with Crown forces was not new —not even in Canada. Indigenous peoples throughout the British empire were employed by the military in a variety of capacities, usually, but not always, as pioneers, or in other labor-oriented battalions. Several hundred black soldiers fought in British units during the American Revolution, and following that conflict most black loyalists accompanied their white counterparts to British controlled territory in Canada.[41] In 1796, hoping to capitalize on the potential pool of manpower, Lieutenant Colonel Charles Stevenson of the 5th Regiment of Foot submitted a proposal for raising a 1,000-man black legion to be comprised of infantry and cavalry. Stevenson intended to deploy his new unit to the West Indies, though service in North America was not ruled out:

> I...offer my services to assist [the government] in raising a Legion of 1000 Blacks, endeavouring to raise them as reasonably as circumstances will permit. I propose...to raise the Legion as follows, to consist of eight companies [of infantry] and 4 Troops [of cavalry]. I [should]...form them into the several following descriptions—As Batteaux [sic] men, as Marines to fight and work the Gun Boats, as Hussar Troops, possibly at some future day [they] may be necessary to oppose the Kentucky Cavalry, the most active Troops of our neighbors, and likewise from their habits of labours may oftimes be usefully employed as pioneers and miners...such a corps...I [should] conceive would be an object that meritted [sic] the attention of Govt.[42]

Although Stevenson's scheme to establish a distinctive black corps was viewed favorably by no less a personage than the Duke of York, the colonel's enterprise failed to engender sufficient support within the military to become a reality. Nevertheless, by the War of 1812, one small unit of black troops had been formed, and a number of black militiamen were serving in various other Canadian units.

Unique among Canadian militia organizations was an outfit designated in unit returns as the Colored Corps, sometimes referred to as Captain Runchey's Company of Colored Men, after its original commander,

Robert Runchey, Sr., a militia captain and tavern owner. The Colored Corps was the vision of Samuel Pierrepont, a Canadian veteran who had served with Butler's Rangers during the American Revolution, and who was an early black settler in St. Catharine's, Upper Canada. Apparently the company was a provisional outfit formed with volunteers from several different militia regiments; the largest of any one group to join the Colored Corps emanated from the 3rd Regiment of York Militia, when, in October, 1812, Sergeant William Thompson and 13 of his compatriots volunteered to transfer to the company. The Colored Corps differed organizationally from average Canadian sedentary militia units in that the men were promised six months severance pay when their term expired, an allowance akin to that offered to incorporated militia units.[43]

Reasons for the company's formation as an all black unit are unknown. Possibly the British army hierarchy was attempting to instill *esprit de corps* by establishing a unified command. Then again, Canada was no different from its southern neighbor. Prejudice was a common attribute in Canada, and the same trait held true in the King's forces:

> The British Army did not institutionally discriminate against Black soldiers, and the employment of local and native soldiers was an established practice throughout the garrisons of the British empire. The nature of employment of such troops, however, was indicative of British social norms. Throughout Upper Canada both racism and slavery were prevalent features of society, and these beliefs were likewise reflected in the Canadian militia.[44]

Along with the bulk of British forces lining the Niagara River's west bank on the morning of 13 October 1812, Runchey's company was unsure of American intentions. Van Rensselaer's plan called for a large number of invasion craft to be assembled at Lewiston, New York, where the American regulars and New York militiamen would embark, cross the Niagara, and overrun the meager British force. But plans and their execution seldom coalesced in the War of 1812. Confusion reigned on the U.S. side as the operation was launched. Sufficient boats and boatmen were lacking, but in spite of the muddle, Van Rensselaer and about 600 regulars and militiamen crossed over to Queenston. Van Rensselaer was wounded early in the engagement, and Captain John E. Wool, from the

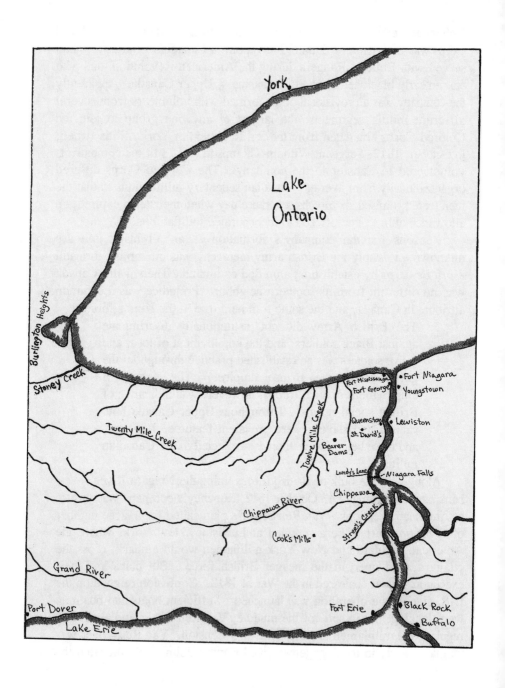

13th U.S. Infantry Regiment, assumed temporary command. After hard fighting and heavy casualties, U.S. troops discovered a little-used track which enabled them to outflank the fiercely resisting British and Canadian soldiers, scale the summit of Queenston Heights, and capture the critical high ground. General Brock, asleep in Fort George when the action commenced, hurriedly gathered all available troops and rushed towards Queenston Heights. Arriving on the scene, Brock chose not to await additional reinforcements, with which he could have executed a planned, coordinated counterattack. Instead, the dynamic general precipitately assaulted the American positions with available troops. Personally leading the charge, Major General Isaac Brock paid for his rash act with his life.

Brock's death was the only consolation for the American cause that day. As the fighting dragged on, Lieutenant Colonel Winfield Scott and a small number of U.S. reinforcements were ferried across the river in the too few available boats, but as more and more British troops double-timed to the scene, American fortunes declined. As the tide began to turn, the New York militia units suddenly refused to cross the river and fight, grumbling that they volunteered solely to defend the State of New York, not to invade a foreign country. Without assistance, the plight of Winfield Scott and his beleaguered men steadily worsened. Scott could only watch helplessly as arriving British troops, led by Major General Sir Roger Sheaffe, congregated below the heights and formed for a headlong assault. Many of the inexperienced American soldiers, forsaken by their comrades and frightened by their bleak prospects, deserted Scott's defensive position on the heights, leaving the American commander hopelessly outnumbered. Sheaffe's assault could not fail:

> The left flank of the British line was of very varied character, consisting of one company of the 41st Regiment, one company of coloured men, and a mixed body of militia and Indians.

> Sheaffe opened the battle at about 4:00 [p.m.] by directing Lieutenant McIntyre, with the Light Company of the 41st on the left of his column, supported by a body of militia, Indians and negroes under Captain Runchey, to fall upon the American right. They fired a single volley with considerable execution, and then charged with a tremendous tumult...The Americans were over-

93

powered by the onslaught and gave way....[45]

About 250 U.S. troops were killed or wounded on Queenston Heights and more than 900 were captured, while the faint-hearted militia sulked on the opposite bank and timorously watched their comrades being crushed by the British assault. Rubbing salt into the wound was General Smyth at Black Rock. As a brigadier general in the United States Army, Smyth snobbishly considered himself superior to officers in the state militia, regardless of rank, and he refused to cooperate in any venture commanded by a militia general. Although American soldiers were fighting and dying a few miles to the north, Smyth peevishly declined to order his regular regiments to march to Van Rensselaer's assistance.

However, Smyth's contribution to the campaign was not yet over. With his brigade of regulars, augmented by sailors from the Black Rock Naval Station, the fickle general plunged ahead with his own invasion plans. On 28 November 1812, Smyth launched the first wave of a 1,200-man assault force across the Niagara River to attack Fort Erie, opposite Buffalo. After meeting some initial success, the American troops on the Canadian shore were appalled to discover that Smyth had skittishly aborted the main crossing, forcing those soldiers who had been transported to the Niagara's west bank to scurry to save themselves. Two days later, Smyth decided to try again. With troops embarked in boats and ready to set forth, Smyth dallied for several hours until he lost his nerve once again and ordered his regulars to disembark to eat lunch. So concluded another invasion attempt of Canada, and along with it, active campaigning along the Niagara River in 1812. The only bright spot for the United States Army in this mismanaged affair was that General Alexander Smyth was relieved of command, never again to lead U.S. troops.

Operations in 1813 commenced on Lake Ontario with a large scale U.S. amphibious raid against York (present day Toronto), the capital of Upper Canada. On 27 April, supported by naval gunfire, ships' boats from Commodore Isaac Chauncey's flotilla landed a force of 1,600 soldiers. Since it has already been established that a significant percentage of Chauncey's crewmen were black sailors, many of the landing craft and guns would have been crewed by black seamen. York was captured, but when Brigadier General Zebulon Pike was killed by an explosion, leaderless American troops went on a rampage, looting and torching public and private buildings alike. Despite the baseless destruction, the raid was still considered a success; the British shipyard at York and a vast array of valuable British naval and military supplies had been destroyed. Since the raid's objective was not to hold or garrison York, the Americans embarked and sailed to the east, returning to their Sackets Harbor base.

No sooner had the successful raid ended than plans were formulated for another amphibious operation, with the target being the British stronghold of Fort George. If the army of Major General Henry Dearborn, with an assist from Chauncey's fleet, could capture and hold strategically-located Fort George, the entire British-held Niagara peninsula might conceivably fall to American troops. Such a sweeping possibility, if consummated, would foreshadow grave consequences for the British supply situation on Lake Erie.

By late May, Dearborn had gathered his 4,000-man army near Fort Niagara, just across the Niagara River from Fort George. Under the operational command of the exchanged and newly promoted Colonel Winfield Scott, the three long waves of invasion craft which constituted the American landing force approached the Canadian shore near Two-Mile Creek, just west of the village of Newark, at dawn on the morning of 27 May. Sweating sailors rowed the ragged lines of soldier-crammed invasion craft awkwardly toward the shoreline, while reddish-yellow flashes and thunderous blasts from the heavy guns of Chauncey's warships served as a turbulent yet reassuring backdrop for the apprehensive American regulars.

Upon discovering American intentions, British General John Vincent insured that Scott's landing would not go uncontested. Swiftly throwing together a mixed bag of regulars and militia, Vincent rushed his troops through the town of Newark to meet the invaders. A British officer remembered the counterthrust:

> The enemy commenced his landing in very great force. Under his galling fire [elements of] the Glengarry [Light Infantry Fencible Regiment], consisting of 90 men, the Royal Newfoundland [Regiment] 40 men, the Black Corps 27 men, a detachment of militia 100 men, and the 8th Regiment [of Foot] 310, advanced to repel the foe, notwithstanding the showers of grape and other shot from his vessels....The contest was severe...The officers and men of the above-mentioned corps fast fell and the

95

contest soon became unequal....Our brave men, compelled to retire, rallied and again charged the enemy at the
water's edge, yet, under the destructive fire from [the
American] ships, which it was impossible to evade, the
enemy was enabled to continue his disembarkation...our
brave troops...[were] reluctantly necessitated to retire to
a ravine a few yards to their rear, where they again
formed....Our brave troops advanced to dispute the
ground but...found themselves still more exposed....A
retreat was most unwillingly resorted to.[46]

For the Crown troops, outnumbered four to one and subjected to a
galling fire from Chauncey's squadron, retreat was inevitable. Unable to
stop the American onslaught, Vincent's overmatched provisional battalion
withdrew, rejoining the British general and his remaining defenders near
the fort. Vincent quickly recognized that his position at Fort George was
untenable. The fort had been heavily damaged by a day-long artillery
bombardment from Fort Niagara's guns two days earlier, so Vincent, with
his troops retreating before the advancing Americans, ordered Fort
George to be abandoned. British losses totaled more than 350 men,
though casualties among Runchey's company are not known. Adding a
note of controversy to the encounter, a U.S. Army officer, penning an
account of the action to a Baltimore newspaper three days later, clearly
remembered seeing "...but one of their Indians and one negro (with the
Glengarry uniform) dead on the field, a proof that neither their black nor
red allies are very potent nor brave."[47]

This American officer's comments are interesting for two reasons.
First, specific reference is made to a black soldier in a Glengarry uniform,
seeming proof that the dead Negro fought with the Canadian-raised
Glengarry Light Infantry Fencible Regiment (a fencible regiment was a
militia unit comprised of men who volunteered for home service only, and
for the duration of the war for which they enlisted). Initially raised in
1807, the Glengarry regiment was composed of Scots volunteers from the
Glengarry region of Canada (extreme eastern Ontario). After war was
declared in 1812, the Glengarries, like many Canadian and American
units, found that volunteers were increasingly more difficult to find. As
a result, the Glengarries recruited far afield, and according to one individual, Glengarry Light Infantry companies "were soon filled up with

runaway sailors, English, Irish, Dutch, Americans, Canadians, and a sprinkling of Africans..."[48] The Glengarry uniform was distinctive for its dark green color, the tunics having black collars and cuffs, white lace, and three rows of white pewter buttons on the breast. Originally the uniform was designed for the British 95th Rifle Regiment, but abundant stocks caused the British government to ship excess uniforms to other countries for distribution to colonial units such as the Glengarries.

The dead man referred to by the American officer was most likely a member of the Glengarry Light Infantry. But it is also possible that some of the spare rifle regiment uniforms were issued to Runchey's company, and the green-uniformed casualty could have been a member of the all-black militia unit. Then again, on 1 January 1813, militia units in Upper Canada were authorized to wear an official uniform consisting of green coats bearing red collars and cuffs with white lace, plus blue trousers and a regulation British felt shako or military hat.[49] Runchey's company may have been issued the specified militia uniform by May of 1813 and the American officer could have confused it with the uniform of the Glengarries. However, this is unlikely since few of the authorized uniforms were available at that early date and because of the scarcity, most Canadian militiamen at Fort George in May of 1813 wore civilian clothes.

Second, the American officer's comment that "neither their black nor red allies are very potent" could mean either that they were few in number, or that they did not stand and fight as well as the white troops. If he meant to convey the latter, then the statement is unfounded. The feats of Runchey's company during the battle are not precisely known, but the British defenders as a whole fought well—American dead nearly equaled those of the British—and to malign the fighting capabilities of one group based upon the criterion of a single dead body would be irrational. A more accurate measure might be the courageous and determined resistance offered by the outnumbered British forces, including Runchey's company.

Retreating from Fort George, Vincent moved around the American army and marched westward, taking up defensive positions on Burlington Heights, near present day Hamilton, Ontario. Not until 3 June did General Dearborn dispatch 2,400 troops to pursue what had been a defeated enemy six days earlier. On the evening of 5 June, the Americans reached a small rivulet called Stoney Creek, where, after scattering a British outpost, the troops bivouacked. General Vincent, acting on the advice of an aggressive subordinate who scouted the American camp, boldly advanced 700 men to Stoney Creek, present Stoney Creek, Ontario, where he ventured a risky bayonet assault in the early morning darkness of 6 June. Completely surprising their unprepared and slumbering foe, the attacking British column, Runchey's company included, captured two American generals, three artillery pieces, and upwards of 100 prisoners before conducting an orderly withdrawal. The light of dawn revealed the U.S. regulars still in control of the battlefield. Nevertheless, despite repulsing the attack, inflicting heavy casualties on the British, and rallying to advance and reoccupy their camp, the Americans remained on the scene only long enough to destroy their excess supplies and equipment before retreating.

American caution was partially attributable to the actions of British General Sir George Prevost, Governor General of the Canadas. Commodore Chauncey's preoccupation with the Fort George assault left the American base at Sackets Harbor vulnerable and denuded of ships. Seizing the opportunity, Prevost loaded 800 redcoats on board Commodore Sir George Lucas Yeo's vessels at Kingston, and on 29 May the British launched an attack on lightly defended Sackets Harbor. The specter of British bayonets stampeded most of the New York Militia protecting the base, but a few regulars and one stalwart band of militiamen rallied to blunt the assault. For two hours the red-coated regiments doggedly pressed their attack. One of those determined units was the 104th Regiment of Foot, among whose ranks fought John Baker, a former slave of Solicitor General of Lower Canada R.I.D. Gray.[50] But John Baker, who was wounded in action during the repeated British assaults at Sackets Harbor, was not the only black soldier to fight with the 104th Foot. Attached to every British Army infantry battalion was a section of pioneers consisting of approximately ten men. Pioneers were skilled in the use of tools and normally they were assigned to construction related duties. In an army where uniformity usually assured anonymity, pioneers were distinguished by heavy tan leather aprons worn to protect their red-coated uniforms. In addition to shouldering muskets like every other foot soldier, pioneers also carried one or more of a variety of specialized tools. The 104th Regiment of Foot was raised in New Brunswick, which had a large black population, and it appears that the entire pioneer section of the 104th Foot was comprised of black soldiers.[51]

The gritty defenders of Sackets Harbor held firm, and the efforts of Baker and his fellow British regulars were ultimately unsuccessful. Determination and perseverance led to an American victory, if such a disaster could be labeled a success. Prevost had retreated, but during the heat of battle, Lieutenant Wolcott Chauncey, the frazzled younger brother of the American commodore, incinerated U.S. Navy warehouses containing half a million dollars worth of naval stores. Moreover, Prevost's raid hastened the return of Chauncey's flotilla to Sackets Harbor, dangerously weakening support for the American offensive west of Fort George.

Gains had been made by the United States all along Lake Ontario and the Niagara River during the spring of 1813. York, the seat of Upper Canada's government, had been overrun and sacked. Fort George had been captured and along with it went Fort Erie, which was forced to capitulate when its supply line was severed when Fort George fell. American control of the forts also hobbled British efforts to supply their outposts on the upper lakes. But British audacity checked U.S. efforts to expand their Canadian foothold and effectively polarized American resolve. Following Stoney Creek, General Vincent's troops advanced, squeezing the faltering Americans onto a narrow strip of the Niagara River's west bank. At this time, Runchey's Colored Corps, with a complement of one officer, two sergeants, 20 rank and file, plus four more men who were on the sicklist, was attached to the British force that was slowly creeping closer to American-occupied Fort George.[52]

Endeavoring to resume the lost initiative, American General John P. Boyd selected Colonel Charles Boerstler to lead an expedition of 550 men against a suspected British supply dump at a place known as the Beaver Dams, about 15 miles southwest of Fort George. As they approached the Beaver Dams on 24 June, Boerstler's troops were attacked by a large body of Indians. The Americans staved off the Indians after a sharp fight, but Boerstler, short of ammunition, decided to abort his mission. Boerstler had barely begun his retreat back to Fort George when a British officer, Lieutenant James FitzGibbon, leading a mounted company of 50 scouts, approached under a flag of truce. Convincing Boerstler that his command was outnumbered and surrounded, the wily Britisher deluded the American colonel into surrendering his entire regiment to a force only one-tenth its own size.

After the Beaver Dams debacle, the increasingly irresolute Dearborn allowed his army to be contained within a constricted band of captured territory. Henry Dearborn's unmitigated bungling, combined with repeated military defeats, finally led to the ineffective general's downfall. Dearborn was relieved of command and replaced by Major General James Wilkinson—an unsavory and greedy conniver, it was later discovered that Wilkinson, while in overall command of the United States Army, was being paid by Spain to spy upon his own country. In conjunction with higher authority in Washington, Wilkinson put into effect a new strategy which called for American efforts to concentrate on the capture of Montreal. Consequently, American forces in the Niagara region were steadily transferred to Sackets Harbor for redeployment, leaving the remaining U.S. forces on the Niagara's west bank in a precarious position.

Taking instant advantage of American vulnerability, the British raided across the Niagara River on 10 July and seized the Black Rock naval depot. Consternation reigned in nearby Buffalo until General Peter B. Porter mobilized the local militia. Catching the British at Black Rock loading their booty on barges, the energetic Porter attacked, pressuring the British to retire across the river after a brisk skirmish. For the British, the Black Rock raid was a material and morale-boosting success.

Just when it appeared as though the British and Canadians might be gaining ascendancy, a decision was made to send two British regiments of foot to Kingston to help repel Wilkinson's thrust on Montreal. News of Perry's victory on Lake Erie and Harrison's triumph at the Thames River gave added pause for reflection and further cooled British ardor. Vincent's force had been weakened, and there was some concern that Harrison's army might advance eastward from Detroit, but at least the British general need not concern himself with his opponent along the Niagara River. By late September, all but a tiny detachment of American regulars had been shunted eastward, leaving Fort George garrisoned principally by an unenthusiastic body of New York militia commanded by General George McClure, who soon found himself in a virtual state of siege by Vincent's army. Among those tightening the grip on the hapless Americans was Runchey's Colored Corps, located at the nearby village of St. David's.[53]

When the American Montreal offensive collapsed in November, General McClure's position at Fort George became even more perilous. Rather than have troops isolated for the winter on the Canadian side of the river, the nervous McClure chose to evacuate Fort Erie and Fort George after destroying everything that might be of use to the enemy. Somehow McClure concluded that the town of Newark, adjacent to Fort George, fell into that category. On 10 December 1813 he reduced the town to ashes, throwing the dispossessed onto the snow-filled streets, including an ill, elderly woman still on her sickbed. That same night McClure abandoned Fort George. Incongruously, having destroyed Newark, McClure left all but one of Fort George's magazines untouched, failed to destroy the fort or most of its heavy artillery, and overlooked enough tentage to shelter 1,500 enemy soldiers.

Retaliation for McClure's brutality and negligence was not long in coming. Just after sunset on 18 December, new British commander Lieutenant General Sir Gordon Drummond crossed more than 550 British regulars and Canadian militiamen over the Niagara River to Youngstown and tramped northward to Fort Niagara. Achieving complete surprise, the redcoats rushed through the unsuspecting fort's open gates and captured the post after a brief firefight, killing 65 Americans with the bayonet and handily capturing more than 350, along with a huge quantity of arms, ammunition, and supplies. At the same time, other British units forayed to the south, cleaving a wide swath of destruction. Accompanied by a number of their Indian allies, Drummond's troops burned and ransacked everything in their path, including the towns of Youngstown, Lewiston, Manchester, and Buffalo. Reprisals effectively administered, Drummond hoped that the Americans would accept his not-so-subtle warning and refrain from future aggression against non-military targets. On such an ignoble note, the 1813 Niagara campaign ended.

The spring of 1814 revealed that U.S. military leaders had learned few lessons from the previous December. On the afternoon of 14 May 1814, 800 Americans debarked from the Lake Erie flotilla near Port Dover, Upper Canada after crossing the lake from Erie, Pennsylvania. No opposition was expected or encountered, so the next morning, U.S. troops plundered and burned the town. Then, guided and assisted by a small number of Canadian volunteers, the Americans roamed the countryside, looting, burning, and killing farm animals. British revenge for Port Dover, plus other real and perceived atrocities, would be exacted later that summer farther to the east.

It was also during the spring of 1814 that the United States Army finally came of age. Preparing for the upcoming summer campaign, an army of regulars commanded by Major General Jacob Brown was being assembled near Buffalo. But this time the training of that force was entrusted to the capable and talented Brigadier General Winfield Scott. Now that the no-nonsense Scott had finally acquired the rank and authority to do so, he took the disjointed elements of what had previously passed for an army and remorselessly drilled them day in and day out for three months. By molding the two brigades into a competent fighting machine, Scott insured that if the Americans experienced future failures, the cause would not be attributable to a lack of training or discipline among his U.S. Army regulars.

At long last, the U.S. Army officially opened the ranks of its regiments to black recruits. The army's liberalism was not a progressive attempt at integration but a reaction to poor results with white recruitment. It was no secret that the war was unpopular, made more so by bungling leadership and botched military campaigns. Indeed, there was even talk of secession at one point among the New England states. With the country in such a somber mood, only the most nationalistic and public-spirited men were willing to join an army having a reputation for repeated failure, and the United States can be thankful that many black patriots were inclined to enlist.

A troop of U.S. Light Dragoons, eight infantry companies from the 5th Pennsylvania Militia Detachment, and a contingent of about 400 Indians would accompany General Brown's army into Canada, but the Americans' real striking power lay with Brown's two brigades of regulars. Commanding the first brigade was Winfield Scott, with the 9th U.S., 11th U.S., and 25th U.S. Infantry Regiments, plus a few companies of the 22nd U.S. Infantry. Brigadier General Eleazer Ripley led the second brigade, consisting of the 21st U.S. and 23rd U.S. Infantry Regiments, along with attached companies of the 19th U.S. Infantry. Ripley's brigade would later be augmented by several companies from the 1st U.S. and 17th U.S. Infantry Regiments. Winfield Scott was proud of the force he had honed to a fighting edge. He was anxious to put his regulars to the ultimate test to discover if they truly were a match for England's best.

During the 1814 Niagara campaign, black regulars fought with the 1st U.S., 11th U.S., 23rd U.S., and 25th U.S. Infantry Regiments, and also with the U.S. Corps of Artillery.[54] And it is not beyond reason to assume that black soldiers marched among the ranks of General Jacob Brown's other regular regiments. Black troops incorporated within the units of Brown's army were new and untried, but then Brown's army as a whole had yet to prove its mettle.

On 3 July 1814, after crossing the Niagara River from Black Rock, the Americans quickly invested Fort Erie and intimidated its small garrison into surrender. After securing Fort Erie, Brown's army marched north along the river, with Scott's brigade in the van. Late on the afternoon of 5 July, the U.S. advance encountered a British force between Street's Creek and the Chippawa River. Without delay, Scott's regulars crossed Street's Creek and formed line of battle, pressing forward against the troops of British General Phineas Riall. Riall was not about to fight a defensive battle; he chose to attack at precisely the same moment as Scott. Nearly equal in size, about 2,000 men each, the forces clashed on open ground using European-style linear tactics, or opposing lines of battle. Standing less than 100 yards apart, the long lines of infantry exchanged volley after volley of musketry. The fierce fighting was terminated when a contingent of Americans penetrated the woods on the British right flank, subjecting Riall's troops to a brisk enfilading fire and forcing the redcoats from the field. When compared to many of the titanic Napoleonic battles that were fought in Europe, Chippawa was but a skirmish—American casualties exceeded 180, British losses were around 200—but for the first time during the War of 1812, American regulars defeated British regulars fighting toe-to-toe in European-style line of battle. It was a crucial turning point in U.S. Army history.

One of the American regulars who formed Scott's line at Chippawa was Private Jacob Dexter. A "colored man" who enlisted in the 25th U.S. Infantry on 28 March 1814, Dexter helped Winfield Scott demonstrate that American soldiers could stand firm in the face of fearsome musketry and artillery fire while comrades were being shot down around them. Jacob Dexter, wounded in action at Chippawa, was one of many who shed blood to prove Scott's point.[55]

Brown followed up his victory by dogging Riall's retreat all the way to Fort George. In another of those regrettable incidents perpetrated by U.S. troops, a detachment of advancing New York militiamen, without Brown's knowledge or approval, burned the village of St. David's. In the meantime, Riall wisely chose not to allow his small army to become bottled up in an untenable position, so he withdrew the bulk of his forces westward toward Twenty Mile Creek after leaving strong garrisons at Fort George and nearby Fort Mississauga. Fort Mississauga was still being built at this time, and among the units selected to defend the fort and complete construction was the Colored Corps, redesignated in 1814 as the Corps of Provincial Artificers and placed under the command of James Robertson.[56]

Deciding not to attack the British fortifications without naval support, and unwilling to initiate siege operations, the Americans, not having a well-defined objective for the campaign, retraced their route to Chippawa Creek. Uncertain about American intentions, Riall nevertheless reversed his steps, tailed his enemy, and established a strong defensive position at Lundy's Lane, a narrow dirt track running westward from Niagara Falls through gently rolling terrain. British reinforcements, led by General Drummond, were hurriedly marching to join Riall.

Concerned by the proximity of Riall's force, General Brown, on the afternoon of 25 July, ordered Winfield Scott to move his brigade forward to reconnoiter the enemy position. Just as Scott was deploying his brigade in front of Lundy's Lane, the first of Drummond's men arrived on the scene to brace the British line. Despite being outnumbered, Winfield Scott aggressively advanced to the attack.

As the warm afternoon shadows lengthened, British and American reinforcements double-timed to the scene, both sides feeding more and more fodder into the bloody maw of combat. Black and white men in blue and red coats grimly scrambled to ready their death-dealing instruments of war. Artillerymen bustled about the cumbersome cannons, feverishly cramming linen bags of black powder and loathsome payloads of deadly iron into the ugly snouts of their unwieldy guns. Tightly-closed double ranks of sweating infantrymen in heavy wool coats leveled their muskets and quickly jerked on resisting triggers, spewing showers of lethal lead from the five-foot-long smoothbore flintlocks. Rancid clouds of dirty white gunsmoke from incessant cannon fire and repeated musket volleys shrouded the battlefield, nearly blotting out the fading sunlight. Officers trying to maintain control frantically waved their swords, like mad conductors orchestrating a deafening cacophony of battle. Facing the music, combatants were exposed to a piercing crescendo of mind-numbing noise which dazed even the most battle-hardened veterans.

AFRICAN-AMERICANS AND THE WAR OF 1812

Plum-sized grape shot and solid iron cannonballs larger than a man's fist sickeningly dismembered everything and everyone in their paths. Soft lead one-ounce musket balls the size of large marbles, mushrooming on impact, punched through pliant flesh and brittle bone, wreaking gruesome damage. The yellow fields and beautiful green shades of surrounding foliage were being crazily splashed with ugly red blotches, as if spattered by a lunatic's macabre paintbrush.

Attack was followed by counterattack succeeded by flank attack checked by bayonet attack. Vicious hand-to-hand fighting ensued. Powerful thrusts by muskets fixed with 18-inch-long triangular bayonets inflicted ghastly wounds; empty muskets were converted into 10-pound clubs, and metal-capped musket butts hammered down unwary opponents; razor sharp swords cleaved through leather, cloth, flesh, and bone. Incoherent screams and agonized shrieks from horribly maimed and mutilated men pierced the dismal gloom.

Rapidly enveloping shades of dusk failed to stop the sanctioned bloodletting. Confusion reigned as disoriented troops continued to struggle in the hideous blackness. Flashes from musket volleys exposed fleeting images of powder-blackened faces twisted into impassioned masks of fear, anger, hatred, and horror. Excited troops eager to lash out at the enemy mistakenly fired into their own comrades. Men stumbled blindly into their opponent's lines, to be mercilessly cut down or captured.

After Scott's first determined attack was repulsed, an equally tenacious assault by General Ripley's brigade managed to overrun a battery of seven British artillery pieces which anchored Drummond's line—General Riall had been wounded and captured just after dark. Ripley's American regulars then braced themselves to beat back three equally obstinate British attempts to recapture the guns. Scott regrouped his decimated regiments and advanced again, only to suffer a serious wound as his spent brigade recoiled from a solid curtain of British musketry. Back and forth the fighting swayed until after 11:00 p.m. when, each army having exhausted the other, the firing finally fizzled out.

As the smoke of battle slowly dissipated, it was revealed that the bloodied American regulars were in possession of the original British line, though the veteran red-coated regiments, battered but unbroken, remained on the field facing their adversary. Generals Brown and Scott were both seriously wounded during the course of the engagement, so command of

105

the U.S. forces devolved upon General Ripley. Concerned with the heavy American casualties and worried about the prospect of a follow-up British attack, the new American commander chose to withdraw to Chippawa Creek. Ripley abandoned both the battlefield and the captured guns for which so much American, British, and Canadian blood had been shed.

Arguments persist concerning which army triumphed at Lundy's Lane, but regardless of victory or defeat, the engagement was indisputably the bloodiest battle of the war for the United States, and no less costly for the British: each side suffered nearly 900 casualties. Robertson's Corps of Provincial Artificers were still in garrison at Fort Mississauga when the summer battles were fought, but black troops did serve with other British units during the campaign. Among them was John Baker and the pioneer section from the 104th Regiment of Foot. The 104th Foot fought at Chippawa, Lundy's Lane, and also at the siege of Fort Erie. Baker later campaigned with the Duke of Wellington's army at Waterloo, and his service for England subsequently earned him a military pension.[57]

Documentation is scarce, but sources suggest that many black soldiers served in various Canadian militia regiments during the war. The Canadian Militia was not that different from its U.S. equivalent in that military service was not always a desirable option. In the summer of 1814, while the battles raged along the Niagara River, an American naval force threatening York caused the local militia to be called out. Luckily for the residents of York, the scare proved false because the response by white and black militiamen fell far short of the need. Among measures initiated to rectify the situation was an order "to take all the black men within the beat of [Captain Hamilton's] Company who have not enrolled themselves, and cause them to be enrolled immediately."[58] Apparently the order met with only limited success since the initial directive had to be followed-up two weeks later with another, which mentioned that, "...a certain number of black men...[did] abscond from the Town of York, having refused to pay due obedience to the Orders of their superior...."[59] By no means can it be inferred from these orders that black Canadians were any less willing to fight than white Canadians since militia musters often experienced notoriously low turnouts, even in times of peril. Instead, it is indicative of the war's unpopularity on both sides of the border.

After Lundy's Lane, General Ripley found himself in an exposed position confronting a reinforced and powerful foe, so he fell back to the protection of Fort Erie. On 4 August, under criticism for yielding the field at Lundy's Lane, Ripley was superseded in command at Fort Erie by Major General Edmund P. Gaines.

Drummond took his time pursuing the Americans, and not until 2 August did he commence siege operations to reduce Fort Erie's shored-up fortifications. Establishing a cordon around Fort Erie, Drummond blasted the American citadel with his artillery, hoping to soften the defensive works. Finally, at 2:00 a.m. on 15 August, Drummond launched a complex three-pronged assault against the stone bastion and the stout defenses which the Americans had extended westward from the fort for about 800 yards. All three of Drummond's attack columns pressed forward unflinchingly in the face of brutal American musketry fire. Reaching Fort Erie's fieldworks, the intrepid British infantrymen hoisted crudely-hewn scaling ladders against the sturdy defenses, but on the American left and center the embattled redcoats simply could not penetrate the scrappily defended fortifications. Only at the towering stone walls of Fort Erie itself were the British successful. Surging atop the fort's northwest bastion, the attackers were on the very brink of success when a magazine under the embattled bastion suddenly exploded, hurling blue and red-coated bodies and body parts in every direction. All cohesion lost, the shocked and dazed British survivors, unable to sustain their impetus after the paralyzing blast, straggled back to their siege lines. General Drummond lost over 900 men during the bloody assault, while Gaines's casualties amounted to 62 killed and wounded.

For the next month, General Drummond's siege operations dragged on, his trenches creeping slowly forward as the tedious and dangerous process wore down the nerves and strength of all concerned. Neither the digging nor the killing seemed to end. General Gaines, wounded by an artillery round on 28 August, was replaced by General Jacob Brown, who was still recovering from a wound suffered at Lundy's Lane. As the siege progressed, Drummond's weary redcoats experienced more and more difficulty maintaining momentum. The British general persisted, until an American foray finally showed Drummond the writing on the wall. At noon on 17 September, American regulars sallied forth against the British right flank in an effort to forestall Drummond's advancing siege lines. Partially successful, the attacking U.S. column captured and spiked (to render artillery pieces temporarily useless by jamming spikes or large nails into the vents) two batteries of siege guns before being repulsed by a spirited British counterattack. It was a costly sortie for the Americans and the British, with slightly more than 500 men lost by each side. Of the British total, about 400 were captured. For Drummond, who was already considering a withdrawal, it was the final straw. Four days later he conceded, abandoned his siege lines, and retreated back to Chippawa.

The siege of Fort Erie unfolded as a bloody meat grinder for both the British and the Americans. Intermittent battles produced heavy casualties, but it was the seemingly non-stop artillery bombardment and ceaseless sniping with small arms that proved both demoralizing and deadly. An endless stream of broken and bloodied bodies flowed either to hurriedly established hospitals or to hastily dug shallow graves. Private Peter Simpson, a "mulatto" serving with the 23rd U.S. Infantry, was among the former. Having been wounded in action, Simpson was recuperating at the Buffalo General Hospital at the end of September.[60]

Three weeks after the siege was lifted, Major General George Izard reinforced Fort Erie with two brigades of regulars, about 4,000 men, hastily marched from Plattsburg, New York. Augmented with 2,000 regulars from Brown's army—Izard outranked Brown—Izard moved north on 13 October to confront Drummond. One day later, the two armies faced each other across the old Chippewa battleground. Instead of assaulting his outnumbered enemy, Izard dawdled for four days before sending a force of 1,200 men on a foray to reconnoiter Drummond's right flank and to destroy British supplies stored at Cook's Mills, about six miles west of Chippawa. Discovering Izard's flanking maneuver, Drummond dispatched 750 men to parry Izard's thrust, and a sharp skirmish ensued near Cook's Mills. Each side suffered about 65 casualties before the Americans withdrew. Deciding not to risk another engagement, even with superior numbers, Izard retreated back to Fort Erie.

So concluded the fighting in what turned out to be the bloodiest summer of the war. On 5 November 1814, the final pointless act of the campaign was perpetrated. With winter approaching, the American toehold on the Canadian side of the river was considered too tenuous to maintain. Fort Erie, paid for with the blood and toil of the U.S. Army's finest soldiers, was abandoned and blown up by General Izard, highlighting the futility of both the campaign and the War of 1812.

10

LAKE CHAMPLAIN AND THE ST. LAWRENCE RIVER

African-American participation in the campaigns along the St. Lawrence River during the early part of the war appears to have been limited. Documentation is scarce, but like the Detroit River and Niagara River areas in 1812 and early 1813, African-Americans were employed mostly as servants, teamsters, and laborers. Undoubtedly there were black Americans tramping through the hardwood forests and fording the lakes and rivers alongside their white counterparts, but as with other campaigns along the Canadian border in 1812, African-Americans were essentially spared the humiliation and defeat endured by U.S. armies during the war's first two years.

Operations along the St. Lawrence River were slow to develop in 1812. While fighting raged along the Detroit and Niagara Rivers, the United States and Canadian border, where it was divided by the St. Lawrence River, witnessed only a few haphazard raids which inflicted minor casualties and little material damage. Farther to the east, Major General Henry Dearborn was amassing an army of 6,000 men, including seven regular regiments, at Plattsburg, New York. Dearborn's objective was to sever the British St. Lawrence River supply artery by capturing Montreal. The American general, in a situation not dissimilar to that encountered by Union General George B. McClellan on the Virginia peninsula 50 years later, commanded a vastly superior force which he was reluctant to commit to battle.

Not until 19 November 1812 did Dearborn begin a cautious march on Montreal. Dearborn's army traveled only 20 miles to the village of Champlain, New York, about one mile from the Canadian border, before encountering and exchanging a few shots with a mixed force of Canadian militia, voyageurs, and Indians. Real bullets fired by a real enemy persuaded most of Dearborn's reluctant militia units, which constituted about half of the general's force, that they lacked strong motivation to cross into Canada. Unsure of how to proceed, Dearborn retreated to Plattsburg and ordered his troops into winter quarters.

In the spring of 1813, Dearborn and most of his regulars were diverted to Sackets Harbor to cooperate with Commodore Isaac Chauncey in an attack on Fort George. Command at Plattsburg eventually reverted to General Wade Hampton, who began raising troops for future operations. Meanwhile, Dearborn's ineffectiveness in the Niagara region resulted in his being relieved of command in July of 1813, whereupon General James Wilkinson was appointed his successor. Wilkinson, along with the strategists in Washington, finally came to the realization that Montreal, and not British forces in the lakes region, should be the focus of American efforts. Accordingly, Wilkinson assembled a large army at Sackets Harbor and ordered Hampton at Plattsburg to cooperate with his campaign and coordinate movements against Montreal. One problem with this scenario was that Wilkinson and Hampton harbored a seething hatred for each other, and their mutual resentment precluded harmonious collaboration. Relations between the two generals were so strained that they would communicate with each other only through Secretary of War John Armstrong. The secretary complicated matters further because he had no clear plan of action for the campaign, as a result of which he passed vague and contradictory orders to his subordinates.

Hampton's feelings for Wilkinson were insufficient reason to disobey orders, so on 19 September 1813 the South Carolinian placed his 4,000 men in motion. As per Secretary Armstrong's wishes, Hampton attempted a diversion at Odelltown, a small Quebec village about five miles north of Champlain, New York, on 21 September. When the diversion failed, Hampton shifted his army 70 miles westward to Four Corners, present day Chateaugay, New York, in an attempt to confuse his opponent. Hampton then wasted three critical weeks at Four Corners while awaiting further instructions from Armstrong. Orders were at last received from the Secretary of War, and Hampton's inexperienced troops crossed into Canada and plodded northward, paralleling the Châteauguay River. Near the Canadian village of Spears the Americans encountered an enemy force under the command of Lieutenant Colonel Charles-Michel d'Irumberry de

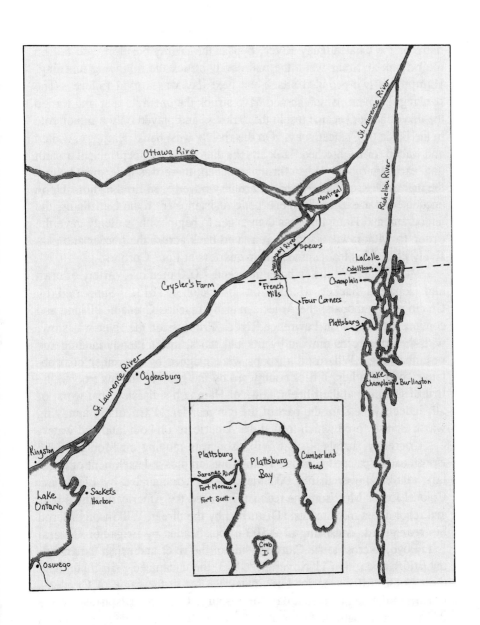

AMONGST MY BEST MEN

Salaberry. With only 1,400 Canadian militiamen, de Salaberry's men confronted an army three times their number. On the evening of 25 October, Hampton ordered the 4th U.S. Infantry Regiment to cross to the east bank of the Châteauguay River, bypass the enemy position, and fall on their flank and rear when the main body struck the following morning. Hampton's two-pronged attack the next day was a total failure. The flanking regiment, which should have struck the enemy's rear and turned the tide of battle, became lost in the darkness and played only a minor role in the Battle of Châteauguay. On the river's west bank, Hampton waited and waited for the botched flank attack, thus delaying his principal assault until early afternoon. When finally launched, there was little spirit behind the main attack, and the American artillery never even fired a shot. Upon encountering unexpected and energetic resistance from the Canadians, the temperamental Hampton, less than eager to begin with, sullenly gave the order to withdraw. Hampton retreated back across the border and passively placed his troops into winter quarters at Four Corners.

Meanwhile, Wilkinson had embarked 7,000 men in a variety of craft and departed Sackets Harbor on 19 October 1813. Supported by Chauncey's gunboats, the American army reached Grenadier Island and continued down the St. Lawrence River. Progress on the river was slow, with the Americans moving by fits and starts, intermittently landing and re-embarking. Wilkinson's troops were plagued by a number of problems: bad weather, illness contracted by the general and his troops, the British snapping at their heels, news of Hampton's disaster, and worst of all, indecisiveness on the part of the commander. Particularly annoying was a British force which trailed the Americans on both land and water.

Correctly surmising that Wilkinson was moving on Montreal, the British had dispatched gunboats from Kingston plus a detachment of regulars totaling fewer than 1,000 men. Ably commanded by Lieutenant Colonel Joseph Morrison, the redcoats hounded the American army's rear and reported its movements. Disturbed by the threat, Wilkinson ordered his rear guard, consisting of 2,500 troops headed by Brigadier General John Boyd, to cross to the Canadian side of the river and brush the annoying British aside. On 11 November 1813, the undaunted British humbled their numerically superior but amateurish foe at the battle of Crysler's Farm, fought near present day Morrisburg, Ontario. Dispirited by the defeat—even though less than half of his army had been engaged—and also

112

exasperated by Hampton's lack of initiative and cooperation, Wilkinson crossed back into New York and put his army into winter quarters at French Mills, present day Fort Covington, New York. America's foremost opportunity to achieve its wartime objective ended in disgraceful and humiliating defeat.

In late March, 1814, depressed by recent setbacks and fearful of being relieved of command, Wilkinson experienced a resurgence of commitment and purpose. Having moved his starving and disease-riddled army from French Mills to Plattsburg, Wilkinson outfitted 4,000 troops and again ventured across the Canadian border. On 30 March, at Lacolle Creek, modern day Lacolle, Quebec, Wilkinson stumbled upon 200 British regulars who had fortified themselves in a stone grist mill. The British were supported by a small detachment of Canadian fencibles in a nearby blockhouse, and by two small gunboats on the Richelieu River. For two-and-a-half hours the inept Wilkinson unsuccessfully pounded away at the mill's stubborn defenders. Unable to conquer 200 plucky redcoats in a stone mill, or to brush aside a small group of fencibles and two tiny gunboats with his vastly superior numbers, Wilkinson turned tail and timidly marched back to Plattsburg. It was a vain effort in all respects for the disaffected American commander. Wilkinson had been relieved of command by the Secretary of War three days before his final battle.

The United States can only be thankful that the British army in North America nurtured its own version of Henry Dearborn and James Wilkinson. Following Napoleon's abdication in March 1814 and the transfer of British troops to North America, General Sir George Prevost had at his command in the Montreal area 17,000 of the world's best soldiers. Under pressure to take action, Prevost considered his options and decided that an offensive campaign into New York via Lake Champlain offered the best hope for success. Amassing 11,000 of his seasoned veterans, the Swiss-born British general departed Montreal on 31 August 1814. Prevost's plan called for a coordinated attack by both his land forces and the British Lake Champlain flotilla; his objective was the American defensive positions at Plattsburg, New York.

Facilitating the British operation was, of all people, U.S. Secretary of War John Armstrong. After Wilkinson had been relieved, Major General George Izard was appointed to command the sizeable U.S. army at Plattsburg. An engineer by training and mindful of the importance of

Plattsburg and the menace that Prevost represented, Izard had prepared elaborate defensive positions along the south bank of the Saranac River. Secretary Armstrong, however, knowing the threat posed by Prevost, ordered Izard and the cream of his army, two brigades of regulars, to march westward to assist the battle-weary American forces on the Niagara frontier. Izard obeyed unquestioningly, leaving at Plattsburg Brigadier General Alexander Macomb and about 3,000 troops, most of whom were newly raised, ill-prepared recruits. To increase his numerical strength, Macomb urgently issued a call-up of New York and Vermont militia, which raised his numbers to about 5,000 men. It was a sizable force by War of 1812 standards, but when Prevost's 11,000-man army appeared in front of Plattsburg in September, Macomb was far from comfortable with his hodgepodge units.

American operations in Canada and upstate New York during late 1813 and into 1814 included a number of black soldiers. Black musketmen were sprinkled among the ranks of the 30th U.S., 31st U.S., and 34th U.S. Infantry Regiments, units which fought at Lacolle Mill and during the Plattsburg campaign. The 11th U.S. Infantry, which saw service at Crysler's Farm and Lacolle Mill, also mustered black regulars. Most black infantrymen, like Private Solomon Sharp of the 11th U.S. Infantry, performed their duties and served with distinction. The 15 April 1814 muster roll for the 11th U.S. discloses that Sharp, having been captured by the enemy, was absent from the regiment as a prisoner of war, although he was exchanged the following month.[61] Not all black soldiers were as duty-bound as Solomon Sharp. At least one regular, Private George Bolton, a 27-year-old Massachusetts farmer, deserted from the ranks in September 1814.[62] Whether Bolton fled before or after the engagement at Plattsburg is unknown, but his case was far from being an isolated one. Desertion rates were very high among white troops in both regular and militia units during the War of 1812. For example, 28 men deserted from Captain Samuel White's company of the 5th Detachment of Pennsylvania Militia on 5 July 1813, the same day that the Battle of Chippawa was fought. In fact, between 12 March and 28 July 1814, 57 out of 118 privates in White's company deserted.[63] Prevost's appearance before Plattsburg and the long odds facing Macomb's army undoubtedly made the prospect of desertion a desirable option to many an American soldier manning the beleaguered Saranac River defenses, regardless of

114

whether or not they followed through with it.

Prevost launched his combined attack on 11 September. A ford had been found a mile upriver which would enable the British to outflank Macomb's line. British units would conduct a feint on the American right to keep U.S. troops in the Saranac River line occupied while the brigades of Generals Frederick Robinson and Manley Powers, a total of 6,000 men, forded the river, crushed Macomb's left flank, and rolled up the entire American position. For some reason, though, Prevost's assault was slow in developing and it was not coordinated with Commodore George Downie's naval attack. Robinson's brigade had just succeeded in crossing the river when Downie's British flotilla suffered total defeat. Prevost, demoralized by the naval disaster, ordered his army to cease its attack before the red-coated regiments could exploit what appeared to be an exceptional opportunity.

Armchair strategists have long since debated the consequences of Prevost's decision. Not much doubt exists that the confident British veterans who flanked Macomb's position would have forced the inexperienced American regulars and militia to evacuate the Saranac River line. From that point, however, without the flotilla's logistical support, British troops would have faced serious obstacles sustaining the campaign. But in all likelihood, Prevost's retreat averted a major military and political disaster for the United States.

Conditioned to victory and aggressive leadership under Lord Wellington in Spain, the angry and nearly mutinous British regiments sullenly trudged back to Montreal. Prevost's decision to withdraw denied him more than just military success. A court-martial board convened to review the campaign eventually cost Prevost his career. Time would not allow the British to regroup for another offensive before winter set in and peace terminated hostilities.

11

THE MID-ATLANTIC THEATER

When the United States declared war on Great Britain in 1812, England's focus on European operations could not be distracted by a major campaign against America's east coast cities. Mustering sufficient resources for the defense of Canada proved to be difficult enough. Even so, the Royal Navy's dominance of the Atlantic Ocean offered certain opportunities. Along the east coast of the United States, the coastal rivers and inland waterways, particularly the Chesapeake Bay and Delaware Bay regions, furnished ideal inroads for the British to raid, plunder, and harass the upstart Americans. The British also hoped to ravage the lairs which harbored those detested American privateers. Incursions into the Chesapeake and Delaware Bays commenced in January, 1813 and culminated with the Washington-Baltimore campaign the following summer. Of course, any British operation conducted in the southern United States introduced a singular and, what was for southerners a frightening element, into the equation—slave revolt.

Mere mention of a slave uprising struck fear into the white population of every southern state. Slavery was still legal in some northern states, but it was a dying institution and not generally practiced above the Mason-Dixon line, thus northerners did not experience the same trepidation as southerners. The potential for a slave revolt was never far removed from the white southern consciousness prior to 1812, and the declaration of war only served to compound apprehensions. Plans concocted to suppress a possible uprising in coastal North Carolina counties were typical. As state militia units were being mobilized around Wilmington during the summer of 1812, General Thomas Brown thought to have several companies of cavalry ready "...to guard against a rebellion of the blacks, so probable, and so much to be dreaded in this section of the State."[64] Arms and ammunition were cached at strategic locations throughout the state, primed for immediate use in the event of an "insurrection among the Blacks."[65]

AMONGST MY BEST MEN

The sudden appearance of any British warship off a southern state's coast only served to heighten anxiety that the enemy would incite a long-feared uprising. Knowing the psychological advantages and opportunities tendered by the situation, Great Britain was equally aware that fomenting a slave revolt could beget disastrous political repercussions; the whole matter would have to be managed adroitly. Official British policy was promulgated by the Secretary of State for War, The Right Honorable Henry, Earl Bathurst, who communicated instructions to his commander of land forces in the region, Colonel Sir Thomas Sidney Beckwith:

> You will on no account give encouragement to any dispo-sition which may be manifested by the Negroes to rise against their Masters....If any Individual Negroes shall in the course of your operations have given you assistance, which may expose them to the vengeance of their Masters after your retreat, you are at liberty on their earnest desire to take them away with you. You are authorized to enlist them in any of the Black Corps if they are willing to enlist; but you must distinctly under-stand that you are in no case to take slaves away as Slaves, but as free persons whom the public become bound to maintain. This circumstance as well as the difficulty of transport, will make you necessarily cautious how you contract engagements of this nature, which it may be difficult for you to fulfill.[66]

Bathurst's policy was all too clear. Slaves were to be encouraged to desert their masters and join the liberating army to fight against their former oppressors. If slaves were not inclined to enlist, they should be discouraged from escaping because the British would have to assume the burden of care and provide transport from the United States to a safe haven. Bathurst conceded that the army might encounter obstacles implementing his directive, but he equivocated on providing solutions for dealing with the problem.

Several towns and villages in the Chesapeake and Delaware Bays suffered from enemy depredations during the spring and summer of 1813: Lewes, Delaware; Havre de Grace, Frenchtown, Fredericktown, George-town, and Kent Island, Maryland; and Hampton, Virginia all felt the Royal Navy's wrath. British craft infiltrated the Potomac, Rappahannock, York, and James Rivers, and one daring expedition on the Potomac River ventured

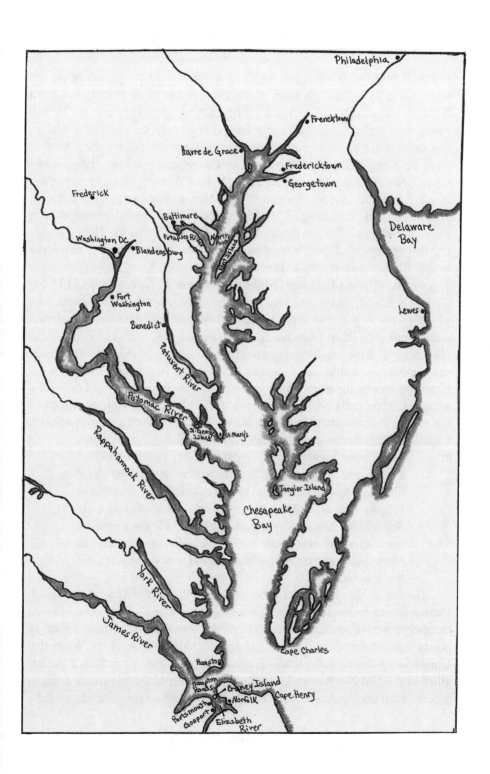

within 25 miles of Washington, D.C. Several of the enemy raiding parties were aided by a small number of slaves who served as guides, but Lord Bathurst's aspirations of recruiting large numbers of slaves into the British Army were dashed. Although more than willing to slip the yoke of bondage, few slaves were eager to trade those circumstances by risking their lives to serve the King, and the British were otherwise reluctant to care for runaway slaves. Nonetheless, Admiral Sir John Borlase Warren, commander of the North American Station, deemed his summer raiding campaign a success, despite his failure to destroy the blockaded U.S. Frigate *Constellation* at Norfolk, Virginia. Warren reported that he had weakened the United States and that he had sailed away with about 600 slaves, most of whom, unwilling to enlist, were transported to Bermuda.[67]

Another British fleet entered the Chesapeake in November, 1813. St. George's Island, Maryland was occupied, and several of the squadron's vessels were engaged in suppressing U.S. privateers. One heavily armed cutting-out expedition from the flagship *Dragon* (74) and the sloop *Sophie* (18) captured three small American merchant vessels in the Potomac River near St. Mary's, Maryland. Not unexpectedly, the British presence furnished an opportunity for many slaves in the region to slip away. Several of the escapees, apparently wishing to please their new benefactors, conveyed to the enemy exactly what the British hoped to hear. Expedition commander Captain Robert Barrie encouragingly reported to Admiral Warren:

> The Slaves continue to come off by every opportunity and I have now upwards of 120 men, women and Children on board....Amongst the Slaves are several very intelligent fellows who are willing to act as local guides should their Services be required in that way, and if their assertions be true, there is no doubt but the Blacks of Virginia & Maryland would cheerfully take up Arms & join us against the Americans.[68]

The fall of Napoleon enabled Great Britain to transfer large numbers of Crown forces to North America, insuring that Britain's 1814 Chesapeake campaign would be much more determined than previous efforts. British policy toward the slaves did not change, although at one point, when the United States threatened to retaliate against depredations by Britain's Indian allies in the Old Northwest, Lord Bathurst countered that he would issue a proclamation urging American slaves to revolt.[69] But recruiting slaves into

Britain's armed forces remained Bathurst's primary goal, a view that was shared by the North American Station's new commander, Vice Admiral Sir Alexander Cochrane. Confidently believing that he need only issue a simple proclamation to induce slaves to swarm to his standard, Cochrane embraced some fanciful stereotyping when he declared to Bathurst:

> The Blacks are all good horsemen. Thousands will join upon their masters' horses, and they will only require to be clothed and accoutered to be as good Cossacks as any in the European army....[70]

Less optimistic was Cochrane's subordinate, Rear Admiral George Cockburn. After conducting operations for three months in the Chesapeake region, Cockburn managed to entice only 120 black recruits. Responding to Cochrane's bombast, Cockburn rebutted:

> If you attach importance to forming a corps of these Blacks to act against their former masters, I think, my dear Sir, your Proclamation should not so distinctly hold out to them the option of being sent as free settlers to British settlements, which they will most certainly all prefer to the danger and fatigue of joining us in arms. In the temptations I now hold out to them, I shall therefore only mention generally our willingness and readiness to receive and protect them....[71]

Cockburn's assertion addressed the root of the matter. Freedom was the only motive that would encourage slaves to flock to Britain's standard. A few slaves might be persuaded to fight, but their overriding concern was liberty for themselves and for their families. Should the British offer solely a military option, then a slave would simply trade one master for another, and most refused to be misguided by British guile. Understandably cautious, slaves trusted neither the British nor the Americans, but they also realized that remaining with their American masters offered nothing but continued bondage. Any hope for freedom the slaves might have lay with the British.

Great Britain's August, 1814 Chesapeake invasion, for which the American-hating Admiral Cochrane controlled considerable military resources, had several objectives. Washington and Baltimore would be made to pay for American insolence and for having the effrontery to challenge the world's premier power. Just as important, American troops would have to be diverted to face the invaders, forestalling the U.S. War Department from sending reinforcements to counter the main British thrust by General Sir George Prevost on Lake Champlain. Raising black recruits locally, another vital element of the campaign, would have far-reaching consequences. After the campaign's successful completion, black units would be detached in the Chesapeake region to continue the previous British policy of harassment in the bay area. Other newly-raised black regiments would be transported south to raid North Carolina, South Carolina, and Georgia. Black troops roaming and plundering freely would enhance the fear of slave rebellions and force the affected states to react, thereby preventing regular and militia regiments in the threatened areas from responding to Cochrane's next objective, the gulf coast of the United States.[72]

Sweeping through the Virginia capes on 11 August 1814, Cochrane's imposing invasion fleet pointed its bowsprits up the Chesapeake Bay. Commodore Joshua Barney's small American flotilla, comprising the cutter *Scorpion* and 16 small gunboats, was the first obstacle in Cochrane's path. Withdrawing into the Patuxent River, Barney soon found himself hemmed in by Cochrane's powerful fleet. Rather than surrender his ships and men to the enemy, the steadfast commodore blew up his hopelessly outgunned vessels. Undeterred by the setback, Barney attached his remaining 400 flotillamen to an amalgamation of units, mostly militia, being collected to defend the U.S. capital.

Meanwhile, on 19 August, Cochrane landed a force 4,500 British soldiers, sailors, and Marines, commanded by Major General Robert Ross, at Benedict, Maryland. As Ross marched toward Washington, panicked leaders in the capital scrambled to improvise a defense. Troops from the District of Columbia, Maryland, and Virginia were called out to respond to the emergency. Civilians were not excluded from playing a role. On 21 August, Washington Mayor James Blake issued a proclamation requiring every able-bodied person, including "all free men of color," to help build defensive works. *The National Intelligencer* reported the next day that:

> An immense crowd of every description of persons
> attended to offer their services....It is with much pleasure
> also we state that on this occasion the free people of color
> in this city acted as became patriots...conducting them-
> selves with the utmost order and propriety. [73]

Response to the emergency by military personnel was also impressive. On the morning of 24 August, approximately 6,000 Americans clustered on a series of modest hills just west of Bladensburg, Maryland, about five miles northeast of Washington, to meet the oncoming enemy. Included among that multitude were President James Madison, Secretary of State James Monroe, and Secretary of War John Armstrong. The American force was more than adequate numerically, but their state of preparation was not, and much of the blame for what occurred at Bladensburg, and for that matter many of the American military disasters during the war, can be laid at the feet of John Armstrong. Totally unqualified to bear the critical responsibilities of Secretary of War, Armstrong's tenure as head of the War Department was characterized by mediocrity, mismanagement, and incompetence. As occurred all too often in other theaters of operation, Armstrong's subordinates during the 1814 Chesapeake campaign, military and civilian alike, fumbled along without capable guidance or direction. One of the Secretary's glaring shortcomings at Bladensburg was that U.S. Army and militia units were not properly armed, equipped, or trained to meet their veteran enemy because Armstrong refused to believe that Washington would be a British target. The American debacle at Bladensburg only served to punctuate the ineffectiveness of John Armstrong.

Advancing to confront the Americans and disdaining their opponents seemingly overwhelming numbers, the confident redcoats initiated the engagement by brazenly attacking with only one-fourth of their infantry on the field. Among the outnumbered British troops present at Bladensburg was a 75-man company of Colonial (West Indian) Marines.[74] The Colonial Marine company appears to have been a unit that Cochrane raised from runaway slaves who agreed to serve in the British Army. One source suggests that the company was comprised of "Negro and mulatto recruits to the Royal Marines who eventually settled in Trinidad."[75] An article written for a British military journal in 1840 indicates that the Colonial Marine company was composed of escaped slaves, who:

> ...after voluntarily serving for a few months in a sort of provisional battalion, called the 'Colonial Marines' obtained grants of land in Upper Canada, where they and their descendants are now happy and loyal settlers....[76]

The Battle of Bladensburg, as witnessed by the Colonial Marines, was by no means an American military showpiece. One example of the chaos that permeated the American high command was the actions of Secretary of State James Monroe. Inflamed by the martial spirit of the moment, but

123

having no real military authority to act, Monroe galloped about the battlefield issuing orders and changing troop dispositions without consulting the commanding general, William H. Winder. A few American units faced the British assault and fought well, but confusion was such that when the British attacked, most of the defenders offered only minor resistance. The vast majority of the terrified American militia, not to mention the high ranking dignitaries, fled when the British launched a few flashy and noisy Congreve rockets which, though impressive, were virtually harmless. One of Joshua Barney's black seamen later scoffed that, "The militia ran like sheep, chased by dogs."[77] Recognizing the situation as irretrievable, the disconsolate General Winder ordered remaining U.S. troops withdrawn from the field.

Barney's sailors were among the few who persevered after the militia retreated. A portion of Barney's men, joined by the 120-man U.S. Marine detachment from the Washington Navy Yard, crewed five artillery pieces positioned on a rise behind the main American line. The remaining seamen and Marines supported the guns by serving as naval infantry. Barney's flotillamen included a number of black sailors, among whom was Caesar Wentworth, who mustered as a cook. Also with Barney was Charles Ball. Ball was a native Marylander born in bondage. Purchased by a slave trader in 1805, Ball was transported to South Carolina and from there he was taken to Georgia. Somehow Ball managed to escape and make an incredible journey back to Maryland, where he managed to evade slave catchers. When the British threatened the Chesapeake region, Ball sought a berth with Barney's flotilla.[78] Another of Barney's black sailors was Ordinary Seaman Gabriel Roulson, formerly attached to U.S. Sloop-of-War *Ontario* (22). Newly built at Baltimore, the *Ontario* had been imprisoned by the British blockade, so 120 of her crewmen, including Roulson, were transferred to Barney's flotilla in the spring of 1814. Apparently Roulson was not too pleased with his new duty assignment—he deserted on 25 May.[79]

With the help of black sailors like Ball, the crusty commodore's contingent of seamen and Marines stemmed the redcoat tide until, flanked on the right, deserted on the left, and ammunition expended, Barney bitterly ordered his men to retire. Sadly, Barney's valiant stand was futile. The British entered Washington that same evening and proceeded to burn public buildings and property.

With their objective achieved, the victorious British troops withdrew the next day to rejoin the fleet. As the redcoats tramped through the hot and dusty Maryland countryside, slaves along their line of march took advantage of the opportunity. One British recorder of the campaign wrote:

> A great number of negroes, delighted at the unhoped-for freedom our expedition had placed within their reach, followed the army from Washington, and were, of course, received on board the fleet. Some of these were engaged as private servants by officers, and the remainder were sent off to Tangier Island, in the Chesapeake [Bay], which had been taken possession of by Rear-Admiral Cockburn, and used as a depot for such of these poor refugees as, from time to time, made their escape to our ships. Perfect freedom—that freedom which the vaunted 'Land of Liberty' denied them—was guaranteed to all....[80]

The ease with which the American capital fell encouraged Cochrane to hasten to his next objective, the port of Baltimore, Maryland. The third largest city in the United States, Baltimore was a notorious haunt for American privateers, and for the British, the port city was a much sought-after prize. Bulging warehouses and docks teeming with all sorts of goods added extra incentive for Cochrane and his men. One particular location slated for British attention was the Fells Point shipyard, where new hulls for the U.S. Navy and the privateering fleet were feverishly being constructed. According to an 1810 Baltimore directory, 220 free men of color, many of them skilled carpenters, caulkers, shipriggers, and sailmakers, were helping to build those sleek predators.[81]

Like the capital before it, Baltimore's citizens rallied to repel the invader. The city's Committee of Vigilance and Safety mobilized the white and black civilian populations to prepare fortifications. On 3 September, the Committee issued an order requiring:

> That all free people of color be, and they are hereby ordered to attend daily, commencing with Wednesday, the fifth instant, at the different works erected about the city for the purpose of laboring thereon, and for which they shall receive an allowance of fifty cents a day, together with a soldier's rations.[82]

Along the city's east flank, in an area known as Hampstead Hill, the city's main fortifications were prepared. Free black citizens were not the only people of color to respond to the call for assistance. When writing about Baltimore's preparations, a young resident of the city reported:

> They are throwing up entrenchments all around the city
> ....White and black are all at work together. You'll see a
> master and his slave digging side by side. There is no
> distinction whatsoever.[83]

Troops from Maryland, Pennsylvania, and Virginia poured in to man the Baltimore defenses. Most were militia units, but included were the 12th U.S., 36th U.S., and 38th U.S. Infantry Regiments. In early September, the 38th U.S. was stationed at Hampstead Hill, and one of the youthful musketmen manning the entrenchments was 22-year-old William Williams. A one-time resident of Prince Georges County, Maryland and a former slave, Williams escaped from bondage in the spring of 1814, changed his name, and enlisted in the U.S. Army. Although slaves by law "could make no valid contract with the government," Williams' recruiter apparently asked no questions when the young "mulatto" enlisted, and Williams seems to have volunteered no details.[84] Yet even as he was serving his country and placing his life in jeopardy, Williams was a wanted fugitive in constant danger of being returned to slavery. A notice placed in a Baltimore newspaper on 18 May 1814 emphasized Williams' peril:

> Forty Dollars Reward
>
> For apprehending and securing in jail so that I can get him
> again,
>
> NEGRO FREDERICK:
>
> Sometimes calls himself FREDERICK HALL a bright
> mulatto; straight and well made; 21 years old; 5 feet 7 or
> 8 inches high, with a short chub nose and so fair as to show
> freckles; he has no scars or marks of any kind that is [sic]
> recollected: his clothing when he left home, two months
> since, was home made cotton shirts, jacket, and Pantaloons
> of cotton and yarn twilled, all white. It is probable he may
> be in Baltimore, having a relation there, a house servant to
> a Mr. Williams, by the name of Frank, who is also a mulat-
> to, but not so fair as Frederick.
>
> Benjamin Oden,
> Prince George's County, May 12th[85]

AFRICAN-AMERICANS AND THE WAR OF 1812

Men like Charles Ball and William Williams deserve the utmost praise and recognition. Their courage and patriotism were unsurpassed by any soldiers who fought during the War of 1812 or any American war. Incredible as it may seem, here were men who, when the occasion arose to escape an evil institution imposed by their own countrymen, chose not to seek protection among those who provided that opportunity but instead jumped at the chance to fight for the very people that enslaved them. Obviously, by enlisting in the Army or Navy a former slave's lot in life improved enormously. Regular rations of food and spirits, plus a steady, if paltry, wage were nothing to scoff at for someone who had lived in slavery. But even so, they risked their brittle freedom knowing that at any time they could be exposed as runaway slaves, clapped in irons, and returned to a lifetime of servitude.

What inspired intrepid men such as these? Escaping the dreaded lash and the unremitting toil of picking tobacco and cotton was a powerful motivation, but fighting for a country which did and would treat them and their sacrifice so deplorably was more than anyone could expect. Easily bandied about are trite phrases such as unbridled patriotism and lofty ideals, but could the answer be so uncomplicated? Slaves who fought for the United States during the War of 1812 did not record their motivation since most who joined the army changed their names when they enlisted, and, like their white counterparts, most black soldiers and sailors were illiterate. It will never even be known how many brave men there were like Ball and Williams. We can only marvel at their sacrifice and sense of duty and honor.

The Baltimore defenses were also manned by a large number of naval personnel. In addition to the previously mentioned *Ontario,* two other vessels were also fitting out at Baltimore, although neither yet berthed a full crew: the U.S. Frigate *Java* (44) and the U.S. Sloop-of-War *Erie* (22), the former commanded by Captain Oliver Hazard Perry. Supplementing the naval contingent at Baltimore was the 350-man crew of the Philadelphia-based U.S. Frigate *Guerriere* (44), under the command of Commodore John Rodgers. As soon as he heard about the invasion threat, Rodgers took immediate steps to have his men transferred to the seat of action. The Bladensburg survivors from Joshua Barney's flotilla also straggled in to Baltimore, and even the remnants of the exchanged U.S. Frigate *Essex* (32) crew, including Captain David Porter, were in the city. If the standard explored in Part I of this work holds true, between 10% and 20% of the naval contingent manning the city's fortifications were black sailors. By the time Cochrane's invasion fleet anchored off North Point on the night of 11 September, the Baltimore defenses were garrisoned by somewhere in the vicinity of 12,500 regulars, militiamen, and sailors.

In the pre-dawn hours of 12 September, Cochrane began off-loading the first of 4,700 troops at the tip of North Point, 10 miles southeast of the city. Cochrane's blueprint called for a two-pronged attack: Ross's troops would approach Baltimore on Patapsco Neck along the south bank of the Back River and assail the city from the east, while ships from the fleet would maneuver up the Patapsco River and decimate Fort McHenry, the brick bastion which guarded the harbor entrance.

Maryland militiamen were advanced from the Baltimore defenses to slow the oncoming redcoats. In the ensuing Battle of North Point, the Americans were forced to retreat after skirmishing with the British for nearly two hours, but not before a Maryland musketman succeeded in killing the British commander, General Robert Ross. Ross's death was a devastating blow, yet it did not stop the British advance. Continuing to move forward, the British force tramped within two miles of the Hampstead Hill fortifications. There the British went into camp to await Fort McHenry's destruction by Cochrane's fleet.

Shortly after dawn on 13 September, a few small British vessels eased within range and opened fire on the fort. Before long, five bomb ketches, a rocket ship, and a schooner were heaving a continuous stream of shot, shells, and rockets towards Fort McHenry. Answering fire from the fort compelled the schooner and rocket ship to retire, but the extensive range of those monstrous mortars which crouched on the bomb ketches' decks enabled the hybrid vessels to shoot with impunity from two miles away, while the largest guns from the fort's batteries fell a half-mile short. Hour after hour, exploding bombs terrorized the fort's defenders as they cringed in trenches and behind thick brick walls for protection. Most were lucky, some were not. Three days before the attack, four companies from the 38th U.S. Infantry were moved from Hampstead Hill to Fort McHenry, where they could help repel any attempt by a naval landing force to storm the fort. During the bombardment, Private William Williams, attached to one of those companies, had "his leg blown off by a cannonball."[86] The young volunteer's wound proved mortal.

AFRICAN-AMERICANS AND THE WAR OF 1812

By 3:00 p.m., several of the bomb vessels, under the mistaken impression that they had reduced the fort's ability to respond, crept closer to the brick bastion. When within range, Fort McHenry's commanding officer, Major George Armistead, opened with every gun that would bear, damaging two of the bomb ketches before they could haul out of range. As the day wore on, the bomb vessels, firing from a safer distance, failed to make any discernable impression on the fort. Cochrane eyed the operation closely, feeling deeply that Baltimore would not fall unless Fort McHenry was captured first. Continuing resistance from Fort McHenry further eroded the admiral's confidence, which began to fail when General Ross was killed the previous day. An unsuccessful diversion by a naval landing party on the night of 13 September heightened the British admiral's misgivings. In the end it was Cochrane's uncertainty which doomed any real hope for British success. Fort McHenry continued to feel the bomb vessels' wrath until 4:00 a.m. on 14 September, but Cochrane's inability to reach a decision and his lack of confidence in the ability of British ground forces to breach the Baltimore defenses had led to a recall of the red-coated infantry regiments at 2:00 a.m.

Glimpsed through the murky dawn of 14 September was the sparking and sputtering fuse of an occasional bomb still being lobbed toward the fort. More importantly, revealed through the mist to temporary British prisoner Francis Scott Key was the huge stars and stripes streaming from the peak of Fort McHenry's lofty flagpole. From his perch on the deck of a flag-of-truce vessel about eight miles from the fort, Key watched the British fire slowly taper off. At 9:00 a.m., the bomb vessels hoisted their anchors and floated down the Patapsco River, soon to be joined by the remainder of Cochrane's fleet.

The British Chesapeake campaign of 1814 was not one of conquest and occupation, but a series of large-scale raids. British intentions were to humiliate the American political machine, punish the United States military establishment, gain revenge for atrocities perpetrated along the Canadian frontier, generate panic and consternation among the populace, and acquire booty for the victors. At Washington, the first four goals were achieved, though it was at Baltimore where the British hoped to win it all—and failed.

Another major British objective was to mobilize large numbers of black recruits and lay the groundwork for future operations. By enlisting black soldiers from the invaded countryside, Cochrane hoped to instill panic and confusion among the white population, and despite considerable fear of slave revolts in Maryland and Virginia—rumors abounded in Washington during August, 1814 that a slave conspiracy had been uncovered in Frederick, Maryland—nothing materialized.[87] To the contrary, at both Washington and Baltimore the black populace flocked to the cause in large numbers, serving in the regular army and militia or otherwise helping to dig fortifications to protect the threatened cities. Admiral Cochrane's scheme for recruiting slaves and disaffected free men of color failed miserably. Cochrane intended to use his new black regiments to raid the southern coastal states as a diversion during his next operation along the gulf coast, a plan he was forced to abandon due to a lack of sufficient recruits. During his entire summer campaign, Cochrane was able to add no more than 300 new black recruits to his forces. About 1,000 more slaves who attached themselves to his army, but refused to enlist, were eventually transported to Halifax, Nova Scotia.[88]

Cochrane must have been dumbfounded by the refusal of the slave masses to join his standard. How could people enslaved in chains not seek freedom at any cost when presented a golden opportunity? Why did slaves in the Chesapeake region not fight for King George III against their oppressors, the United States? Unable to formulate an answer for this seemingly imponderable mystery, Cochrane decided to move on.

12

THE SOUTH AND
THE GULF COAST

Emboldened by the ease with which Washington capitulated and dismissing his repulse at Baltimore, Admiral Cochrane felt heartened enough to extend operations to the Gulf of Mexico, part of an overall plan long ago submitted to Lord Bathurst. In collusion with Spanish authorities, the British hoped to establish fortifications at Pensacola and Apalachicola in western Florida. From his newly established bases in Spanish Florida, Cochrane intended to move further westward and capture Mobile, Alabama. Once Mobile was secured, the British would attack the prime target—New Orleans. American commerce and military operations could be seriously disrupted by the capture of New Orleans, which would cork the Mississippi River. Whether intentioned or not, the vast stores of cotton and other goods which lined the wharves of New Orleans would also fatten the purses of Cochrane and the British government. Lord Bathurst had named Major General Sir Edward Pakenham, brother-in-law to the Duke of Wellington, to replace General Robert Ross, who was killed at Baltimore. To insure success, Bathurst shipped several thousand infantry reinforcements to join Cochrane's force. The British gulf coast expedition would incorporate considerably greater military resources than did their Chesapeake Bay campaign.

Although British plans concerning the gulf coast gelled during the summer of 1814, military operations in the southeastern United States heated up long before Cochrane focused his interest in the area. During the first months of 1812, several key members of President Madison's government, knowing that war with Great Britain was imminent, believed that United States interests would be better served and that the war could be more easily prosecuted if Florida could first be wrenched from the clutches of Spain. Control of Florida would also preclude the British from using the Spanish colony as a jumping off point for operations against the United States. But the President and his followers would have to overcome considerable opposition before any such endeavor could be initiated. One of Madison's most vocal opponents in his quest to cede Florida was Rhode Island Senator William Hunter. Hunter conjectured that military intervention in Florida would provoke a counter-invasion of the United States by Spain and that Spanish authorities might use black military units from Florida and other Caribbean possessions to incite a slave rebellion. Spelling out his concerns, Hunter warned that slaves in the United States:

> ...that unhappy species of population, which prevails in our southern country, aroused to reflection by the sight of black soldiers and black officers, may suspect themselves to be fellow men, and fondly dream they likewise could be soldiers and officers....Take care, that while you are pursuing foreign conquest, your own homes are not devastated.[89]

Hunter's caution was shared by many of his fellow Congressmen, and while their voices carried sufficient weight to limit military operations to northeastern Florida, Madison's opponents could not muster enough support to completely block the incursion. So the United States would invade Spanish territory, and because the men who later volunteered to participate in the offensive were called patriots, what ensued in eastern Florida became known as the Patriot Rebellion of 1812.

The Patriot Rebellion of 1812 could be referred to as the war before the War of 1812, and once war was declared against Great Britain in June of 1812, the rebellion became a war during the War of 1812. In March of 1812, a mixed force of U.S. regulars, Georgia militiamen, and Georgia patriots, supported by a small number of U.S. Navy gunboats, sailed south of the Georgia border into Florida waters. Altogether the little American army totaled fewer than 1,000 men. Several bases were first established at strategic locations: at the town St. Mary's on the Georgia border; at the village of Fernandina on Amelia Island; at Goodby's Creek, a tributary of the St. John's River; and at Davis Creek, also a tributary of the St. John's. Once the bases were firmly rooted, a column of troops set out to capture Florida's capital city and the invasion's primary objective: St. Augustine.

Guarding the approaches to St. Augustine was the Castillo de San Marcos, a substantial stone fortress dating to 1695. All available Spanish troops were mobilized to garrison the Castillo and St. Augustine's other defenses, and one of the units called upon to meet the invader was a body of troops known as Florida's black militia company.

Florida's black militia company boasted a long and proud history, with the company's origins being traced to the genesis of slavery in North America. Spanish Florida, like its neighboring British colonies to the north, favored the institution of slavery, albeit with a more benign attitude. Spanish slaves enjoyed many rights not tendered to English slaves. Perhaps the most amazing privilege granted to Spanish slaves was the right to own property. This paradoxical entitlement evolved into a complex system whereby slaves could actually purchase their own manumission. Another controversial Spanish protocol, accorded intermittently during the late 1600's and early 1700's, awarded freedom to runaway English slaves who would submit to baptism and conversion to the Roman Catholic faith.[90] Spain's indulgent stance regarding slavery in general, and its position relating to escaped English slaves in particular, provided strong inducement for English slaves to flee to Florida. Spanish policy affecting escaped English slaves developed haphazardly and it changed often in order to meet shifting military, diplomatic, and economic interests. But regardless of what policy was in effect, the lot of the average slave was considerably better in Spanish Florida than it was in British North America.

The liberal policies and forbearing attitudes adopted by Spanish officials, combined with their refusal to return escaped English slaves, were contributing factors to periodic military clashes between the Spanish and British colonies. Manpower resources in Florida were limited and, since the colony claimed a large slave population, the government in St. Augustine organized a slave militia company to help defend Spanish territory during periods of conflict with the English. Unlike their northern neighbors, Spaniards in Florida little feared an armed slave rebellion because of the tolerant and humane relationship they maintained with their slaves. Established around 1683, the slave militia company was originally comprised entirely of Spanish slaves. However, after the slave company was formed the Spanish conceived another compact which permitted slaves to secure freedom by virtue of military service, and within a few years the militia company's ranks included both slaves and free men of color. The ability of Spanish slaves and runaway English slaves to purchase or otherwise acquire freedom led to the development of a large free black society in Florida.[91]

Georgia

St. Mary's

Cumberland
Island

St. Mary's River

Fernandina

Florida

Amelia
Island

Atlantic
Ocean

Goodby's Creek

Davis Creek

St. John's River

Mose

Castillo de San Marcos
St. Augustine

Lotchaway Towns

AFRICAN-AMERICANS AND THE WAR OF 1812

When the black militia company was first constituted, Spanish leaders envisioned that it would serve as a first line of defense for St. Augustine. Consequently, the town of Gracia Real de Santa Teresa de Mose, usually referred to as Mose, was founded and located two miles north of the capital city. Mose was unique in that it was the sole example of a free black town in the colonial south. Primarily a fortified garrison town, almost all of Mose's male inhabitants were members of the black militia. In due course, the town and the black militia company grew in size and function, and both were expanded by the influx of escaped English slaves. The town's newer residents were also promised freedom if they volunteered for armed service in the black militia company and pledged their allegiance to Spain. Mose's black militia proved their worth time and again during the thirteen decades preceding the War of 1812. One of their crowning achievements was the company's service in the defense of St. Augustine during the British invasion of 1728.[92]

St. Augustine was again under siege, but the invader was now the United States. In April of 1812, Lieutenant Colonel Thomas A. Smith, heading a force of approximately 300 U.S. regulars, Georgia militiamen, and patriots, entrenched near the Castillo de San Marcos and the adjacent city. Spanish Governor José de Estrada refused to surrender the fort and city, so instead of an easy victory, Smith confronted the prospect of an extended siege. Governor Estrada was replaced in June, 1812 by Sebastian Kindelan, who inaugurated diplomatic efforts to have the occupation force removed. But, in the meantime, Governor Kindelan was challenged with a difficult military situation.

Mose's importance as a military outpost dwindled during the latter half of the 1700's, and by 1812 the town had faded into a memory. Such was not the case with the black militia company, which had remained an integral part of Florida's small military community. The black militia company, consisting of 52 men in 1812, was called up at the first sign of American aggression. Word of the U.S. thrust soon spread to Cuba, the seat of Spanish government in the Caribbean, and an additional two companies of black troops from the 3rd Battalion of the Regiment of Cuba were ordered to reinforce St. Augustine. This relatively large number of black troops fighting for the Spanish became a matter of great concern to the Americans, and more U.S. leaders began express reservations similar to those of Senator Hunter. Georgia Governor David Mitchell was so worried that he advised

AMONGST MY BEST MEN

President Madison:

> They have armed every able-bodied negro within their
> power, and they have also received from the Havana [sic]
> a reinforcement of nearly two companies of black troops!
> [If black troops]...are suffered to remain in the province,
> our southern country will soon be in a state of insur-
> rection.[93]

Governor Mitchell's concern was mimicked by John McIntosh, a
Georgia supporter of the invasion. McIntosh cautioned James Monroe that
should the fighting spread north of the Florida border, the Spanish black
militia might readily find willing allies:

> Our slaves are excited to rebel, and we have an army of
> negroes raked up in [Florida], and [other black soldiers]
> brought from Cuba to be contended with...from [Florida]
> emissaries...will be detached to bring about the revolt of
> the black population of the United States.[94]

A potential slave uprising was the least of the problems that vexed U.S.
troops besieging St. Augustine. Severe heat and humidity, illness, and logistical difficulties plagued the small American force. Having too few troops
to begin with, sickness further shriveled Colonel Smith's numbers until he
could muster fewer than 200 effectives. The besiegers found themselves
outnumbered by the besieged. Raids against U.S. positions and supply con-
voys, often conducted by the black militia, likewise weakened the Americans
and eroded morale. It was one such raid that served as the catalyst which
finally broke the siege of St. Augustine.

On 12 September 1812, two U.S. Army wagons brimming with supplies
were journeying to St. Augustine from the base at Davis Creek. Escorting
the wagons were approximately 20 U.S. Marines and Georgia militiamen
under the command of Marine Captain John Williams. As the tiny convoy
traversed Twelve Mile Swamp, northwest of St. Augustine, it was ambushed
by "a mixed unit of Negroes and Indians, organized and led by a free black
named 'Prince'."[95] A one-time slave, Prince—whose real name was Principe
Huiten—escaped from South Carolina in the late 1700's. Huiten procured
his freedom, and by 1812 he was a property owner and a skilled carpenter
who not only had achieved status in the black community but had recently
been elevated to the rank of lieutenant in the black militia. Leading a force
of between 50 to 70 of St. Augustine's black militiamen, along with a small

number of Seminole Indians, Huiten infiltrated American lines and carefully laid an ambush in the confining swamp.[96] When the ambush was sprung, Captain Williams was shot down in the first volley and his only sergeant was killed instantly. Although hard hit, the convoy escort rallied, counter-attacked, and saved their mortally wounded captain from immediate death, but not before the attackers destroyed one of the wagons and hauled the second away.[97] The Spanish officially credited Lieutenant Principe Huiten with lifting the American siege of St. Augustine.

In actuality, Huiten's raid did render the *coup de grâce* to Colonel Smith's St. Augustine operation. Hampered by the elements, crippled by disease, and unable to maintain an open line of communications, Smith was compelled to abandon his siege lines. Assisting Smith and his debilitated command as they withdrew to the American base at Davis Creek was Colonel Daniel Newnan and a detachment of 250 Georgia patriots. Newnan had arrived at the American fieldwork on Goodby's Creek, named Camp New Hope, on 15 August 1812. There he was issued orders to attack the Seminole Indian towns situated on the Lotchaway River, northeast of present day Gainesville, Florida. Logistical problems and other disruptions, such as safeguarding Colonel Smith's retreat, delayed Newnan's march against the Seminoles, and not until 24 September was he able to begin his expedition. Newnan was beset by numerous difficulties from the start, not least of which was the fact that his ranks had been reduced to only 117 men.

Four days later, having marched to within six or seven miles of the Lotchaway Towns, Newnan's column encountered a force of Seminole Indians led by Chief Payne. Two-and-a-half hours of skirmishing exacted light losses on both sides, but the Seminole casualties included Chief Payne, who was mortally wounded. When Payne was shot down, the Indians broke off the engagement, though they remained near the battlefield. Newnan recorded that a few hours later, just before dark, his opponents "obtained a considerable reinforcement of Negroes and Indians from their towns... approached within two hundred yards of us, when they halted and com-menced firing..."[98] Fighting dragged on well past dark before Newnan again repulsed his foe. The surrounded Georgians then built a stout log breast-work and settled in for a siege.

The Negroes that Newnan alluded to were runaway English and Spanish slaves and the descendants of runaway slaves who, over the previous cen-tury, had cast their lot with the Seminole Indians. Through the years so

137

many runaways intermingled with Indian society that the make-up of some Seminole villages was more than 25% black. Spanish authorities had turned a blind eye towards escaped slaves who found refuge among the Indians, a situation that had intensified animosity between the English and Spanish. In 1812 the enemy of the Seminole's was American instead of English, but the incentive to fight was just as strong for the ex-slaves since all that awaited if Newnan achieved success was a return to chains. The assimilated Seminoles resisted fiercely, and Newnan was so impressed with the fighting capabilities of the ex-slaves that he later wrote, "...in the second engagement, [the enemy's] number, including negroes who were their best soldiers, was double ours..."[99]

Newnan and his men remained barricaded and besieged for an entire week. Seven men successfully escaped the crude fort during the siege's first night, so Newnan expected help to arrive at any moment, but there was no relief for the hungry band of Georgians, who were reduced to killing and eating their horses. In desperation, Newnan opted to fight his way back to Camp New Hope. For four days the patriots slogged through the woods and swamps, harried by Seminole snipers at every turn. Newnan chronicled that during one of the frequent firefights "...the enemy fired upon our advanced party, and shot down four of them, one, a Spaniard, died on the spot, and two survived a few days; my negro boy was one of them..."[100] On the evening of the fourth day, one of the many messengers who Newnan had dispatched for help finally appeared with reinforcements, and Newnan's ragged column of patriots straggled back to Camp New Hope without further incident, minus about 20% of their original force.

Newnan's expedition proved to be the last offensive operation in what was a questionable campaign from the very beginning. Military failure, combined with increased pressure from sources within and outside the U.S. Government, convinced President Madison to abandon efforts to cede Florida, at least for the moment. By May, 1813, all U.S. forces had been plucked from eastern Florida.

If the Patriot Rebellion of 1812 might be called the war before the War of 1812, the Creek Indian War of 1813 could be labeled the war within the War of 1812. What began as civil strife between rival bands of the Creek Indian Nation in the summer of 1813 spread to open warfare with the United States. One of the conflict's early encounters involved a fortified settlement called Fort Mims. Situated on Lake Tensas about 20 miles north of Mobile,

Alabama—then part of the Mississippi Territory—Fort Mims was constructed as a small frontier palisade in July, 1813. Following an incident at Burnt Corn Creek on 24 July 1813 between a force of Mississippi militiamen and a group of the separatist Creek faction known as the Red Sticks, settlers from the surrounding area gathered at Fort Mims for mutual protection. Sent to augment the civilian defenders was a detachment of about 120 Alabama militiamen. By late August the Fort Mims defenses had been strengthened, and the site embodied a stockade surrounding 17 buildings. The bastion was so strong that the inhabitants were confident the Indians would not dare attack.

Warning signs seemed to suggest otherwise. Intelligence received from different sources indicated that a large number of Creeks were poised to attack several of the Tombigbee River settlements. Then, on 29 August, the commander of the Fort Mims militia, Major Daniel Beasley, reported to his superior:

> Two negro boys belonging to Mr. Randon were out some distance from the Fort minding some beef cattle and told that they saw a great number of Indians painted, running and hallooing on towards Messrs. Pierce's Mill [one mile distant from Fort Mims]. The conclusion was that they knew the mill fort to be more vulnerable than [Fort Mims] and that they had determined to make their attack there first....What gave some plausibility to the report of the negro boys at first was some of Mr. Randon's negroes who had been sent up to his plantation for corn and reported his plantation to be full of Indians committing every kind of Havoc....[101]

A mounted scouting party sent to investigate could not confirm the slaves' excited report, so Beasley discounted the sighting. For their efforts, the two slaves were strung up and whipped for lying and fomenting panic. Another reported sighting the following morning, 30 August 1813, was likewise ignored by Beasley—one account purported the major to be drunk at the time. No precautions had been instituted by Beasley. The gate guards apparently were playing cards when a Creek scouting party reconnoitered the fort the night before the attack, and the stockade's main gate was wedged in the open position by drifting sand and debris.

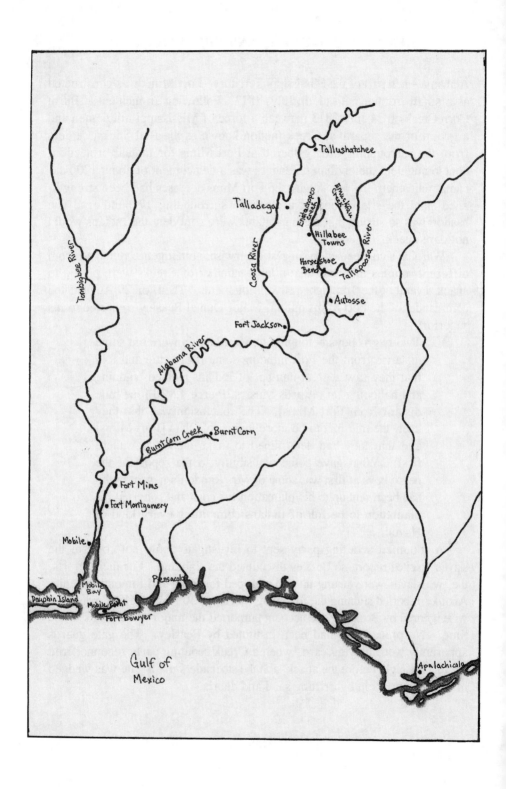

AFRICAN-AMERICANS AND THE WAR OF 1812

During the mid-day meal at Fort Mims on 30 August, as many as 1,000 Creeks rushed the stockade and swarmed through the blocked-open gate. Among the first killed were the two slaves who had been flogged by Beasley and left helplessly trussed to the whipping posts. Despite being surprised, the fort's defenders organized a spirited defense. Creek casualties were heavy, but fierce hand-to-hand fighting could not save the outpost from being overwhelmed. Estimates vary, but of the roughly 300 soldiers, settlers, and slaves sheltering in the fort, about 250 were killed. A small number managed to escape, and several of the fort's black occupants were spared and kept as slaves by the Creeks. Few whites were taken captive. Appalled by the carnage, the officer who led a burial party ten days later reported, "Indians, negroes, white men, women, and children lay [dead] in one promiscuous mass."[102]

For the next seven months, the Alabama country was embroiled in a full-scale frontier war. Numerous small battles and skirmishes were fought at places like Tallushatchee, Talladega, Hillabee Towns, Autosse, Emuckfau, and Enotochopco. Finally, on 27 March 1814, Major General Andrew Jackson cornered about 1,000 Creeks at a fortified camp on the Tallapoosa River in eastern Alabama. Located on a river bend called Tohopeka—from a Muskogee word meaning fort or fence—the site was known to the separatist Red Sticks as Cholocco Litabixee, or Horse's Hoof. The white man called it Horseshoe Bend.

Aptly named, the Tallapoosa's nearly circular Horseshoe Bend forced General Jackson to execute a frontal assault against a stout log breastwork. Shrewdly constructed, the Creeks emplaced the sturdy fortification where it would bisect the river bend's narrow neck. Preceded by a brief bombardment from two artillery pieces, Jackson's attack was spearheaded by regulars from the 39th U.S. Infantry Regiment, supported by Tennessee militia on both flanks. Ferocious no-quarter hand-to-hand fighting eventually wrested the log barrier from the fiercely resisting Red Sticks. Among those wounded at the breastwork, his leg pierced by an arrow, was a young Army ensign named Sam Houston.

With their main line of defense overrun, many of the Creek warriors attempted to escape by swimming the Tallapoosa River. Anticipating such a move, Jackson had sent mounted Tennessee riflemen to circle behind and surround the Indian position. Hundreds of Red Stick warriors, struggling against the river current, were shot in the water and swept away.

Altogether, between 800 and 900 Creeks were killed, while approximately 350 women and children were captured by Jackson's Cherokee allies. Considered spoils of war, the prisoners were turned over to the Cherokees, who enslaved them. Jackson's frontal assault cost the lives of 49 U.S. soldiers, with an additional 154 wounded.

Among the Tennesseeans' ranks at the Horseshoe was at least one slave, Americus Hammock. Hammock took part in the engagement as a musician, and following the battle he played a dirge over the grave of 39th U.S. Infantry Major Lemuel Montgomery, who was killed at the breastwork. In 1839, Hammock helped locate the burial site of Major Montgomery—after whom Montgomery County, Alabama was named. Hammock, along with another veteran of the Horseshoe named Samuel Barrett, "gave a short account of how the battle was conducted—how the charge was made, and where Montgomery fell."[103]

His success at Horseshoe Bend propelled Andrew Jackson, previously a relatively obscure general in the Tennessee Militia, into the national spotlight. Jackson's crushing victory, while not totally subjugating the Red Sticks, compelled most of the insurgent Creeks to surrender unconditionally within the next 30 days. Signed on 9 August 1814 was the Treaty of Fort Jackson, the provisions of which, in addition to terminating hostilities, required the Creeks to relinquish black captives taken at Fort Mims.[104] The Treaty of Fort Jackson was heavily slanted to favor the area's white settlers, so its terms were not completely acceptable to the Indians, especially the Lower, or White, Creeks who served with Jackson during the Creek War. Fleeing south, numbers of Upper Creeks joined with the Florida Seminoles, with whom they maintained close tribal ties. Because of that staunch relationship, Creek dissatisfaction with the treaty also caused unrest among the Florida Indians, a phenomenon which the British fully intended to exploit.

Thinking ahead to future operations after the Chesapeake campaign, Admiral Cochrane sent British officers into northwestern Florida in May, 1814 to contact the Seminoles and Creeks. Secret negotiations were already underway with Spanish authorities in Cuba regarding British use of Spain's western Florida outposts. Angered by what he considered to be United States aggression against Spanish territory, the senior Spanish official, the Governor of Cuba, made no objection to British activity in the area. Spain had long considered Mobile its own, but the U.S. claimed the region as part of the Louisiana Purchase. As a result, Mobile, later to become the State of Alabama's premier port city, had been incorporated into the Mississippi Territory. But as late as 1813, Spain still maintained a garrison at Mobile, and in an effort to further buffer its territory, Spain had been providing assistance to the Indians in their conflicts against the United States. However, an American military expedition forced the bloodless capitulation of Spanish Fort Charlotte at Mobile in April, 1813, compelling Spain's troops to withdraw to Florida. Because of these transgressions, not to mention America's recent incursion into northeastern Florida, Spain would willingly turn a blind eye when viewing British operations within its territorial boundaries.

Receiving favorable reports from initial British contacts with the Indians, Admiral Cochrane dispatched Royal Marine Major Edward Nicolls and 100 men to Florida. Nicolls was given orders to raise a 500-man battalion of Indians and escaped slaves, many of the latter having been assimilated into Seminole society. After making contacts at Apalachicola, Nicolls moved on to Pensacola, where he recruited about 500 Indians and 100 black troops; the latter were mostly runaway American and Spanish slaves. Unsuccessful overtures were also made by Nicolls to Jean Lafitte and his Baratarian pirates. Though Nicoll's force played no role at Mobile Point during the unsuccessful 12 September 1813 British attack on Fort Bowyer, some of his troops were present during the engagement. [105]

During the British retreat from Mobile Point, a number of Spanish slaves were forcibly impressed into Nicoll's black unit. Upon their return to Florida, a continuation of British strong-arm tactics expanded the black battalion by more than 100 men. [106] To reach the desired numbers, devious methods were employed by a small number of Royal Marines who:

> ...visited the negro cabins in [Pensacola], attended their
> meetings and by every means that the genius of seduction
> could invent endeavoured to entice the slaves of the Spanish
> citizens to join them—whenever they succeeded, the evasion
> of the slave [from his Spanish master] was easy, he had but
> to walk to the fort, at noon day or at night, he was sure of
> [a good] reception.... [107]

Following the attack on Fort Bowyer by the Pensacola-based British forces, Spanish claims of neutrality were nullified as far as the United States was concerned. In response, Andrew Jackson mobilized his 4,100-man

143

army and marched from Fort Montgomery in the Alabama country to Pensacola. Arriving before the town, Jackson sent a message to the Spanish commander offering surrender terms. Relations at Pensacola between the Spanish and the arrogant British had deteriorated by this time. British provocation had not only incurred an American invasion, but the English had treated the Spanish people and property with contempt. Nevertheless, pride and politics demanded that the Spanish commander, though largely over-matched, refuse to surrender.

On 7 November 1814, Jackson's troops assaulted Pensacola. What role Nicolls' force played in the Spanish and British defense of Pensacola is uncertain. Overall resistance was light. Initially, the British supported the Spanish garrison with naval gunfire, but they eventually abandoned their Spanish allies, allowing the Americans to capture the town with little effort. Before sailing away, the British completed their alienation of the Spanish by blowing up nearby Fort Barrancas and taking with them most of Pensacola's slaves along with 200 black troops whom the Spanish had maintained as a labor battalion at Apalachicola.[108] British designs to occupy Mobile had been thwarted, at least for the time being.

It was while Andrew Jackson was still in Pensacola following the town's capture that he learned of Admiral Cochrane's movements toward New Orleans. The New Orleans campaign constitutes the best known and documented instance during the War of 1812 where black troops fought in larger, cohesive units. New Orleans was also the only campaign during the War of 1812 where organized black units faced each other in battle.

With its multi-cultural and multi-racial make-up, New Orleans was one of the most cosmopolitan cities in the young nation. An 1805 New Orleans census recorded 3,551 whites, 3,105 slaves, and 1,566 free people of color, to which were added 1,977 black refugees who fled the 1809 Santo Domingo rebellion.[109] By 1810, people of color in New Orleans outnumbered whites by two-to-one. The racial imbalance was alarming among those whites who had arrived after the Louisiana Purchase and who were unfamiliar with and unused to the city's sophisticated style. Soon to become part of the State of Louisiana, New Orleans would eventually succumb to the restrictive and repressive vagaries of the Old South. Among those directly affected by the new order was Louisiana's long-serving black militia companies.

Black soldiers had served in an organized military capacity in Louisiana beginning in 1729, first under the Spanish and later for the French. An excellent 1965 work—*Honor And Fidelity, The Louisiana Infantry Regiment And The Louisiana Militia Companies, 1766-1821*—details the history of Louisiana Militia companies and reveals that:

> By 1801, the negro militia of New Orleans included a commandant, first and second lieutenants, a sergeant first-class, three sergeants-second-class, 8 corporals first-class, 5 second-class, and 125 soldiers. They were stationed in sections of New Orleans and from St. Louis to the Attakapas post. The mulatto militia had a commandant, lieutenant, two sublieutenants, 8 sergeants, 17 corporals, and 348 militiamen scattered throughout Louisiana and West Florida....The Battalion of negro Militia included a company of grenadiers and a company of infantry. The mulattoes had a company of grenadiers and three companies of infantry militia.
>
> By 1802, there was also a company of negro and mulatto infantry militia stationed in the Mobile District under Captain Carlos Lalanda, which included 2 officers, a sergeant and 21 men.[110]

No serious problems were encountered with Louisiana's black militia units until the territory was purchased by the United States. On that day in 1803, when Louisiana was transferred from French to United States control, the status of Louisiana's black militia companies changed drastically. Louisiana had just become part of a system that urged the enslavement of the very men who had served the territory in a formal military capacity.

When Louisiana became a U.S. territory, Governor William C. Claiborne recommended that the already established free men of color units be incorporated into the territorial militia. A Virginian raised in a culture which endorsed slavery, Claiborne was broad-minded where Louisiana's black population was concerned. But many whites, in and out of the new territory, were resentful and fearful of Louisiana's organized black troops. Among those who expressed an opinion on the subject was U.S. Secretary of State James Madison, who wrote Governor Claiborne:

> ...my principal difficulty arises from two large companies of people of Colour, who are attached to the service, and were esteemed a very serviceable corps under the Spanish government. Of this particular Corps I have reflected with

much anxiety. To recommission them might be considered as an outrage on the feelings of a part of the Union and as opposed to those principles of policy which the safety of the Southern States had necessarily established. On the other hand, not to recommission them would disgust them, and might be productive of future mischief. To disband them would be to raise an armed enemy in the very heart of the Country, and to disarm them would savour too strongly of that desperate system of Government which seldom succeeds.[111]

Madison's backhanded support helped Claiborne prevail, despite considerable opposition. The black companies were formally mustered into the Louisiana territorial militia, but the standard of treatment experienced under American rule was a different matter. Under Spanish control, black soldiers were treated the same as white troops, but American behavior toward the black militiamen was less agreeable. Disregard for their rights fostered discontent among the black companies. Performance suffered, and it was not long before their reliability was called into question by the white establishment. Even Claiborne, a staunch supporter, was concerned, and he recorded that "this neglect has soured [the black militia] considerably with the American Government, and it is questionable how far they would in time of danger, prove faithful to the American standard."[112] Among those who thought to gain advantage from the unsettled situation was the Spanish minister to the United States, who informed an acquaintance in August, 1805:

There are in New Orleans more than two thousand mulattoes and negroes who composed a corps of mixed troops when that province belonged to the King, and inasmuch as all of them love our government, they could easily be persuaded to move to Florida where they could form two Regiments.[113]

The Spanish minister's sentiment was premature, the free men of color endured despite poor treatment. Claiborne's flagging faith was eventually restored when the black militiamen helped subdue a slave insurrection in January, 1811. Feeling vindicated for his decision to retain the black militia companies, the governor wrote: "The free men of color...manifested the greatest zeal for the public safety. Their services were tendered and one

Company...performed with great exactitude and propriety...."[114]

Two months after the war's outbreak in 1812, the Louisiana Legislature passed a new militia bill which, in addition to authorizing 2,200 new troops, also empowered the Governor to enlist "Certain Free People of Color."[115] As a result of the militia bill authorization, Claiborne organized four companies of black militia, with each company mustering 64 men. The new unit was designated as the Battalion of Free Men of Color. One provision of the bill specified that the new black units be commanded by white property holders. However, Claiborne defied the Legislature's restriction concerning white officers. Among the battalion's newly commissioned officers were three black second lieutenants: Isadore Honoré, Jean Louis Dolliole, and Étienne Saulet.[116] But officers and men alike received no opportunity to test their mettle during the war's first two years.

When Andrew Jackson began marshalling his forces to combat British operations in the gulf region during the late summer of 1814, Governor Claiborne encouraged the general to embrace Louisiana's free men of color units. Old Hickory readily accepted Claiborne's advice. He responded to the Governor's plea when he stopped at Mobile on his way from Pensacola to New Orleans:

> The free men of color in your city are inured to the
> southern climate and would make excellent soldiers. They
> will not remain quiet spectators of the contest. They must
> be either for or against us. Distrust them, and you make
> them your enemies. Place confidence in them, and you
> engage them by every dear and honorable tie to the interest
> of the country by extending to them equal rights and privi-
> leges with white men.[117]

Although an ardent proponent of slavery, Jackson recognized the expediency of utilizing all available manpower. For this reason he welcomed the Battalion of Free Men of Color into his army. Knowing he would need every man who could shoulder a musket, Jackson issued a proclamation seeking additional black recruits. Arguably, Old Hickory's sincerity could be called into question, but his need for soldiers outweighed any personal qualms he might have held:

> Through a mistaken policy, you have been heretofore
> deprived of a participation in the glorious struggle for
> national rights in which our country is engaged. This no

longer shall exist.

As sons of freedom, you are now called upon to defend our most inestimable blessing. As Americans, your country looks with confidence to her adopted children for a valorous support, as a faithful return for the advantages enjoyed under her mild and equitable government. As fathers, husbands, and brothers, you are summoned to rally around the standard of the eagle to defend all which is dear in existence.

Your country, although calling for your exertions, does not wish you to engage in her cause without remunerating you for the services rendered. Your intelligent minds are not to be led away by false representations. Your love of honor would cause you to despise the man who should attempt to deceive you. With the sincerity of a soldier and the language of truth I address you.

To every noble-hearted freeman of color volunteering to serve during the present contest with Great Britain, and no longer, there will be paid the same bounty, in money and lands, now received by the white soldiers of the United States....

Due regard will be paid to the feelings of freemen and soldiers. You will not, by being associated with white men in the same corps, be exposed to improper comparison or unjust sarcasm. As a distinct independent battalion or regiment, pursuing the path of glory, you will, undivided, receive the applause and gratitude of your countrymen.[118]

Even though Governor Claiborne supported the concept of raising a black regiment, he did not immediately publish Jackson's proclamation, fearing the response it might evoke from Louisiana's white population. White opinion generally presupposed that by "...putting arms in the hands of men of color, we only add to the force of the enemy...."[119] When Claiborne finally summoned the nerve to present Jackson's overture to the New Orleans Committee of Defense, their response was, at least to the governor, gratifyingly positive. The Committee would approve Jackson's proposal "provided there would be a guarantee against retention of the regiment when the war was over."[120] In other words, when it was no longer necessary to sacrifice their lives to protect the white citizenry, free men of color soldiers would be returned to their second-class status.

Ultimately, two free men of color battalions served under Jackson. Commanded by Major Pierre LaCoste—a white planter whose plantation would serve as the field of battle on the night of 23 December—the first battalion of approximately 280 men incorporated the original companies of free men of color. The second battalion of about 200 men was comprised almost entirely of refugees from Santo Domingo. Prior to the British invasion, Santo Domingans had been precluded by law from serving in the militia, but Jackson's proclamation removed the barrier and enabled them to enlist. Raised by Colonel Jean Baptiste Savary, a man of mixed blood from Santo Domingo and formerly an officer in the French Army, the second battalion was actually led in battle by Major Louis D'Aquin. Colonel Michel Fortier, a wealthy white merchant and planter who commanded the Battalion of Free Men of Color when it was first formed in 1812, was placed in overall command of the combined battalions. A separate company of 45 men led by Captain Ferdinand Listeau, a free man of color, was sent on detached duty to Fort St. Philip. Additionally, at least two other black companies served in the Louisiana Militia. With the 15th Louisiana Regiment was a 50-man company headed by Captain Alexandre Lemelle and a 31-man company commanded by Captain Charles Forneret, who was also a free man of color. Both of these companies served primarily as garrison troops. A number of individual black soldiers also appear to have fought among various other regular and militia outfits.[121]

Jackson's dealings with his black volunteers during the campaign were scrupulous. Black or white, Jackson insured that any soldier serving with his army was treated fairly and equally. At one point, the assistant paymaster of Jackson's 7th Military District hesitated before paying cash money to black troops. Jackson angrily chastised his subordinate:

> Be pleased to keep to yourself your Opinions upon the
> policy of making payments to particular corps. It is enough
> for you to receive my order for the payment of troops...
> without enquiring whether the troops are white, Black or
> Tea.[122]

Black troops did not fight exclusively for the United States at New Orleans. Two units, the 1st West India Regiment and the 5th West India Regiment, were attached to Sir Edward Pakenham's army during the New

Orleans campaign. The British government first authorized the raising of black troops among its Caribbean colonies in 1795. Two black regiments, the 1st West India and the 2nd West India, were formed to suppress a slave rebellion on the islands of St. Lucia and Guadeloupe. So successfully did they stand the test that additional West India regiments were raised, and over the next fifteen years West Indian troops fought for the crown on more than a dozen Caribbean islands. Failing to leave well enough alone, the British government initiated a misguided program to increase the number of black soldiers by purchasing slaves from the Gold Coast of Africa and incorporating them into the 2nd West India Regiment. The experiment proved a miserable failure. After being issued weapons, the slaves revolted and two white officers were bayoneted. Discounting this single aberration, the West India regiments performed very well on behalf of Great Britain.[123]

When the New Orleans campaign was being planned, the British leadership, uninformed about local conditions, tragically assumed that the gulf coast climate would be ideally suited for West Indian troops. However, instead of being greeted by tropical weather when the invasion force arrived off the gulf coast, the British encountered torrential rains and temperatures so cold that nightly frosts were not uncommon. Lacking proper clothing and equipment, British troops suffered terribly, particularly the West India Regiments, who were unused to and unprepared for the bitter conditions. Recalling their adversity, the historian of the 1st West India Regiment wrote:

> ...during the voyage [to New Orleans] the regiment had been much scattered in small craft, where the soldiers were obliged to sleep on deck, exposed to the torrents of rain which fell by day and the frosts that came on at night; and being unaccustomed to the severity of an American winter, large numbers of them died from cold and exposure, the 5th West India Regiment suffering equally with the 1st.[124]

After British troops landed below New Orleans, George Gleig, a lieutenant with the 85th Regiment of Foot, recorded in his journal that many of the West Indian troops, "to whom frost and cold were altogether new fell fast asleep and perished before morning."[125] Approximately 200 soldiers from the 1st and 5th West India Regiments succumbed to the intemperate conditions, and many more were too ill either to join the main army when the campaign got underway or to fight when the army arrived before New Orleans.

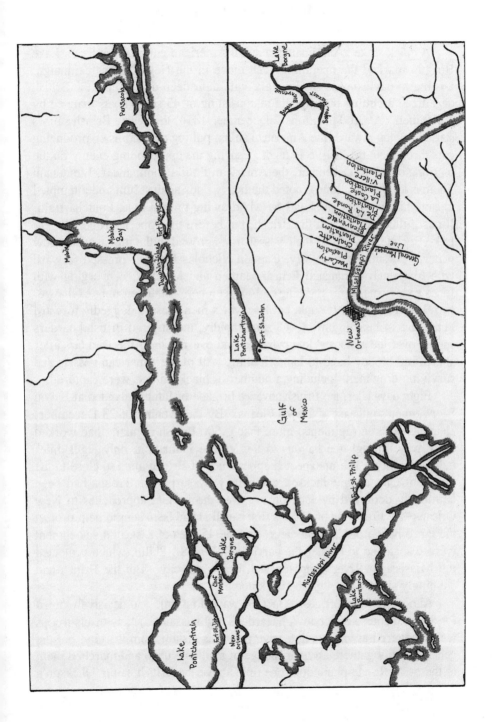

AMONGST MY BEST MEN

A quick strike to eliminate the small American gunboat flotilla on Lake Borgne marked the opening British move in the New Orleans campaign. Unable to navigate the shallow lake with their deep-draft ships, the British organized a cutting-out expedition consisting of 45 small boats manned by 1,000 men. At 3:00 p.m. on 12 December 1814, the hearty British sailors started rowing towards the American ships, pulling on the blister-producing oars throughout the long, cold night. Espying the approaching enemy on the morning of the 13 December, the American flotilla commander, Lieutenant Thomas ap Catesby Jones, noted the heavy odds against him and attempted to save his five little gunboats by withdrawing toward Lake Pontchartrain. Jones pulled away from the British, but before the Americans could clear Lake Borgne, several of their vessels ran aground in the unseasonably low water. Pursuing relentlessly, Captain Nicholas Lockyer pressed forward with his nearly exhausted British seamen and Marines, converging with Jones's gunboats on the morning of 14 December. In the ensuing exchange, two British barges were sunk, but Lockyer's men pressed doggedly forward in the face of heavy gunfire. Closing rapidly, the inspired British boarders surged over the gunboats' low bulwarks and overran the American tars after sharp and bloody hand-to-hand fighting. All of the American vessels and surviving crewmen, including a number of black sailors, were captured.

Eight days later, the British advance brigade of infantry landed at Bayou Bienvenue, southeast of New Orleans. By the evening of 23 December, elements of three regiments, more than 1,600 British regulars, had worked their way through the bayous to the Villeré Plantation, only eight miles below the city. The unexpected appearance of British units so close to the Crescent City caught Jackson completely by surprise. Troops had been cautiously deployed by Jackson to cover the normal approaches to New Orleans—the Free Men of Color's first battalion had been sent to help protect the large bayou of Chef Menteur, and the 45 men of Listeau's detachment were dispatched to bolster the garrison at Fort St. Philip, which protected the Mississippi River approach well below the city. But the British had cunningly slipped through the back door.

Although caught off guard, Jackson wasted no time and decisively opted for the bold course of action, a hazardous night assault. Many of his troops were scattered at various defensive positions distant from the city, but the general hastily gathered a hodgepodge of available units and marched them to the de la Ronde plantation, one mile above the British camp. Jackson's force totaled around 2,100 men, including the Free Men of Color's second battalion. Launching the American attack at 7:30 p.m. was the gunboat *Carolina* (14), which opened fire after silently floating downriver on the current. Following a 30-minute bombardment, Jackson advanced his infantry in line of battle across the open ground of the LaCoste Plantation, which adjoined the de la Ronde property. Reacting quickly, disciplined British regulars formed line to meet the oncoming Americans. In the confusion of darkness and fog, the battle quickly degenerated into a melee of tangled small unit actions.

Near the river levee on the American right, the 44th U.S. Infantry Regiment advanced beyond their supports and found themselves outflanked by the British 95th Rifle Regiment. In danger of being cut off, the U.S. regulars were saved when Plauché's Battalion of Orleans Volunteers and the Free Men of Color advanced and poured devastating volleys into the flank of the green-coated riflemen. At the other end of Jackson's battle line, the 7th U.S. Infantry Regiment had moved forward to support the advancing Tennessee brigade. Marching among the ranks of the 7th U.S. was 14-year-old Jordan Noble, a black drummer boy. One account of the battle reported:

> At eight o'clock [p.m.], when the fog became particularly heavy, it was this boy's drum, rattling away in the thick of battle, 'in the hottest hell of fire,' that helped to serve as one of the guideposts for the fierce battling American troops.[126]

The battle lines swayed back and forth for several hours. Much of the tumultuous fighting was at close-quarters with bayonets and clubbed muskets. Finally, around 4:00 a.m., British reinforcements began arriving on the field and Jackson realized it was time to retire. British casualties were nearly 300, while Jackson lost slightly more than 200 men; the Free Men of Color had seven men wounded.[127] In his report of the engagement to Secretary of War James Monroe, Jackson wrote:

> I was resolved to attack [the enemy's] first position, with Major [Thomas] Hinds' dragoons—General [John] Coffee's brigade—part of the 7th and 44th Regiments—the uniformed company of militia under the command of Major [Jean Baptiste] Plauché—200 men of color, chiefly from St. Domingo, raised by Colonel [Jean Baptiste Savary] and acting under the command of Major [D'Aquin]....General

Coffee was ordered to turn their right, while with the remainder of the forces, I attacked his strongest position on the left near the river....In this affair the whole corps under my command deserve the greatest credit....[Savary's] Volunteers manifested great bravery.[128]

No clear-cut victor emerged from the night battle of 23 December, though the American attack had served its purpose. Unsettled by Jackson's audacity, Major General John Keane chose to await additional reinforcements before making further advances on New Orleans. Keane's caution was sparked by the fact that he was only in temporary command of British forces until General Pakenham arrived, and he had no intention of risking any major moves before his superior assumed control. Meanwhile, Jackson had withdrawn about two miles to establish a defensive line along the Rodriguez Canal, the glorified name given to a narrow ditch which served as the boundary between the Macarty and Chalmette Plantations. Taking every advantage of his enemy's pause, Jackson used the time to begin construction of a sturdy mud and fencepost rampart. Extending from the Mississippi River on the American right, the rampart stretched more than half a mile into a cypress swamp which anchored Jackson's left. Cotton bales were hauled in to buttress the eight American artillery emplacements spaced intermittently along the line. To further enhance the position's defensive strength, the Rodriguez Canal, just in front of Jackson's line, was widened, deepened, and then flooded.

Major General Sir Edward Pakenham arrived at the British camp below New Orleans on 25 December 1814, but not until three days later, five crucial days after the night battle, did the aristocratic general feel sufficiently strong to conduct a reconnaissance in force. On the morning of 28 December, arrayed in line of battle, Pakenham advanced his entire army in two wide columns against Jackson's partially completed defensive works. Near the Mississippi River, the British left encountered immediate difficulties when their artillery either bogged down in the swampy ground or was disabled by American fire. The gunboat *Carolina* had been sunk the previous day when British cannoneers built a furnace and hurled hot shot at the wooden schooner's dry timbers, but the guns of another American schooner, the *Louisiana* (16), enfiladed Pakenham's exposed infantry while Jackson's artillery pelted the British from the front. Pakenham's left column was stopped cold, but the British right achieved a near breakthrough when the commander of a Tennessee detachment was killed and his panicked men retreated in confusion, leaving a dangerous gap in the unfinished American line near the edge of the cypress swamp. Luckily for Jackson and New Orleans, Pakenham missed the opportunity. Troubled by the determined resistance encountered near the river and surprised by the deadly ferocity of Jackson's heavy guns all along the line, the general issued orders to withdraw, unaware of his near success on the right but convinced that more artillery would be needed to breach the American line.

Over the next three days, in what can only be described as an incredible display of industry, tenacity, and perseverance, British soldiers and seamen, through blinding sweat and backbreaking drudgery, manhandled several ponderous naval guns, including eight 18-pounders and four 24-pounders, through the treacherous bayous to Pakenham's line. To supply the large guns with shot, each British soldier traveling from the fleet to the front carried a heavy cannonball in his pack. A number of those soldiers perished horribly when they slipped or fell into the bayous' cold waters, unable to surface because of their heavy loads.

Emboldened by the additional artillery support, Pakenham heralded the new year with an attempt to smash Jackson's line using the iron from his big guns. For a period of three hours on the morning of 1 January 1815, the thunder of cannons reverberated across Chalmette plain. Numerous problems hampered the British gunners' efforts, one being the soft ground on which the cumbersome guns were emplaced. Another complication was the hogsheads of sugar which had been positioned around the artillery pieces for protection. American shot pierced the sugar barrels and the sticky substance seeped into the soupy mud, causing one recorder to state that, "this was the first battle fought in molasses."[129] Particularly troublesome to the British was the fire from the single American 32-pounder cannon which constituted battery number 4, near the center of Jackson's line. Removed from the gunboat *Carolina* before she was sunk, the massive gun was manned by a contingent of the schooner's seamen, at least one of whom was a black sailor. A British observer of the artillery duel remembered:

> Their gun, a 32-pounder, was a most bitter antagonist to
> our principal battery. This happened to be erected in front
> of that part of the line where this gun was situated, and
> when it fired, its shot always struck [our] battery at the first
> bound, then ricocheted into the redoubt where I had taken

up my post...any of the other guns seemed like child's play to the unceasing and destructive fire of this heavy piece of ordnance. I could distinctly see that they were sailors that worked it—one of whom, a large mulatto with a red shirt, [was] always sponging her out after firing.[130]

Although Jackson's mud rampart absorbed most of the British shot, damage was inflicted to American guns and personnel. Eventually, their limited ammunition supply forced the British to cease fire before any appreciable results could be achieved; Pakenham was frustrated once again. Each side suffered about three dozen casualties during the duel. Because the Free Men of Color battalions were posted in Jackson's line supporting battery number four, three black soldiers suffered wounds during the exchange.[131]

During the next week the British brought up two more infantry regiments as reinforcements, while at the same time toiling to transport additional artillery ammunition from the fleet on Lake Borgne. Jackson used the same interval to strengthen his own position behind the Rodriguez Canal. When finally completed and fully manned, the main American line embodied slightly more than 4,500 men, braced by eight artillery positions. LaCoste's first battalion of Free Men of Color had been replaced at Chef Menteur on 26 December and incorporated into Jackson's Rodriguez Canal line alongside the second battalion. Together the two battalions defended a section of Jackson's right center between batteries three and four. Battery number three comprised two 24-pounders served by Jean Lafitte's Baratarian pirates (from the Barataria region northwest of the Mississippi River's mouth), and battery number four mounted the 32-pounder crewed by *Carolina* sailors. In the event his main defenses were breached, Jackson also prepared two additional lines: the first, Line Dupré, was constructed one-half mile above his principal Rodriguez Canal line, and the second, Line Montreuil, was built one mile behind that. About 900 slave laborers were conscripted to construct the backup defenses.[132]

Pakenham's patience, along with his common sense, expired on the morning of 8 January. The British commander's battle plan called for simultaneous attacks on both banks of the river at the crack of dawn. However, Packenham's plan miscarried when the men responsible for conveying the assault units across the river to the west bank underestimated both the engineering difficulties of getting boats onto the river and the actual strength of the river current. By the time the attack force's boats touched shore, the river current had carried the craft well below their intended land-ing point, and it was already past the scheduled time for the attack. The west bank assault would be delayed about an hour.

Totaling about 1,100 men, the west bank formation originally included the 5th West India Regiment minus its light company, which had been detached and ordered to Pakenham's right flank (light companies were often used for skirmisher duties). At first light, when Pakenham was tardily in-formed that only about half of the designated force had managed to cross the river, he ordered the 5th West India, which was still on the east bank, to remain behind.[133]

Meanwhile, in anticipation of launching the east bank attack at first light, Pakenham's regiments had been marched onto Chalmette plain in the pre-dawn darkness and formed into line of battle. As the sky brightened the red-coats were completely exposed and within range of the murderous American artillery batteries. Pakenham faced a difficult dilemma. He could not delay the assault until the west bank formation maneuvered into position because his east bank regiments were exposed to Jackson's lethal artillery fire. His choices were to either cancel the attack, march his troops back to camp and try again later, or continue without the desired coordination. Rather than postpone his attack once again, Pakenham, placing the utmost confidence in the abilities of his veteran regiments, decided to drive his 5,000 already deployed troops through Jackson's line on the east bank.

Using the same tactics he employed on 28 December, Pakenham formed his regiments into two columns. Near the river bank the smaller British formation, including several companies from the 1st West India Regiment, would assault the American right, but the attackers' main effort would strike Jackson's left near the cypress swamp, at the very spot where the 28 December attack almost succeeded. At the verge of the cypress swamp, the extreme British right flank was supported and protected by the light companies from four different regiments, including that of the 5th West India Regiment.[134] The balance of the 5th West India, recalled from the west bank attack, remained with the British reserve.

Pakenham's plan began to crumble even before the attack started. The regiment earmarked to carry the scaling ladders and fascines (bundles of bound together sticks which would be used to fill in the Rodriguez Canal) failed to carry out its assignment. Ignorant of the oversight, the British assault regiments advanced without the crucial tools needed to breach the

American defensive line.

Subjected to heavy American artillery fire from the outset, the British troops near the swamp bogged down almost immediately, and the supporting attack by the river encountered equally heavy fire. Marching forward with courageous precision, Pakenham's veterans encountered a wall of grape and canister shot. Then, when the British had advanced to within small arms range, American rifle and musketry fire added to the bedlam, creating an almost impenetrable barrier of lead. Bending forward as if in the face of a hail storm, the orderly red columns soon fell into disarray as British regulars stumbled over ever-increasing numbers of their own dead and mutilated comrades. Compounding the confusion were the heavy casualties suffered among senior officers. The flat, open plain of Chalmette plantation was transformed into a grisly slaughter pen.

On the British left, a few valiant and determined regulars fought their way into the American line, but supporting units were stopped in their tracks, leaving those who had breached the line to be either shot down or captured. On Pakenham's right, men falling at every step, the tenacious British veterans advanced as far as flesh and blood could possibly go before reluctantly giving ground, leaving a red carpet of bodies littering Chalmette plain. In less than 30 minutes, Great Britain's proud regiments lost 2,000 men killed and wounded. Pakenham himself, who rushed forward to rally his already broken assault columns, paid for his folly with his life.

In later years, there was great debate over the identity of the sharpshooter who felled Pakenham. Such were the number of men shooting, combined with the confusion of battle, that any number of soldiers could have been responsible. Andrew Jackson was of the opinion that the credit belonged to a free man of color (not necessarily a member of the Battalion of Free Men of Color). In a letter written some time afterwards to President James Monroe, Jackson avowed:

> I heard a single rifle shot from a group of country carts we had been using, and a moment thereafter I saw Pakenham reel and pitch out of his saddle. I have always believed he fell from the bullet of a free man of color, who was a famous rifle shot and came from the [Attakapas] region of Louisiana.[135]

So sudden was the British repulse that many Americans found no opportunity to discharge their weapons. Several accounts reported that the Free

Men of Color battalions, situated between the two advancing British columns, never fired a shot. However, a private from Plauché's Uniformed Battalion of Orleans Volunteers, the unit in line next to the Free Men of Color, remembered that:

> D'Aquin's so called mulatto corps was next to us and the New Orleans colored regiment were so anxious for glory that they could not be prevented from advancing from over our breast works and exposing themselves. They fought like desperadoes and deserved distinguished praise.[136]

For Andrew Jackson and the United States, it was a dramatic and stunning victory. Immediately after the British retreat, Jackson could have thrown his ill-trained, hybrid battalions against the wounded British lion, but he prudently declined to chance a risky counterattack. American troops had performed extremely well from behind the protection of a mud rampart, but if Jackson had pushed his men to fight on open ground, where the tough British regulars excelled, disaster could very well have resulted for the Americans.

Pakenham's assault regiments had been decimated in the attack. Three out of four general officers were shot down and eight colonels had fallen. A lack of overall coordination had doomed the assault to failure. Belatedly for the British, the attack on the west bank cleaved through the defending ranks of Louisiana and Kentucky militiamen, and the 16 artillery pieces protecting Jackson's flank on the east bank were captured without difficulty. In spite of this tardy success, Major General John Lambert, by default finding himself in command of a demoralized army facing an uncertain future, ordered a withdrawal from the west bank. Had Pakenham's assault been properly coordinated, the British breakthrough on the right bank would have flanked Jackson's line on the left bank. The 16 cannons in British hands would have enfiladed Jackson's line and, in all likelihood, would have compelled the Americans to abandon an untenable position at Chalmette plantation. Faulty British timing and ineffective British leadership saved New Orleans.

But the Crown forces did not submit easily. One final effort to capture New Orleans involved an untimely attempt to overwhelm strongly reinforced Fort St. Philip, located on the Mississippi River's east bank about 30 river miles below the city. On 9 January a British flotilla, including two bomb ketches mounting four heavy mortars, eased within range of the fort and opened a concentrated fire. That night, under cover of the bombardment, several ships from Cochrane's fleet attempted to slip past the fortification. Ably assisted by Listeau's company of black militiamen, Fort St. Philip's heavy guns thwarted the effort. For eight more days the British persisted with their bombardment of Fort St. Philip, failing to make any impression whatsoever. Finally, on 18 January, having achieved no success in any quarter, the debilitated British forces retreated from New Orleans.

In circumstances similar to that of the British withdrawal from Washington, nearly 200 slaves sought sanctuary with His Majesty's forces. Already overburdened and facing critical supply shortages, the British did not welcome the slaves but neither did they turn them away. Since the British tarried in the Gulf of Mexico region after retreating from New Orleans, a six-week dispute ensued, with letters being exchanged between Jackson and General Lambert. Toward the end of the period, Lambert, refusing to yield on the matter, wrote:

> If those negroes belonged to the territory or city we were actually in occupation of, I should conceive we had no right to take them away; but by their coming away, they are virtually the same as deserters....I am obliged to say so much in justification of the right; but I...have used every persuasion that they should return to their masters, and many have done so; but I could not reconcile it to myself to abandon any, who...joined us during the period of hostilities, and have thus acted in violation of the laws of their country, and besides become obnoxious to their masters.[137]

In an effort to salvage something from the campaign, the British again attacked Fort Bowyer at the entrance to Mobile Bay. This time the weight of the much larger combined British force easily accomplished what they had failed to achieve several months earlier. The 375-man Fort Bowyer garrison, plus three black servants, capitulated on 11 February. On the very next day, a British frigate sailed into Mobile Bay bearing news that the Treaty of Ghent had been signed.[138] Remaining in the area, the British regiments camped on Dauphine Island until word arrived on 14 March that the Treaty of Ghent had been ratified. Embarking on troop ships the following day, the last British army ever to invade American soil sailed over the horizon.

AFTERWORD

For the United States, hostilities ceased at an opportune time. Despite the decisive victory at New Orleans, the country's outlook was bleak. The prospect of continued operations against the greatest military power in the world left little room for optimism, especially following the abdication of Napoleon. Prior to Napoleon's defeat, Great Britain's involvement in the American War of 1812 would have been analogous to the United States being bogged down with the Viet Nam conflict while at the same time trying to fight a global war with another world power. The balancing act was indeed dangerous, and England's mastery of the oceans was the principal factor that enabled the island nation to survive. After the threat of Napoleon was eliminated, Great Britain had the option of channelling all of its military resources into the North American continent. If that choice had been made, the United States would have faced an uncertain future at best. The settlement negotiated at Ghent, Belgium, which dictated *status quo ante bellum*—everything to return as it was before the war—was probably the best that the United States could expect.

It could be argued that Great Britain would have confronted many challenges in the coming year, challenges that would have obligated England to redirect its resources back to Europe. Such arguments have merit. Europe, in a continual state of unrest at the best of times, was seething in political and military turmoil. In March, 1815, Napoleon's resurgence forced Great Britain to mobilize frantically for a nerve-wracking 100-day campaign that culminated in the cataclysmic encounter at Waterloo. Even after Waterloo, with Napoleon finally defeated, Great Britain, as a world power, had to maintain military readiness and be constantly vigilant for any contingency—not unlike the superpower United States in current times.

During the final months of the War of 1812, Great Britain was consumed by internal dissention. Until the fall of 1814, most British citizens staunchly supported their government's policy regarding the prosecution of the North American war, especially where it concerned the rights of the Royal Navy regarding impressment. But the triple failures at Baltimore, Lake Champlain, and Fort Erie caused many an Englishman to re-evaluate their views. Huge costs, reduced trade due to captured merchant shipping, an increasing number of military defeats, and long casualty lists influenced the British government to change its tactics at the Ghent peace talks, which had been initiated more than a year earlier. Previously pursued by the British peace commissioners at Ghent was the policy of calculated delay, at least until such time as military victories over the Americans would enable Great Britain to attain all of its demands.

In late 1814, British military failures in North America caused London's rhetoric at Ghent to become less strident. First to be discarded were England's claims against large tracts of United States territory; the British would settle instead for *uti possidetis*—each side to keep its captured territory—which would give the British Fort Niagara, Fort Mackinac, and much of Maine. As time wore on, pressure on the government was intensified by an increasingly disgruntled British public, who were frustrated and discontented with heavy taxation, ever-increasing costs for goods, and the loss of jobs and income. The Duke of Wellington tossed the final straw. In 1814, Lord Wellington was tendered the overall command of British forces in North America, an offer he declined, stating his belief that a continuation of the American conflict would be futile. Wellington's advice was to counsel peace with the United States. Internal and external pressures alike finally convinced the British government to negotiate in earnest and to accept *status quo ante bellum*.

Had the war been prolonged, the United States could have continued to fight. Recent military successes had gelled the United States Army. Younger and more competent commanders were coming to the fore and new recruits were flocking to the standard as a result of Washington, D.C. being burned. Yet there was little purpose in continued fighting. By 1814, not one of the three reasons for which the United States had declared war were still extant. England had virtually abandoned its Indian allies after the Thames River defeat, and thereafter retracted its demands on the Indians' behalf. Napoleon's abdication terminated the European blockade and eliminated any need to impress seamen to crew fleets of blockading ships. And finally, in one of the war's great ironies, Great Britain, attempting to appease its American cousins in 1812, had repealed the economic sanctions imposed by the Orders in Council two weeks before the United States declared war. However, news of Great Britain's policy reversal did not reach North America until after the United States had declared war, and the U.S. Congress stubbornly refused to back down. Also, it had become patently obvious to American leaders as the war progressed that Great Britain was not about to allow Canada to be annexed by the United States. Thus, if the primary military objective of the U.S. was unattainable, then there was no reason to waste additional lives in a hopeless gesture. Nonetheless, the United States could have continued to resist on land in 1815 with success depending largely upon the number of troops Great Britain consigned to North America, and the continued ability of United States forces to oppose the British Army.

It was the war at sea where the U.S. would have faced the greatest challenges. U.S. Navy commerce raiders and American privateers were, to a large degree, successful in their efforts, but it was Great Britain's economic blockade against the United States that would have been the country's undoing. Napoleon's 1815 uprising had little impact upon the British Navy, so regardless of other commitments England might have faced, the Royal Navy possessed the naval assets to strangle the United States. Great Britain ruled the waves and would continue to do so for another 100 years. The U.S. Navy—its heart, determination, courage, defiance, and daring not-withstanding—simply did not command the resources to sustain a continued conflict against the world's most powerful navy. There was no question that the U.S. Navy would fight. Victories would be gained and new ships would be launched and fitted. Yet 20-to-1 odds would be virtually impossible to overcome. For the United States, a maritime nation with its lifeline cut and little hope of staying afloat, the best option was peace.

The War of 1812 should never have been fought. There was not one point of contention between the United States and Great Britain that could not have been resolved by negotiation or arbitration. More than 6,000 deaths could have been avoided. But this does not mean that America's efforts were a total waste. The seeds for the modern U.S. Navy and U.S. Army were planted during the War of 1812, seeds that grew and were carefully nurtured by committed people through hard times and harsh conditions. The United States emerged from the War of 1812 a stronger nation, sending a forceful message that a new power was on the rise.

Throughout the War of 1812, the morale and indomitable fighting spirit of the U.S. Navy remained high. Confronting heavy odds, ships of the infant sea service gained amazing victories and spawned fear, panic, vexation, and confusion among its enemies far out of proportion to its own scanty numbers. Since the United States failed to achieve its military goal of annexing Canada, it can be argued that the U.S. did not win the War of 1812. This fact does not nor can not belittle the efforts of those valiant men in their fragile ships. They dared challenge the most powerful fighting force on earth and in a one-on-one fight, all factors being equal, the United States Navy prevailed more often than not. George Washington said, "Without a decisive naval force we can do nothing definitive, and with it everything honorable and glorious."[1] During the War of 1812, the United States Navy, outnumbered and overmatched, proved that it could function decisively. Sailors of the frigate navy—black and white—boldly and courageously ventured forth in frail vessels, establishing a proud tradition which molded the modern United States Navy.

Unlike the U.S. Navy, which started and ended the war as a competent, professional fighting force, the U.S. Army marched down a much tougher path. Beginning the war as a nationally unpopular organization, the Army was encumbered with stuffy, incompetent leaders, low morale, and substandard equipment. Lacking numbers, training, and discipline, it was quickly established during the war's first year that the pre-war leadership and pre-war methods were unequal to the task. Not until younger, professional officers such as Harrison, Scott, Brown, Macomb, and Jackson emerged did the Army transform itself into a professional fighting force. With the proper training and discipline and led by capable and effective officers the United States fighting man was, one-on-one, equal to his British Army counterpart.

But neither the Army nor the Navy was responsible for America's entry into the war, only for carrying out the less than perceptive policies of the country's political leadership. Wielding far too much direct influence and operational control before and after war was declared, the men in Washington severely hampered efforts by America's military leaders to prosecute the war. A few irresponsible political leaders, motivated by greed and ambition, propelled the country blindly into a war that, if not won in an immediate, overwhelming attack, had very little chance to succeed at all.

Such does not diminish nor detract from the role of the Americans, Canadians, and British who served during the War of 1812, including the service of black soldiers, sailors, and civilians; in fact, just the opposite. Black volunteers in large numbers stepped forward to defend homelands which paradoxically deprived them of the basic freedoms for which they fought. Not only were men of color treated abominably, they were generally considered to be less than manly. An influential southern writer of the period expressed the opinion that the black man was "...wholly destitute of courage...Cowardice is a principal of his soul, as instinctive as courage is

164

in the white man."[2] Time and again during the War of 1812, black soldiers and sailors proved the fallacy of that absurd notion.

In spite of overt prejudice, discrimination, and hatred, African-Americans stepped forward to serve, either in a civilian or a military capacity. Many who fought were former slaves, while others incredibly were still officially in bondage when they volunteered to serve. Sadly, it was mostly due to the desperation of circumstances that the United States allowed black volunteers to enlist in the Army and Navy. Those same circumstances compelled the United States armed forces to experiment with integration, an experiment that was both viable and successful. The U.S. Army and U.S. Navy were integrated, even if for a short time only, during the last year of the war. It is unfortunate that the country was neither progressive nor mature enough to improve upon gains that had been made by 1815.

After the War of 1812, the U.S. Navy did not prohibit black sailors from serving, but as the years passed black recruitment was severely curtailed. By 1842, the percentage of black seamen in the Navy had declined considerably, and Navy Secretary Abel P. Upshur related to members of the U.S. House of Representatives that "not more than one-twentieth part of the crew of any vessel is allowed to consist of negroes."[3]

Many black soldiers who served in the regular army during the War of 1812 were treated shamefully once the war was over and it was perceived that their services were no longer required. Some black regulars served until their tours of enlistment expired in 1817 or 1818, but in the First Military District, headquartered in Boston, black soldiers in regular regiments were summarily discharged once notification was received that the Treaty of Ghent had been ratified. Adding insult to injury, many entries in the discharge register for black regulars bore the offensive remark, "Being a Negro [he] is deemed unfit to associate with the American and on account of being a negro...not fit to accompany American soldiers."[4] Treated with equal contempt was a black cannoneer in the U.S. Corps of Artillery, discharged on 2 March 1815 because he was "a Negro and not [a] fit companion for the American soldier."[5] Black soldiers who enlisted in the 26th U.S. Infantry were not subjected to derisive remarks, but the result was the same when, in the spring of 1815, they were "Discharged under an order of [the] War Department directing that soldiers of color be discharged."[6] The final indignity was inflicted on 18 February 1820, when a general order was issued from the Army's Adjutant and Inspector Generals Office directing that, "No Negro or Mulatto will be received as a recruit of the Army."[7]

It would take another war nearly 50 years later—when once again the bodies of youthful fighting men would pile up grotesquely on bloody fields of battle, when the U.S. armed forces would again experience considerable difficulty enticing a sufficient number of young men willing to die for their country—before black soldiers and sailors would be actively invited to wear their country's uniforms.

Slaves also served in the country's defense in the War of 1812, labor which they had no choice but to perform. Uncounted numbers of individuals toiled for others who cared not. One can only imagine the conflicting loyalties and emotions experienced by slaves finding themselves in territory occupied by an invading army, loyalties torn by responsibility and duty to self, family, and country—a country which also cared not how they lived or if they died. Can some of them be blamed for assisting an enemy when their own countrymen treated them as chattel and their very freedom from a brutal and inhumane institution was at stake? Surely no censure can be leveled at those slaves who simply requested that the British transport them to a place where they could live as free people, to seek that liberty which their masters fought so desperately to retain and perpetuate for themselves.

Slave and free, African-Americans served, fought, suffered, and died for their country before, during, and after the War of 1812. The vast majority did so willingly in what can only be described as a noble display of patriotism. Their sacrifice was particularly compelling because African-Americans were fighting to preserve the fundamental rights of the United States of America; rights they themselves were not privileged to enjoy.

NOTES

Part I: NAVAL OPERATIONS

1. Joseph T. Wilson, *The Black Phalanx; A History Of The Negro Soldiers Of The United States in the Wars Of 1775-1812, 1861-'65* (Hartford: American Publishing Company, 1889), 73-74; Philip T. Drotning, *Black Heroes In Our Nation's History* (New York: Cowles Book Company, Inc., 1969), 35-36.

2. Christopher McKee, *A Gentlemanly and Honorable Profession, The Creation of the U.S. Naval Officer Corps, 1794-1815* (Annapolis: Naval Institute Press, 1991), 101; Theodore Roosevelt, *The Naval War of 1812* (New York: G.P. Putnam's Sons, 1882), 42-43; William S. Dudley (ed.), *The Naval War of 1812: A Documentary History* (Washington, DC, Naval Historical Center, 1985-1992), Volume I, 62—two volumes of a projected three volume series have been published to date. Estimates for the number of men pressed into the Royal Navy vary dramatically depending on the source. Roosevelt reports the U.S. State Department had records for 6,257 cases of impressment at the beginning of the war, but he further asserts that those were probably only a portion of the total, which likely amounted to 20,000. Dudley relates: "A conservative estimate of the number of American seamen impressed from 1796 to 1 January 1812 is 9,991..." Dudley also states that contemporary sources estimate between 10,000 and 50,000 impressments.

3. Quoted in Drotning, *Black Heroes In Our Nation's History*, 37.

4. Martha S. Putney, *Black Sailors: Afro-American Merchant Seamen and Whalemen Prior to the Civil War* (New York: Greenwood Press, 1987), 1.

5. W. Jeffrey Bolster, "'To Feel like a Man': Black Seamen in the Northern States, 1800-1860," in the Journal of American History, Volume 76, Number 4, March 1990, 1174.

6. William J. Brown, *The Life of William J. Brown of Providence, R.I., with Personal Recollections of Incidents in Rhode Island* (Providence: 1883), quoted in Bolster, "To Feel like a Man," 1182.

7. Putney, *Black Sailors*, 53, 79-80, 162-63.

8. Ibid., 120-123.

9. Bolster, "To Feel like a Man," 1174.

10. Putney, *Black Sailors*, 2, 49-53.

11. Frederick Douglass, *Life and Times of Frederick Douglass, Written By Himself: His Early Life As a Slave, His Escape From Bondage, And His Complete History*, quoted in Bolster, "To Feel like a Man," 1173.

12. Bolster, "To Feel like a Man," 1173.

13. Putney, *Black Sailors*, 33-38.

14. Ibid., 38-42, 142-143.

15. Henry E. Gruppe, *The Frigates* (Alexandria, Virginia: Time-Life Books, 1979), 77, 114-115; excerpt from "Ships in Sea Pay, Admiralty Office, 1 July 1812," in Dudley, (ed.), *The Naval War of 1812*, Volume I, 180-182. Warships were rated by the number of guns carried: 1st rate, 100-120 guns; 2nd rate, 90-98 guns; 3rd rate, 64-80 guns; 4th rate, 50-60 guns; 5th rate, 32-46 guns; 6th rate, 14-30 guns.

16. Gruppe, *The Frigates*, 14-17. The carronade was a type of cannon invented in the 1770's in Carron, Scotland. With a thinner molding and a shorter tube, or barrel, the carronade weighed considerably less than a standard long gun, meaning that a greater number and heavier caliber guns could line a ship's broadside, and those guns could be mounted at a higher level without having to worry about disturbing the ship's stability. In other words, a 32-pounder carronade weighed about the same as a 12-pounder long gun. Carronades took fewer men to load and fire, used less powder, and could be fired at a much faster rate. Range was the carronade's principal disadvantage. Because of its thinner molding the attenuated barrel perforce used less powder, which by extension rendered the carronade's range less than half that of a long gun with the same caliber. Deadly at close range, carronades were virtually useless at long range. Whether or not a ship carried carronades was a major factor in deciding the tactics a ship captain would employ.

17. Frederick S. Harrod, "Jim Crow in the Navy (1798-1941)," in U.S. Naval Institute Proceedings, September 1979, 47. Harrod attributes the quote to Secretary of the Navy Samuel Southard, but the Secretary of the Navy from the formation of the department in 1798 until 31 March 1801 was Benjamin Stoddert.

18. Tyrone G. Martin to the Author, 5 January 1995.

19. Perow Newzer to the Secretary of the Navy, 10 November 1806, Records of the Department of the Navy (RG45), Letters Received by the Secretary of the Navy, Miscellaneous Letters, 1801-1884, Volume 13, Number 48, National Archives and Records Service (NARS). On 31 October 1803, the U.S. Frigate *Philadelphia* (36) was in pursuit of two Tripolitan vessels off Tripoli harbor when it ran aground on an uncharted reef. After the frigate surrendered, the Tripolitans refloated the ship and moored it inside the harbor. In a daring raid on the night of 16 February 1804, Lieutenant Stephen Decatur and 75 volunteers slipped into the harbor unnoticed on board the ketch *Intrepid*. Decatur's men boarded the captured frigate, quickly subdued the sleepy Tripolitan crew, and set the *Philadelphia* ablaze. The U.S. Brig *Siren* (16)—sometimes spelled *Syren* in contemporary documents—supported the *Intrepid* during the entire operation, and *Siren's* smallboats helped tow the *Intrepid* out of harm's way.

20. William M. Fowler Jr., *Jack Tars & Commodores, The American Navy 1783-1815* (Boston: Houghton-Mifflin Company, 1984), 129.

21. Baltimore *Federal Gazette & Commercial Daily Advertiser*, 15 March 1813.

22. Tyrone G. Martin to the Author, 5 January 1995.

23. McKee, *A Gentlemanly and Honorable Profession,* 333.

24. William Jones to Surgeon Edward Cutbush, 23 May 1813, quoted in Dudley (ed.), *The Naval War of 1812*, Volume I, 124-125.

25. McKee, *A Gentlemanly and Honorable Profession*, 219.

26. Quoted in Bolster, "To Feel Like A Man," 1179.

27. Usher Parsons to George Livermore, 18 October 1862, quoted in Wilson, *The Black Phalanx*, 78.

28. Putney, *Black Sailors*, 90.

29. Tyrone G. Martin to the Author, 5 January 1995.

30. Quoted in Charles F. Adams, "Wednesday, August 18, 1812, 6:30 P.M.: The Birth of a World Power," in the American Historical Review, Number 18, April 1913, 519-520.

31. Quoted in Roosevelt, *The Naval War of 1812*, 287; C.S. Forester, *The Age Of Fighting Sail* (Garden City, NY: Doubleday & Company, Inc., 1956), 134.

32. Kenneth Poolman, *Guns Off Cape Ann* (London: Richard Clay and Company, Ltd., 1961), 46-47.

33. Ibid., 86-125.

34. Ibid., 145-160.

35. Ibid., 48.

36. Quoted in James E. Valle, *Rocks & Shoals, Order And Discipline In The Old Navy 1800-1861* (Annapolis: Naval Institute Press, 1980), 153.

37. Ibid.

38. Poolman, *Guns Off Cape Ann*, 169.

39. A Wanderer [Noah Johnson], *Journals Of Two Cruises Aboard The American Privateer Yankee* (New York: The Macmillan Company, 1967), xvi-xvii.

40. Charles F. Grandison to Paul Hamilton, 7 November 1812, in Dudley (ed.), *The Naval War of 1812*, Volume I, 596-597.

41. Sarah McCulloh Lemmon, *Frustrated Patriots, North Carolina and the War of 1812* (Chapel Hill: The University of North Carolina Press, 1973), 129.

42. Extract of a letter from Nathaniel Shaler, commander of the private armed schooner Governor Tompkins, to his agent in New York, dated at sea, 1 January 1813, in George Coggeshall, *History of the American Privateers and Letters-Of-Marque, During Our War With England In The Years 1812, '13 and '14* (New York: by and for the author, 1856), 140-143.

43. Excerpt from "Desperate battle, fought between the American Schooner-Privateer *Decatur*, of Charleston...and His Britannic Majesty's Schooner *Dominica*..." in op. cit., 174-175.

44. Charles R. Simpson to Thomas Barclay, 24 August 1813, quoted in Dudley (ed.), *The Naval War of 1812*, Volume II, 214-217.

45. John Drayton to James Monroe, 24 August 1813, quoted in op. cit., Volume II, 214.

46. Johnson, *Journals Of Two Cruises Aboard The American Privateer Yankee*, 62-141.

47. Coggeshall, *History Of The American Privateers*, 319.

48. Johnson, *Journals Of Two Cruises Aboard The American Privateer Yankee*, xvii.

49. Usher Parsons, "A Diary Kept During The Expedition To Lake Erie, Under Captain O.H. Perry, 1812-14," entry of 7 April 1813, Newport, Rhode Island Historical Society. Parsons later served as a Surgeon's Mate on Oliver Hazard Perry's flagship during the Battle of Lake Erie.

50. Commodore Isaac Chauncey to Secretary of the Navy William Jones, 4 June 1813, 8 July 1813, Letterbook of Isaac Chauncey, William L. Clements Library, University of Michigan, Ann Arbor (WLCL); Perry to Chauncey, 9 July 1813, Letterbook of Oliver Hazard Perry, Oliver Hazard Perry papers, WLCL.

51. Perry to Chauncey, 27 July 1813, Perry Letterbook, WLCL.

52. Chauncey to Perry, 30 July 1813, Chauncey Letterbook, WLCL.

53. Perry to Jones, 10 August 1813, Records of the Department of the Navy (RG45), Masters Commandant Letters, NARS.

54. "Account of the Battle of Lake Erie," affidavit by William Taylor, 23 June 1818, Oliver Hazard Perry papers, WLCL. Taylor was the sailing master on board the U.S. Brig *Lawrence* during the Battle of Lake Erie.

55. Diaries of Samuel Hambleton, entry of 12 October 1813, Maryland Historical Society, Baltimore, Maryland. Hambleton was the purser for the U.S. flotilla on Lake Erie.

56. Quoted in *Analectic Magazine*, vol. iii, 255, in "Negroes in the Navy," in Massachusetts Historical Society Proceedings, First Series, Volume VI, 1862, 241. Commander Robert Heriot Barclay was the senior British naval officer on Lake Erie. The *Niagara*, a 20-gun brig and one of two under Perry's command, served as his flagship during the latter stages of the Battle of Lake Erie.

57. "Samuel Hambleton's account of the Distribution of prize money on Lake Erie," in "Documents, Legislative and Executive, of the Congress of the United States," in the *American State Papers* (Washington, DC: Gales and Seaton, 1834), IV:1/566-572; "List of Killed and Wounded on board of the United States' squadron, under Command of O.H. Perry, Esq. in the Battle of 10th September 1813," op. cit., 295-296; Tyrone G. Martin, "The Constitution Connection," in *The Journal of Erie Studies*, Volume 17, Number 1, Fall 1988, 44; Martin, "The Captain's Clerk" data base, file on Jesse Williams; "Correspondence Relating to Medalists 1812-14," in Thomas Lynch Montgomery (ed.), *Pennsylvania Archives, Sixth Series* (Harrisburg: Harrisburg Publishing Company, State Printer, 1907), Volume IX, 289.

58. "List of Killed and Wounded in the Battle of 10th September 1813;" "List of Officers and Men from NewPort R.I. under command of Captain O.H. Perry,"

Perry Papers, WLCL; Putney, *Black Sailors*, 39, 143.

59. "Samuel Hambleton's prize list;" *Nashville Globe*, 29 August 1913 and *The Illustrated Buffalo Express*, 31 August 1813, in the Charles A. Dickson papers, The Western Reserve Historical Society, Cleveland, Ohio (WRHS).

60. "Anonymous and miscellaneous manuscript," no date, in the Oliver Hazard Perry papers, WLCL. Following the Battle of Lake Erie, Perry was promoted to captain and given command of a new ship, the U.S. Frigate *Java*, under construction at Baltimore. Tiffany accompanied Perry in the *Java* on a cruise to the Mediterranean Sea after the War of 1812.

61. "Samuel Hambleton's prize list." Ship's boys were young men, usually between the ages of 10 and 18 who, in normal ship's operations, functioned as officer's servants or messengers. During battle they served as powder monkeys, supplying cartridges to the big guns.

62. Pension application file of Diane Hardy, Records of the Pension Office (RG15), War of 1812 Pension Application Files (PAF), NARS.

63. Benson J. Lossing, *The Pictorial Field-Book Of The War Of 1812* (New York: Harper & Brothers, Publishers, 1868), 538; Vertical file article entitled "Colored Seamen," dated 1882, WRHS; Alfred T. Goodman papers, op.cit. Goodman was an officer with the Western Reserve Historical Society in the 1860's, and he collected information pertaining to survivors of the Battle of Lake Erie. The name appears on Goodman's list as Jesse Wall, and preceding the list Goodman wrote, "...On the occasion of the inauguration of the Statue of Perry, it was ascertained that the following named participants of the battle of Lake Erie were then living." Goodman's monograph further relates the names and dates of death for those survivors who died over the next ten years. At the end of that list is, "Jesse Wall at Erie—date not known."

64. Pension application file of Mary Brown, PAF, NARS.

65. Pension application file of Elizabeth Brown, op.cit.

66. Pension application file of Margaret Boone, op.cit.

67. Jan M. Copes, "The Perry Family: A Newport Naval Dynasty of the Early Republic," in "Newport History," Volume 66, Part 2, Fall 1994, Number 227, 63.

68. Usher Parsons to George Livermore, 18 October 1862, quoted in Wilson, *The Black Phalanx*, 78. Colonel George Croghan, famous for his successful defense of Fort Stephenson on 2 August 1813, led American ground forces during an unsuccessful combined operation to recapture Fort Mackinac in August of 1814.

69. Emily Cain, *Ghost Ships, Hamilton and Scourge: Historical Treasures from the War of 1812* (New York: Beaufort Books, 1983), 99-112.

70. J. Fenimore Cooper (ed.), *Ned Myers; or, A Life Before The Mast* (Annapolis, Maryland: Naval Institute Press, 1989), 60. Reprint of 1843 Lea and Blanchard edition.

71. Ibid., 80-91.

72. Daniel G. Hill, *The Freedom Seekers—Blacks in Early Canada* (Agincourt, Canada: The Book Society of Canada Limited, 1981), 114.

73. Charles G. Muller, *The Proudest Day, Macdonough on Lake Champlain* (New York: The John Day Company, 1960), 155.

74. Ibid., 320.

75. The Negro Soldier, 68.

76. Michael W. Williams (ed.), *The African American Encyclopedia, Volume 6* (New York: Marshall Cavendish, 1993), 1651; Charles H. Wesley, *In Freedom's Footsteps—From the African Background to the Civil War* (Cornwells Heights, Pennsylvania: The Publisher's Agency, Inc., 1976), 150.

77. Robert Ewell Greene, *Black Defenders of America, 1775-1973* (Chicago: Johnson Publishing Company, Inc., 1974), 38.

78. Lossing, *The Pictorial Field-Book Of The War of 1812*, 687.

79. Augustus Thomas to the Secretary of the Navy, 29 January 1814, Records of the Department of the Navy (RG45), Letters Received by the Secretary of the Navy, Miscellaneous Letters, 1801-1884, Volume 68, Number 136, NARS.

80. David Porter to the Secretary of the Navy, 3 July 1814, in Abel Bowen, *The Naval Monument* (New York: Nafis & Cornish, 1816), 97-115.

81. Williams (ed.), *The African American Encyclopedia, Volume 6*, 1651.

82. Tyrone G. Martin to the author, 5 January 1995, 17 February 1995.

Part II: LAND OPERATIONS

1. John K. Mahon, *The War of 1812* (Gainesville: University of Florida Press, 1972), 25.

2. John R. Elting, *Amateurs, To Arms! A Military History of The War of 1812* (Chapel Hill, North Carolina: Algonquin Books, 1991), 2.

3. Mahon, *The War of 1812*, 10-19; Francis F. Beirne, *The War of 1812* (New York: E.P. Dutton & Co., 1949), 65-76; Reginald Horsman, *The Causes of The War of 1812* (Philadelphia, University of Pennsylvania Press, 1962) 217-236. David Webb to the author, 2 December 1995.

4. Quoted in Jesse J. Johnson (ed.), *The Black Soldier Documented (1619-1815), Missing Pages In United States History* (Hampton, Virginia: Jesse J. Johnson, 1970), 64.

5. Robert J. Gough, "Black Men and the Early New Jersey Militia," in "New Jersey History," Volume LXXXVII, Winter, 1990, #4, 231.

6. Ibid., 236.

7. "Reminiscences of John Harmon, Esq.," in *History Of Portage County, Ohio* (Chicago: Warner, Beers & Co., 1885), 262.

8. Johnson, *The Black Soldier Documented*, 61.

9. Ibid., 63.

10. "Judge [Augustus B.] Woodward's Resolutions," in *Historical Collections Made By The Pioneer Society Of The State Of Michigan,* (Lansing: Wynkoop Hallenbeck Crawford Co., State Printers, 1908), Volume XII, Second Edition, 469-470.

11. Johnson, *The Black Soldier Documented*, 61.

12. Ibid., 63-64.

13. Ibid., 65.

14. McBarron, H. Charles Jr., Todd, Frederick P., Elting, John R., "Chatham Light Dragoons, Georgia Volunteer Militia, 1811-1816," in Elting, John R. (ed.), *Military Uniforms In America, Volume II, Years of Growth, 1796-1851* (San Rafael, California: Presidio Press, 1977), 8-9. This work is part of a series produced by The Company Of Military Historians.

15. Mahon, *The War of 1812*, 221; Lemmon, *Frustrated Patriots*, 196.

16. "Receipt Roll of the Field Officers and Regimental Staff of the 17th Regiment of Pennsylvania Militia Doing Duty at Erie," in Thomas Lynch Montgomery (ed.), *Pennsylvania Archives, Sixth Series* (Harrisburg: Harrisburg Publishing Co., State Printer, 1907), Volume X, 209. Among its other service during the war, the 17th Pennsylvania Militia Regiment was called up for a two-week period from 24 July to 8 August 1813 to help protect the American flotilla at Erie from a possible British attack.

17. Gough, "Black Men and the Early New Jersey Militia," 234.

18. Lemmon, *Frustrated Patriots*, 196.

19. Ira V. Brown, *The Negro In Pennsylvania History* (Harrisburg: Pennsylvania Historical Association, 1970), Booklet 11, 13.

20. Wilson, *The Black Phalanx*, 82-83.

21. Ibid.

22. Ibid.

23. William Lee to the War Department, Jasper County, Georgia, 5 September 1814, quoted in Johnson, *The Black Soldier Documented*, 67-68.

24. Greene, *Black Defenders Of America*, 29-40. Greene's data was derived from a number of sources, but primarily he used the Register of Enlistments in the United States Army 1797-1815, found in the U.S. National Archives. Quite often a number of personal traits relating to the enlistee are recorded in the Register of Enlistments, such as age, occupation, height, hair color, eye color, and complexion. Greene's study of the register revealed more than 65 individuals who may have been African-American. In several cases the references as to race are specific; i.e., mulatto, Negro, colored, black or a free man. More often than not the description reads: black or curly hair, black or brown eyes, and black, brown, or chestnut complexion. Greene assumes that such listings denote the individual to be African-

American, and in the vast majority of cases he is undoubtedly correct, but there is room for doubt in a few instances. Particularly questionable are those individuals Greene cites as having enlisted in 1812 and early 1813. Unfortunately, sufficient information is not provided in the register of enlistments to offer definitive proof.

25. Mahon, *The War of 1812*, 9.

26. Hill, *The Freedom Seekers*, 113; Daniel L. Crossman, "Early French Occupation of Michigan," in *Collections and Researches made by the Michigan Pioneer and Historical Society* (Lansing: Wynkoop Hallenbeck Crawford Company, State Printers, 1908), Volume XIV, 659. Although still legal, slavery was not a commonly practiced institution in Canada, which finally abolished legal bondage on 28 August 1833.

27. James Askin to Charles Askin, 18 August 1807, quoted in Milo M. Quaife (ed.), *The John Askin Papers, Volume II: 1796-1820* (Detroit: Detroit Library Commission, 1931), 566. The John Askin Papers are part of the Burton Historical Collection.

28. Lieutenant Colonel I. Grant to James Green, Esquire, 17 August 1807, quoted in *Collections and Researches made by the Michigan Pioneer and Historical Society* (Lansing: Wynkoop Hallenbeck Crawford Co., State Printers, 1909), Volume XV, 41-43. Captain William Elliott was the son of Colonel Matthew Elliott, head of the British Indian Department in Upper Canada, and a cousin of Master Commandant Jesse D. Elliott of the U.S. Navy, who commanded the U.S. Brig *Niagara* at the Battle of Lake Erie.

29. Hill, *The Freedom Seekers*, 113-114.

30. Nelly Kinzie Gordon (ed.), *The Fort Dearborn Massacre* (Chicago: Rand McNally & Company, 1912), 26. Among other items, this book contains personal accounts of the fight by Lieutenant Linai T. Helm, Fort Dearborn's second in command, and Mrs. John Kinzie, who published her complete reminiscences in pamphlet form in 1836.

31. Ibid., 15-26, 64-66.

32. G. Glenn Clift (ed.), "War of 1812 Diary of William B. Northcutt, Part II," in "The Register," the quarterly of the Kentucky Historical Society, Volume 56, Number 3, July 1958, 257.

33. "Muster roll of a troop of volunteer state dragoons, for twelve months, under command of Captain William Garrard," reproduced in Lewis Collins, *History of Kentucky* (Frankfort, 1882), Volume II. Also reproduced as "Captain William Garrard's Troop, 'The Bourbon Blues' 12 Months Kentucky Volunteer Light Dragoons," Muster Roll of 31 December 1812, in *The Battle of the Mississinewa 1812* (Marion, Indiana: Grant County Historical Society, 1969), Volume 2, 45-46.

34. Colonel Orlando Brown, *Governors of Kentucky, 1792-1824*, quoted in G. Glenn Clift, *Remember The Raisin* (Frankfurt: Kentucky Historical Society, 1961), 125.

35. Clift, *Remember The Raisin*, 95. Lieutenant Colonel John Allen was killed in action, Lieutenant Colonel William Lewis became a prisoner of war, and Captain Nathaniel G.T. Hart was among those massacred following the battle.

36. Gordon, (ed.), *The Fort Dearborn Massacre*, 98-99.

37. "Diary of Daniel Cushing," entry of 1 January 1813, in Harlow Lindley (ed.), *Captain Cushing In The War of 1812* (Columbus: The Ohio State Archaeological And Historical Society, 1944), 75-76. Cushing commanded a company of the 2nd U.S. Artillery at Fort Meigs during both sieges.

38. Joseph H. Larwill, "Journal of Joseph H. Larwill Relating to Occurrences Transpired in the Service of the U. States Commencing April 5, 1812," entry of 1 March 1813, in the Burton Historical Collection, Detroit Public Library, Detroit, Michigan.

39. Op. cit., entry of 15 March 1813.

40. Greene, *Black Defenders Of America*, 35.

41. Hill, *The Freedom Seekers*, 111.

42. Lieutenant Colonel Charles Stevenson to Henry Dundas, 1 April 1796, reproduced in *Collections and Researches made by the Michigan Pioneer and Historical Society* (Lansing: Robert Smith & Co., State Printers and Binders, 1896), Volume XXV, 111-113.

43. Ernest Green, "Upper Canada's Black Defenders," in *Papers and Records of the Ontario Historical Society* (Toronto: Ontario Historical Society, 1931), Volume XXVII, 368; Hill, *The Freedom Seekers*, 114-117; David Webb to the author, 2 December 1995. Sedentary militia regiments were the same as American militia units in that every able-bodied man was required to serve, whereas the incorporated militia units of Canada were similar to those American militia regiments that were "federalized," or sworn into federal service for a specified period, usually six months. One such American outfit was the 147th Regiment of Pennsylvania Militia, organized in April 1813 and federalized for six months to protect the U.S. flotilla under construction at Erie, Pennsylvania. Another was Richard M. Johnson's Regiment of Kentucky Mounted Volunteers, which fought with distinction at the Thames River. One major difference between American federalized militia and Canadian incorporated, or provincial, militia units—such as the Incorporated Militia of Upper Canada and the Glengarry Light Infantry Fencible Regiment—was that the Canadian regiments served full-time for the war's duration.

44. Wayne Kelly, "Black Troops In Upper Canada During The War of 1812," in Historic Toronto Magazine, Summer 1994, Issue 6, 9.

45. Quoted in Hill, *The Freedom Seekers*, 114-116. Hill specifies Lossing's *The Pictorial Field-Book Of The War Of 1812*, page 402f as his source. The second paragraph of the quotation is located on page 403 of Lossing, but this author was unable to locate the first paragraph in Lossing's description of the Battle of Queenston Heights.

46. Captain Fowler to Colonel Baynes, 29 May 1813, quoted in Green, "Upper Canada's Black Defenders," 368-369.

47. From E.A. Cruikshank, *Documentary History of the Campaigns on the Niagara Frontier, 1812-14*, Part V, 275, quoted in Green, "Upper Canada's Black Defenders," 369.

48. Quoted in George Sheppard, *Plunder, Profit, and Paroles: A Social History of the War of 1812 in Upper Canada* (Montreal & Kingston: McGill-Queen's University Press, 1994), 45.

49. Jose M. Bueno and Rene Chartrand, "Upper Canadian Militia and Provincials, 1812-1815," The Company of Military Historians Plate Number 430, 1976.

50. Green, "Upper Canada's Black Defenders", 370; David A. Owen, "Black Troops on [the] Canadian Frontier," in "Lock, Stock & Barrel," Volume 2, Number 4, June 1981. "Lock, Stock & Barrel" was a small periodical newsletter compiled for War of 1812 enthusiasts by Mary Jo Cunningham, formerly of Deshler, Ohio and now residing in Custar, Ohio. Owen's article was serialized in the March, May, and June 1981 numbers.

51. Summers, Jack L. and Chartrand, Rene, *Military Uniforms in Canada 1665-1970*, Canadian War Museum Historical Publication Number 16 (Ottawa: National Museum of Man, 1981), 63-65.

52. Green, "Upper Canada's Black Defenders," 369.

53. Ibid.

54. Greene, *Black Defenders Of America*, 30-39.

55. Ibid., 30-31.

56. Green, "Upper Canada's Black Defenders," 369. The location of Fort George was such that it could not adequately cover the Lake Ontario approach to the Niagara River or effectively counteract the guns of Fort Niagara on the opposite shore. Therefore, a stout earthwork fortification, Fort Mississauga, was built at the immediate mouth of the river across from Fort Niagara.

57. Ibid., 370; Owen, "Black Troops on [the] Canadian Frontier."

58. Regimental Orderly Book, 3rd Regiment of York Militia, in the Metropolitan Toronto Library, Baldwin Room, quoted in Kelly, "Black Troops In Upper Canada."

59. Ibid.

60. Greene, *Black Defenders Of America*, 30-39.

61. Ibid., 37.

62. Ibid., 30.

63. "Muster Roll Of Capt. Saml. Whites [sic] Company Of Militia Belonging To The 5th Detachment From Pennsylvania Now In The Service Of The United States At Buffalo, N.Y.," in Montgomery (ed.), *Pennsylvania Archives, Sixth Series*, Volume VIII, 36-40. The instability and indiscipline exhibited by most militia units is displayed by the fact that at the Battle of Chippawa the 5th Pennsylvania reported

a total of only 12 casualties: 3 killed, 2 wounded, and 7 missing.

64. General Thomas Brown to William Hawkins, 14 July 1812, quoted in Lemmon, *Frustrated Patriots*, 122.

65. Op. cit., 196-197.

66. Henry, Earl Bathurst to Colonel Sir Thomas Sidney Beckwith, 20 March 1813, quoted in Dudley (ed.), *The Naval War of 1812*, Volume II, 325-26.

67. Mahon, *The War of 1812*, 122.

68. Captain Robert Barrie to Admiral Sir John Borlase Warren, 14 November 1813, quoted in Dudley (ed.), *The Naval War of 1812*, Volume II, 395-96.

69. Mahon, *The War of 1812*, 313.

70. Cochrane to Bathurst, no date given, quoted in Walter Lord, *The Dawn's Early Light* (New York: W.W. Norton & Company, Inc., 1972), 44-45.

71. Cockburn to Cochrane, no date given, quoted in op.cit., 45.

72. Frank Lawrence Owsley, Jr., *Struggle for the Gulf Borderlands, The Creek War and the Battle of New Orleans, 1812-1815* (Gainesville: University Presses of Florida, 1981), 103.

73. Quoted in Drotning, *Black Heroes In Our Nation's History*, 42.

74. Captain H.B. Eaton, "Bladensburg," in the "Journal of the Society for Army Historical Research," Volume LV, Number 221, Spring, 1977, 9.

75. Philip Haythornthwaite, "Royal Marines In The War Of 1812," in "Empires, Eagles & Lions," Issue #75, 15 October 1983, 51.

76. "Expedition To The Chesapeake And Against New Orleans," in the England "United Service Journal," Number 4, May, 1840, 27.

77. Quoted in Lord, *The Dawn's Early Light*, 140.

78. Ibid., 123-143; Michael Morgan, "A black—one of many— who defended Baltimore," in the Baltimore *Evening Sun*, 12 September 1985. After the war Ball bought a 12-acre farm near Baltimore, where he raised a family and a herd of dairy cows. Seized by slave catchers in 1830, Ball was again sent south, but the incredibly resourceful Marylander escaped again, stowed away on a ship, and made his way to Philadelphia, where he remained for the remainder of his life.

79. Scott S. Sheads, *The Rockets' Red Glare, The Maritime Defense of Baltimore in 1814* (Centreville, Maryland: Tidewater Publishers, 1986), 30, 120-121; Sheads, "A Black Soldier Defends Fort McHenry, 1814," in "Military Collector & Historian, Journal of The Company of Military Historians," Volume XLI, Number 1, Spring 1989, 20; reward notice in the Baltimore *American and Commercial Daily Advertiser*, 25 May 1814. In total the notice reads:

Ten Dollars Reward

Deserted from the U.S. Chesapeake Flotilla

GABRIEL ROULSON, black man. He is about 6 feet high, very black, stout made, small eyes; when spoken to has a down look. Had on when he went away, blue jacket and blue trowsers [sic], white cotton shirt, tarpaulen [sic] hat, striped gingham vest and boots. The said deserter shipped on board [the] U.S. sloop of war *Ontario*, from which he was turned over to the flotilla, he was seen last night by me in Water-street, when he immediately made his escape. It is very likely he is lurking about the negro houses. The above reward with all reasonable charges will be paid by delivering him at either of the rendevouzes [sic] on Fell's Point, or at the Lazaret.

JOHN DAVIS, M[aster] U.S.N.

N.B. The said deserter has said that he has worked for Mr. Reinicker in town.

80. "Expedition To The Chesapeake And Against New Orleans," 27.

81. Sheads, "A Black Soldier Defends Fort McHenry," 20.

82. Quoted in Charles H. Wesley, *In Freedom's Footsteps, From the African Background to the Civil War* (Cornwells Heights, Pennsylvania: The Publisher's Agency, Inc, 1976), 148.

83. Quoted in Lord, *The Dawn's Early Light*, 235.

84. Sheads, "A Black Soldier Defends Fort McHenry," 20.

85. Baltimore *American and Commercial Daily Advertizer*, 18 May 1814, attachment to Sheads, "A Black Soldier Defends Fort McHenry."

86. Sheads, "A Black Soldier Defends Fort McHenry," 21.

87. Lord, *The Dawn's Early Light*, 76.

88. Mahon, *The War of 1812*, 314.

89. Rembert W. Patrick, *Florida Fiasco, Rampant Rebels on the Georgia-Florida Border 1810-1815* (Athens, Georgia: University of Georgia Press, 1954), 251.

90. Jane Landers, *Gracia Real de Santa Teresa de Mose: A Free Black Town in Spanish Colonial Florida* (St. Augustine: St. Augustine Historical Society, 1992), 13-15. Reprinted from *El Escribano*, 1991; Jacqueline K. Fretwell and Susan R. Parker (eds.), *Clash Between Cultures, Spanish East Florida 1784-1821* (St. Augustine: St. Augustine Historical Society, 1988), 92.

91. Landers, *Gracia Real de Santa Teresa de Mose*, 13-21.

92. Ibid.

93. Jane Landers, *Black Society In Spanish St. Augustine, 1784-1821* (Gainesville: University of Florida, 1988), 199-200. A dissertation presented to the graduate school of the University of Florida in partial fulfillment of the requirements for the degree of Doctor of Philosophy.

94. Ibid., 200.

95. J. H. Alexander, "The Ambush of Captain John Williams, U.S.M.C.: Failure of the East Florida Invasion, 1812-1813," in "The Florida Historical Quarterly," Volume LVI, Number 3, January 1978, 293.

96. Landers, *Black Society In Spanish St. Augustine*, 203-205; Fretwell and Parker (eds.), *Clash Between Cultures*, 97.

97. Alexander, "The Ambush of Captain John Williams," 293-294. Williams was struck by eight bullets and died 17 days later. He was only the second U.S. Marine officer to be killed in action. The first was Lieutenant William S. Bush, shot down during the battle between the *Constitution* and the *Guerriere* on 19 August 1812.

98. Daniel Newnan to Governor David Mitchell, 19 October 1812, reproduced in "United States Troops in Spanish East Florida, 1812-1813," in "The Florida Historical Quarterly," Volume IX, Number 1, July 1930, 150.

99. Ibid., 155.

100. Ibid., 153.

101. Quoted in Owsley, *Struggle for the Gulf Borderlands*, 36-37.

102. Ibid., 30-41; James W. Holland, *Andrew Jackson And The Creek War: Victory At The Horseshoe* (University, Alabama: University of Alabama Press, 1968), 8-10; Glenn Tucker, *Poltroons and Patriots* (Indianapolis/New York: The Bobbs-Merrill Company, Inc., 1954), two volumes, Volume II, 448-451; Beirne, *The War of 1812*, 235-238; Lossing, *Pictorial Field-Book of the War of 1812*, 757; Mahon, *The War of 1812*, 234-35. Versions differ concerning the two slaves. One source states the slaves had been released before the battle, while two others purport that one of the slaves again saw the Indians before they rushed the fort, and that he would have shouted a warning but for fear of being whipped again; corroboration would be difficult since both were killed. Lossing quotes the report of Captain Joseph P. Kennedy, who was sent by Brigadier General Ferdinand L. Claiborne to bury the dead at Fort Mims.

103. *The Alabama Journal*, 23 July 1839.

104. Holland, *Andrew Jackson and the Creek War*, 35.

105. Owsley, *Struggle For The Gulf Borderlands*, 99-109.

106. Ibid., 115-116.

107. Ibid.

108. Ibid., 118-119. Many former slaves who served with Nicolls remained in the area. After the war, with weapons and supplies left by the departing British, they formed an alliance with a group of Indians and fortified themselves in a former British outpost, sometimes referred to as Fort Nicolls, on the Apalachicola River. The little bastion became known as the Negro Fort, and served as a refuge for runaway slaves. By 1816 there was grave concern about the enclave among many Americans. It was feared that an armed force of former slaves so near to U.S. territory could lead to a slave revolt. When Spanish authorities, citing a lack of manpower, refused to take action, the United States sent ships and troops to eliminate the perceived threat. On 27 July 1816, after strong resistance, the fort was overrun. As many as 300 men, women, and children, primarily black occupants of

the fort, were killed. Most died horribly when a shot from a naval cannon exploded the powder magazine. Those who survived were sent back into slavery.

109. Marcus Christian, *Negro Soldiers In The Battle of New Orleans* (Chalmette, Louisiana: The Battle of New Orleans 150th Anniversary Committee, 1965), 4.

110. Jack D.L. Holmes, *Honor And Fidelity, The Louisiana Infantry Regiment And The Louisiana Militia Companies, 1766-1821* (Birmingham: 1965), 55. Black Louisiana militiamen were treated the same as white militiamen under the Spanish, but there was self-imposed segregation based upon color, hence the separate Negro and Mulatto units. Black soldiers with darker skin, or *Morenos*, preferred to serve with soldiers of their own darker color, while lighter skinned men, *Pardos*, likewise chose to enlist in units with men of their own lighter color.

111. Quoted in Samuel A. Carter III, *Blaze of Glory, The Fight for New Orleans, 1814-1815* (New York: St. Martin's Press, 1971), 75-76.

112. Quoted in Holmes, *Honor And Fidelity*, 57.

113. Quoted in ibid., 59.

114. Christian, *Negro Soldiers*, 2-12.

115. Quoted in Carter, *Blaze of Glory*, 81.

116. Ibid., 81-82.

117. Ibid., 83.

118. General Andrew Jackson's proclamation "To the Free Colored Inhabitants of Louisiana, Headquarters, Seventh Military District, Mobile, September 21, 1814," in William Lloyd Garrison, *The Loyalty and Devotion of Colored Americans in the Revolution and War of 1812* (Boston: R.F. Wallcut, 1861), reprinted in *The Negro Soldier, A Select Compilation* (New York: Negro Universities Press, 1970), 19-20.

119. Quoted in Carter, *Blaze of Glory*, 84-85.

120. Quoted in ibid., 85.

121. Powell A. Casey, *Louisiana at the Battle of New Orleans* (Chalmette, Louisiana: The Battle of New Orleans 150th Anniversary Committee, 1965), 14-15; Stuart O. Landry, *Side Lights On the Battle of New Orleans* (New Orleans: The American Printing Co., 1965), 34; Christian, *Negro Soldiers*, 36; Greene, *Black Defenders of America*, 344-345.

122. Carter, *Blaze of Glory*, 84.

123. No author, "Campaigns", quarterly journal of the Napoleonic age philatelists, Volume 4, April-June 1988, 67.

124. A.B. Ellis, *History of the First West India Regiment* (London: 1885), quoted in Robin Reilly, *The British at the Gates: The New Orleans Campaign in the War of 1812* (New York: G.P. Putnam's Sons, 1974), 258.

125. George Robert Gleig, *The Campaigns of the British Army at Washington and New Orleans in the Years 1814-15* (London, 1821), quoted in op.cit., 227.

126. Christian, *Negro Soldiers*, 32.

127. Ibid., 35-36.

128. Andrew Jackson to James Monroe, 27 December 1814, quoted in Johnson, *The Black Soldier Documented*, 72.

129. J. Fred Roush, *Chalmette*—National Park Service Historical Handbook Series No. 29 (Washington, DC: Government Printing Office, 1958), 32.

130. William Surtees, *Twenty-five Years in the Rifle Brigade* (Edinburgh, Scotland: 1833), quoted in Carter, *Blaze of Glory*, 225.

131. Christian, *Negro Soldiers*, 36.

132. Reilly, *The British at the Gates*, 279.

133. Tim Pickles, *New Orleans 1815, Andrew Jackson Crushes The British*—Osprey Military Campaign Series No. 28 (London: Reed Consumer Books Limited, 1993), 62-63.

134. Ibid., 70. Robin Reilly, in *The British at the Gates*, page 296, stated that this was the light company from the 1st West India Regiment.

135. Quoted in Drotning, *Black Heroes In Our Nation's History*, 51.

136. *Niles Weekly Register*, 11 February 1815, quoted in Greene, *Black Defenders Of America*, 344..

137. Quoted in Reilly, *The British at the Gates*, 320-321.

138. Ibid., 318-319; William S. Coker, *The Last Battle of the War of 1812: New Orleans. No, Fort Bowyer!* (Pensacola: The Perdido Bay Press, 1981), reprinted from Alabama Historical Quarterly, XLIII, Number 1 (1981), 55-60.

AFTERWORD

1. George Washington to the Marquis de Lafayette, 15 November 1781, quoted in Robert Debs Heinl, Jr., *Dictionary Of Military And Naval Quotations* (Annapolis, United States Naval Institute, 1966), 289.

2. Quoted in Drotning, *Black Heroes In Our Nation's History*, 37.

3. Quoted in Harrod, "Jim Crow in the Navy," 47.

4. Greene, *Black Defenders Of America*, 29.

5. Ibid., 36. The individual in question was James Perry, who had enlisted in November, 1814.

6. Ibid., 29.

7. Quoted in Johnson, *The Black Soldier Documented*, 5.